Divided Europe

WITHDRAWN
FROM STOCK

DATE DUE FOR RETURN

0 - DEC 2007	11 JAN 2002
2 5 FEB 2008	- 5 JUN 20~
2 6 OCT 200 *2008*	
16	

2007

Divided Europe

The New Domination of the East

Adam Burgess

Pluto **Press**
LONDON • CHICAGO, ILLINOIS

First published 1997 by Pluto Press
345 Archway Road, London N6 5AA
and 1436 West Randolph, Chicago, Illinois 60607, USA

British Library Cataloguing in Publication Data
A catalogue record for this book is available from the British Library

Library of Congress Cataloging in Publication Data
Burgess, Adam.
    Divided Europe: the new domination of the east/Adam Burgess.
      p.   cm.
    ISBN 0–7453–1262–4
    1. Europe, Eastern—Civilization—20th century—Foreign public
opinion. 2. Europe, Eastern—Civilization—20th century.
3. Europe, Eastern—Civilization—Foreign influences. 4. Cold war.
I. Title.
DJK51.B868   1997
940'.09717—dc21   97–20419
                                                                CIP

ISBN 0 7453 1262 4 hbk

Designed and produced for Pluto Press by
Chase Production Services, Chadlington, OX7 3LN
Typeset from the author's disk by Stanford DTP, Northampton
Printed in the EC

Contents

Introduction

The peaceful revolution that has swept Eastern Europe is probably the most significant event in global terms of the past 45 years. It represents a challenge and an opportunity to which the EC has given an immediate response ...

The time when Europe was divided into three distinct regions – the Community, EFTA and Comecon is now changing ...

The community is aware of these legitimate aspirations and concerns of its Eastern neighbours. But early membership of the EC will not be possible for a number of reasons ...

For one thing, the countries of Eastern Europe need to consolidate their commitment to pluralist democracy and to a market driven economic system ... . (EC briefing/pamphlet on 'The Community and Its Eastern Neighbours', 1991)

Why 'Eastern' Europe?

This book is about Central and Eastern Europe, and to a lesser extent Russia. More particularly, it is concerned with the perception of that part of the world here in the West, and the impact that the West has had in shaping, or rather misshaping this 'other' Europe. It is customary for books on this subject, and indeed on 'Europe' itself, to begin with a brief discussion of definitions. What is 'Europe'? Where does 'Eastern' Europe begin and end? Who is 'Central' rather than 'East' European? Is Russia a part of Europe, or Asia? And so forth.

Most studies conclude that the definitions to hand are unsatisfactory. There can be no final word on where these boundaries lie. It depends upon who is making the judgment, and from where. Writers from countries like Poland and Czechoslovakia in the 1980s, for example, insisted that their countries be considered a part of 'Central' Europe, and Russia a part of Asia. Here, ostensibly geographical notions provided a means of establishing distance from a hated Soviet Union, and an affinity with the West. In saying that these countries were 'Central' rather than 'East' European, they were telling us in no uncertain terms that they shared more in common with, they were closer to, the West, rather than the Soviet East in the metaphorical, if not the literal sense.

Judgments about the division between East and West lack objectivity. Consequently, experts concede it would be foolish to take them as given. Nevertheless, few studies have attempted to delve further into the question. Most introductions on the subject conclude that precisely what comprises the 'East' may be as imperfect as that which makes up its corollary, 'the West', but this is the only vocabulary available to us. There is perhaps little more that can be said beyond noting these definitions should be treated with caution. This book also resorts to the common sense language of 'East' and 'West' to distinguish the countries of the former Soviet bloc. To do otherwise would be confusing. However, these categories are in many ways also the very object of investigation, as understanding the significance of the East–West divide is the essential prerequisite to placing events within the region, and certainly relations with the wider world, in any proper context.

The existence of a meaningful division between East and West is assumed. This is why so little energy goes into further elaboration beyond the standard perfunctory remarks with which books on the region begin. While opinions differ as to precisely where 'the West' ends and 'the East' begins as we travel across Europe (a voluminous literature testifies to this debate), there remains the conviction that such a distinction is significant. There is no such certainty when it comes to a North–South European axis. Here, geographical shorthand remains just that. Saloon bar wisdom might suggest that climatic differences account for differences in temperament – 'hot headed' Latins as opposed to clinical Nordics – but no one seriously relies upon such prejudice in analysis. A North–South division is certainly not employed as a framework through which European affairs can be better comprehended, as is the case with East and West.

We are left with the curious situation in which everyone relies upon a distinction between East and West, that the very same commentators concede is impossible to properly delineate. Meanwhile, with the end of Soviet domination, there is surely less reason than ever to believe Europe should not be treated as a whole – given that the idea of East and West was so closely bound up with the Cold War division of Europe. Yet, as we shall go on to indicate, the sense of profound difference between East and West has, if anything, intensified with the end of the political division of Europe between communist and capitalist blocs. As it is far from self-evident that the division is merely given, we need to ask the question: *what is the impulse behind the drawing of these conceptual boundaries*? The countries of the region have as much that sets them apart from each other as they have in common. As with 'Northern' or 'Southern' Europe, such descriptions are necessarily inexact. Yet there is a certainty that, unlike with the terms 'Southern' or 'Northern', the idea of 'Eastern' Europe has some real meaning, and is therefore deployed with more confidence. Thus Jowitt, in his influential book, *New World Disorder: The Leninist Extinction*, makes only what he terms a 'necessary genuflection' to the idea that national differences exist.[1] He is certain that the region can be treated as a piece, and that any differences are of little note. As it is at the very least contestable that these countries constitute an homogeneous whole, the conviction that they do, suggests there to be other forces at play: there is something about Ken Jowitt's view of the world here that leads him to make such assertions. It is unlikely that he would only make a 'necessary genuflection' to the idea that national differences existed between Southern European nations such as Spain and Italy. Having accepted this division as a self-evident starting point however, it should come as no surprise that analysts proceed to try and understand 'the East' as a discrete world unto itself.

Understanding 'the East' in Isolation

> ... I believe in the area concept because it insists that people with scholarly interests in a country or region immerse themselves in the languages and culture of the places they study. The view that the universal laws of human behaviour are accessible to the rationalising methodologies of the social sciences seems to me to be quaint, an amusing leftover from a confident eighteenth century, and not one that should be taken seriously.[2]

Thus an American academic expert on Eastern Europe explained the predominant approach in his field. In so doing he has spelled out with admirable clarity its prevailing assumptions. It cannot be understood in relation to 'universal laws of human behaviour', instead we have to 'immerse ... in the languages and culture'. In contrast to the 1970s and 1980s when the academic working principle was precisely the universality of political behaviour – that despite communism, these societies and their peoples should be understood through the same terms of reference as our own – the emphasis now most decidedly rests on what is allegedly unique about the countries of the former Eastern bloc.

At the intellectual level, this book is a heartfelt attack on this view. Of course there is no problem with familiarising oneself with the particularities of these societies, and indeed I have spent much of my adult life doing so. Nor do I wish to champion the more comparative approach which prevailed in the Reagan years. After all, as another American authority, Daniel Chirot, makes clear in the same volume, East European studies in America was saved by that late Cold War offensive, and of course this came at a price. Greater research funds were made available only because of the demands of American foreign policy. And then as now, the largess of the American state was reflected in the type of (invariably useless 'Kremlinology') material that was produced – which even failed in its own terms, as no one anticipated Soviet collapse. What I object to is the idea that the region can be understood 'in itself'; that it is driven by forces of its own making.

Eastern Europe has been continually made and remade by external influences – to the extent that those forces native to the region have played a distinctly secondary role. Most recently of course, this was a zone of Soviet influence. Before that it was decimated by the Nazis. This was after 'enjoying' a brief and difficult period of formal independence with the dissolution of the the the Habsburg and Ottoman empires from which they were largely constituted. The insistence that this region be examined only in itself clearly makes no sense in its own terms. To study Eastern Europe is at the same time to study and understand European and indeed world history, at least of a number of its most decisive moments.

Refusing to situate 'the East' in this global context leads to only isolating elements of difference – to the exclusion of similarity. No wonder another contributor to the same volume finds that it '... is becoming as "exotic" as other parts of the world ...'.[3] Having decided to downgrade any continuities with what happens in the wider world, we are left only with the 'exotic'. Eastern Europe becomes an anthropological zoo where we seek out peculiarities, and it is through these that events are then interpreted. Torn out of context, these peculiarities then even take on a life of their own. The wilful exclusion of the wider forces which shape this part of the world leads to the conclusion that there is some sort of transcendental force – a spirit outside of human action – which dominates the region. Indeed this is the prevailing wisdom, even if it is not made so plain. In particular, 'ethnicity' and 'history' are seen to have a virtually independent existence in this part of the world. They determine the actions of the people almost regardless of will, according to much of academic and popular wisdom.

The consequences of this approach are also objectionable, and perhaps reflect the extent to which ostensibly academic study is governed by the concerns and needs of Western society. In positing autonomous forces which govern the fate of Eastern Europe, responsibility for any problems which befall the region are laid squarely at the feet of people in the region themselves, rather than with the larger determining forces of the international market and great power rivalries. The flip side of this reasoning is that the role of external forces, in particular those of the West, are conveniently taken out of the picture. This is an issue of some significance. As every educated person knows, the history of this part of the world has been shaped and disfigured by competing European powers. The very term 'Balkanisation' describes the process repeated again and again whereby these powers, principally Germany and its rivals, have fought for influence through hapless proxies on these, the fringes of Europe. This aspect is conveniently neglected through a focus on inspecting the region in and of itself.

It is significant in this respect that in relation to the key event in contemporary Eastern Europe, the war in the former Yugoslavia, there remains little serious academic study which unravels the role played by external interference – despite the fact that all Balkan wars in the past were acknowledged to have been driven by these wider rivalries. The few books which highlight the role of the West, such as the recent *The World and Yugoslavia's Wars*, begin from the a priori assumption that Western involvement was not self-interested, merely reactive and bumbling, while the motives of Serbia can only be the opposite – an unexplained abstract desire for territory and aggrandisement.[4] Such is the consensus that we look only at internal factors to understand the region that the overwhelming precedent for Balkan wars being 'made in the West' is ignored. Instead the alleged 'tribal' peculiarities of local actors stand as 'explanation' for conflict.

This is not to say I believe there to be some sort of conspiracy against the region intent on blaming it for anything and everything. Rather, it is both less demanding to avoid teasing out the inter-relations between processes in East and West, and more importantly, it is far more comfortable to stick to terms of discussion which focus only on the alleged problems of others. It is not the intellectual depth nor explanatory powers of the concepts used to understand Eastern Europe, such as the need for 'civil society' for example, which account for their popularity. For academic and politician alike, highlighting the shortcomings of others, and making demands that they make amends, is comfortable and even flattering.

What follows is a critique of the Western view of Eastern Europe. In so doing it suggests an alternative view of the region which, yes, draws upon the rationalising methodologies from a confident eighteenth century. What is the alternative? As Gale Stokes makes clear above, the notion of separate cultural worlds upon which the idea of a unique 'East' depends, requires that we reject the idea of progress. This steers us toward the outlook of cultural pessimism, whereby there is only the decline and fall of discrete civilisations. In the notion of human development still prevalent in the sixteenth century it was assumed that it was in the nature of compound bodies to decline. The ascent of states, prosperity and virtue was something of a miracle, certainly an exception. Renaissance man then still believed in a closed culture that could not indefinitely expand. Here cultures become things with a life and death of their own. In more contemporary times, this is a notion associated with the German irrationalist Oswald Spengler and his infamous *The Decline of the West* – of which more later. Contemporary academic thinking on 'the East' as a closed culture impervious to wider forces, certainly shares more in common with this pre-modern naivete than the notion of a single human civilisation which developed with the progress of the eighteenth and nineteenth centuries. The conceptual alternative is then to go further back, implicitly or explicitly, to what to me is truly 'quaint' and 'amusing' pre-Enlightenment thinking.

Europe Still Divided

This enquiry is an attempt to question the dominant understanding of Eastern Europe. The starting point is the current state and status of the countries of the former communist bloc. More than a decade since the fall of the old regimes, it is evident that these countries have not simply been painlessly absorbed back into Europe. The continent remains divided, symbolised by the fact that even Eastern and Western Germany, despite a massive injection of funds into the former GDR, are far from being one. 'Ossies' and 'Wessies' remain apart, to the extent that of the 16,383 weddings in Berlin in 1995 only 562 were between the two groups. And this in a city where both live side by side.

All agree that special problems remain with the East – despite the improved economic performance noted by authcritative analyses in 1996. It is not simply that their economies and infrastructures remain weighed down by a legacy of inefficiency from the communist era. There is seen to be an even more profound inadequacy. Despite there now being a multi-party system in place, the establishment of democracy since the fall of communism is seen to be, at best, fragile. To varying degrees, an anti-democratic, potentially authoritarian political culture apparently persists. The American political scientist Ken Jowitt, for example, wilfully dismissed the scenario of a transition to democracy. Instead, he (wrongly) sees the failure of economic reform in even the more developed societies like the Czech Republic, and anticipates a growing role for the military throughout the region. Such are the 'Unpleasant Truths about Eastern Europe', as an American journalist more recently entitled his contribution to the journal, *Foreign Policy*. Even in the Czech Republic, frequently held up as a model for others to follow, this same commentator suggests that 'a police state can be preserved in the national mentality'.[5] There remains a problem of 'democratic culture' in even the supposedly more advanced new democracies of the former communist bloc, and it is this which explains the persistence of division as the EC (now EU) suggest in the quote with which we began. Despite the peaceful revolution being the most 'significant global event of the last 45 years' for the EU, surprisingly little seems to have changed, such that a range of 'commitments' need 'consolidating' before the new democracies of Eastern Europe can even hope to be recognised as full Europeans. These 'commitments' are often quite baffling. EU Commissioner Hans van der Broek's visit to Lithuania in April 1997 to discuss their potential membership of the Union, involved his urging the Lithuanians not to reopen a nuclear power plant. What the country's plans for energy production have to do with joining the EU is unclear.

The region apparently remains distinct, different. It has special problems; for the EU, they lack 'commitment' to pluralist democracy and the market. And while written back in 1991, that perspective outlined above has not abated. The countries of Eastern Europe – and the CIS – remain on probation in the judgment of most Western institutions and authorities. The Western jury is still out on their 'commitment' to the market and democracy – despite no one explicitly denying that a market and democracy exist. This means not only that it remains in some sense 'Eastern', but requires special treatment. That special treatment is assistance from the West to establish the rule of law, democracy and human rights, and a free market. This 'assistance' is of considerable significance. It implies a relationship of inequality with the rest of the world; in the language of Jowitt, Western Europe must play the role of 'brother's keeper' if the region is not to 'degenerate in a frightening fashion'.[6] The West represents the East's only salvation; as *The Economist* put it, '... the more the EC gets involved in Eastern Europe, the stronger will grow the democrats on the other side of the fault line'.[7]

Curiously, a Western society acknowledged to be encountering considerable difficulties with even its most basic principles and institutions, is considered equipped and qualified to export them to others in this context. No one questions the basis upon which the United States, where the President was recently re-elected with only 49 per cent of eligible votes cast (meaning only 44.6 million of the country's 250 million citizens voted for him), can interfere in the domestic affairs of numerous countries in Eastern Europe in order to establish a properly functioning democracy and 'civil society'. Yet this is precisely what happens, despite the fact that electoral turnout, a key indicator of the relative health of their democratic systems appears no worse, indeed frequently better, than in the United States.

This, the dominant perspective in contemporary East–West relations, obliges the new democracies of Central and Eastern Europe to organise their societies around satisfying the demands of the West. If evidence of what the West deems democratic is not forthcoming, if the 'democrats do not appear to grow on the other side of the fault line in response to EC involvement', to paraphrase this consensus, societies in the East face exclusion from important bodies like the Council of Europe, and the more general marginalisation that follows. The fortunes of countries in Central and Eastern Europe are thus dependent upon their performance in meeting standards regarding the consolidation of a free market, and an adequate legal and democratic environment. Unlike other European countries, the future of those in 'the East' is not even formally in their own hands – or only in so far as they conform to requirements not demanded of others.

What is at stake in the discussion of the place of post-communist democracies is a new division of Europe, one half of which enjoys the right to set targets for the other. In place of the Cold War political division of Europe, the prospect of a new moral divide constructed around the degree of conformity to idealised standards of conduct. This is a damaging and unjustified development. This book argues that such a dichotomy is not the product of failings on the part of countries in Central and Eastern Europe – either now or in the past. Insofar as these societies have had special problems, they are the product of intense interference in their affairs by the major powers. They have consigned the region to a peripheral status in the world economy, and fought their wars on Eastern soil. The notion of an East–West divide represents an attempt to write off the consequences of this destructive interference by positing a mythical dividing line which separates the 'civilised' from the 'barbarian'. In more contemporary vernacular, it is a contrast between the 'tolerant' West and 'intolerant' East.

Questioning 'Cultures' and 'Westernisation'

The purpose of this work is to probe and question the literature on Eastern Europe and to an extent the former Soviet Union. It became clear to me studying the subject that the continual assumption of this literature was that this part of the world could never be like our own. More than 40 years of what now must be described as propaganda, suggested that only the evils of communism stood between the oppressed peoples of Eastern Europe and their enjoyment of all that was available to their fellow Europeans in the West. The dominant wisdom in the Western understanding of the East now is that it will always remain different. 'East is East, and West is West, and never the twain shall meet' as Kipling famously put it referring to the classical 'East' of the 'Orient'. Undermining this duality is a conscious objective of this work. The goal then, as they now say in Russia, is to gain recognition for this as just a 'normal' part of the world. One of the first tasks here is to demystify the discussion of Western culture and, at the same time, highlight the destructive process of westernisation that is currently under way.

What is it that is said to be so different about the region? What is the problem with these people? Sometimes it is called their lack of 'civil society', but in a word it is their 'culture'. Their habits and traditions are said to act as an obstacle to development. It is for this reason that they remain distinct, still 'Eastern'. I should make clear from the beginning that I do not believe that we are simply all the same; that there are no differences between the habits, customs and even psychology of peoples living in different parts of the world. On the contrary, in some respects I think we can even speak of such a thing as a national mentality. For all sorts of reasons, there are certain American, British, French and yes, Hungarian, Romanian and Russian traits for example. But what conclusions do we draw from such observations?

First, it is important to recognise that cultural stereotypes are usually inaccurate, based as they so often are only on ignorance rather than wide ranging experience – as with the British conviction that the Germans are humourless for example. This is especially striking regarding impressions of Russia and Eastern Europe – for the simple reason that commentators have generally never really got to know or understand what surrounds them on their visits. These peoples are not really 'one of us' in the first place as far as the majority of commentators are concerned. The natural distance that the Western intelligentsia and elite even ordinarily might keep from 'the people' is even more pronounced. Instead of immersing themselves in the different dimensions of the regions' peoples, as one would have to do to draw any sort of cultural judgments, they rely on second hand prejudice. It is summed up for me by the Western businessmen one meets on the plane to Russia. Never having left the hotel throughout their hundreds of business trips for fear of violence, they might just as well be on Mars for all they know about what is around them. Nevertheless, lack of experience and knowledge invariably do not prevent them from pontificating at length (given the chance) on the ways of the mysterious Russians. If such ignorance is understandable for a businessman, it is more grotesque with those for whom knowledge is supposed to be a stock in trade. But there often seems little difference between the ill-informed musings of Western businessmen about the problems of the Eastern character, and the frequently flimsy and impressionistic judgments cast by academics, journalists and officials of one sort or another.

What characterises the shallow diagnosis of cultures is their insistence on singling out only one particular feature. It is rare that one cultural characteristic operates to the exclusion of all others. The demanding and hard boiled 'culture' of Americans for example does not preclude, indeed complements, a general willingness to bend over backwards to help others. It is for this reason that people are rightly much more reluctant to cast firm cultural judgments. With East European culture, however, it is a different matter. The 'collectivist', 'tribal' mind-set operates to the exclusion of all else, if one were to believe the majority of writings on the subject. There is no room here for the fact that, for example, East Europeans and Russians from my experience are generally better educated and more conversant with classical (Western?) culture than their Anglo-American counterparts.

Cultural judgments not only need to be informed, but importantly, even if they contain a degree of truth, we need to realise that they can also be rationalised. 'Culture' is not a mysterious thing passed down through the generations. The greater familiarity with classical culture already mentioned is not 'historic'. 'Mass culture' did not develop in the East as it was excluded from this post-war development in the Western world. Instead, access, even for the working class, to the opera, ballet and theatre had to act as a substitute, and was hailed as a virtue by the authorities. More contemporarily, so too is the 'culture' of hustling for opportunities – perhaps most evident in

Hungary – readily explicable. It is a response to privation combined with the sense of the possibility of escape based on the exodus of people after the 1956 revolution.

Even more important than realising such trends can be explained, is the recognition that they are subject to change. Many apparently timeless cultural traits therefore are actually very recent, and themselves quite different phenomena from their antecedents – even if they formally look the same. Russian culture for example is quite distinctly shaped by the *dacha*, the country cottage which many Russians possess. And this certainly influences society. Witness the desertion of the cities on fine weekends. But this important aspect of life is no ancient Russian tradition, but a social bargain struck by post-Stalinist leaders, which additionally helped supplement a disastrous agricultural sector with privately grown fruit and vegetables. And it is now changing, not least in the fact that as more and more people no longer need to live on the produce of the *dacha*, it is becoming purely recreational. The same process of change is evident with most apparently fixed aspects of Russian and East European culture. Similarly, it is instructive to note the ease with which adaptation to other environments, and the effective abandonment of the 'mother' culture can take place. This is not to say that the extent to which one's original 'culture' remains important does not vary. What is decisive here, however, is the attractiveness of the alternative, and the boldness of particular individuals in taking on new ideas rather than falling back upon the familiarities of 'the way things are done back home'.

Most importantly of all, 'culture' has no explanatory power in itself. It can describe how people react to circumstances, and how that is reflected in their daily routines, but it cannot explain why this is the case. The real pressures and opportunities of social existence determine the patterns of life, not the other way around. When explanations are attempted on the basis of distinct cultures, we invariably learn little more than the prejudices of those making the judgments. What is especially galling is that what is often little more than saloon bar prejudice now comes dressed up as self-important wisdom. It is one thing to hear Czechs mouthing off about gypsies in a bar. There is little pretence it is not really just because 'we don't like them', and it can also (with considerable difficulty) be argued with – precisely because the issue is clearly one of blaming others for wider social problems. It is quite another when such sweeping generalisations are systematised into 'theory', and dressed up as profound academic insight – as is the case with so much written about Eastern Europe.

As a humanist, I have a rule of thumb about anything I read: if you cannot imagine yourself doing it, why believe it of someone else?

A second focus of my critique is related but separate. It is what is referred to in Russia as the problem of 'westernisation'. Before I later explain my objections to this process, I should again explain what I do not object to. To put it crudely, I do not see any great problem with the spread of McDonald's restaurants throughout the region. The problem with westernisation is not one of a valuable native culture being eroded by crass Western commercialism. That 'native culture' is a questionable concept in itself – certainly as some integral and ancient whole. It may be a pity that few East European film-makers are now getting the opportunity to produce films, and instead only Hollywood movies are available, for example. But this is the case in most of the world – that the native film industry cannot compete with the resources of the big American studios. Such matters are best looked at more practically than from the lofty heights of bemoaning the loss of culture. Are there actually any decent directors around? Might not American films just be better – certainly in establishing universal appeal to all of us?

What is important about westernisation is to understand that it is precisely Western forces which have shaped and moulded the East in its most decisive, not merely trivial respects – and continue to do so. It is not the obvious trappings like the availability of Coca-Cola that need to be scrutinised, but the more insidious and hidden processes going on behind the scenes. Of greatest significance here is the way in which the Yugoslav war was fuelled and driven by competing powers. More broadly we can see the siphoning of a new elite through the links established with the West, and the importing of the full range of contemporary 'politically correct' social concerns which bear little relation to the problems of Eastern Europe. These are creating divisions, and it is this destructiveness, rather than abstract neglect of the indigenous culture of the East, which is of concern.

Challenging Apologias

There are clearly real obstacles to the realisation of a unified Europe. Even Western Europe seems more divided than ever, especially from a British vantage point. As for uniting East and West, Europe remains deep in recession and is not about to open up its markets to competition even from East European agriculture. More widely, the fundamentals of what the West has prided itself on – a belief in progress and improvement; freedom from the state; a belief in democracy; etc. – have been undermined. Under these circumstances, it is hardly surprising perhaps that these values cannot be successfully exported. To an extent then, there is a degree of inevitability to the new division of Europe, and it might therefore seem nonsensical to complain.

But it is one thing to recognise that a European Union deep in recession is not going to allow in agricultural produce from Eastern Europe. It is quite another to mask this inequality by raising the 'problem' of their backward political and economic culture. The obvious reason why the latter 'explanation' is preferred is that it shifts responsibility on to the peoples of Eastern Europe. The problem becomes one of their inability to grasp the complexities of competitive capitalism rather than Europe's exclusion of goods. If this literature frankly admitted the problem was with the West rather than the East I would have little cause for complaint, even if a great deal of regret.

As for style of the work which follows, I should point out that it is highly argumentative, even polemical. I do not really make any apologies for that. These are frighteningly uncritical times, and that the writers, politicians and soldiers with which I deal have generally not even qualified their often astonishing arrogance and hypocrisy is testimony to the fact that no one ever questions their assumptions. I hope that challenging these views might at least create some debate of the real problems that need to be addressed.

There are many different strands to this subject, and I flag up and challenge all those which seem most important. In so doing, however, this work is limited in what it can achieve. It is simply not possible in the space of one book to deal with all the issues raised in this work in anything like the detail they deserve. Often I have resorted to only illustrating (albeit with what are usually the most significant examples) the many substantial issues I raise, rather than reconstructing their development, and interaction with other trends. In this respect, it is assertive. I have also emphasised the commonality of approach, rather than dwelling on undoubted elements of difference. This is most obvious in generally speaking of a 'Western' view which does not substantially distinguish between the perspectives of the various powers. Given the nature of this book, I would argue that this is legitimate one-sidedness however.

My purpose is to initiate discussion. In this respect outlining the key dynamic in East–West relations to the neglect of their nuances is important. More particularly I would defend the treatment of

Western views and actions as relatively monolithic on two other grounds. What needs to be grasped first of all, before we move on to other questions, is the essential consensus that 'the East' is a problem and needs to be 'dealt with'. Almost all actors and commentators concur with this perspective, and it is right that this fundamental agreement is emphasised. Second, even where authors and international actors consider they disagree quite substantially, it is invariably a matter of tactics rather than substance. Perhaps the most fundamental division in this discussion is between the more 'liberal' approach which demands vigorous intervention, and the more 'conservative' which is not so sure it even merits our concern being a 'faraway land of which we know (and care) nothing' as the infamous phrase about pre-war Czechoslovakia goes. Both agree there is a special problem however – only one thinks we should bomb the Serbs for example, the other that none of these peoples is even worth the bother. This is no kind of substantial debate, and I think it is quite valid to emphasise the extent to which they concur.

In terms of acknowledgements, thanks go to all the other members of the research association, Bez Hranic with whom I have been developing ideas for some years now. Special thanks to Ed Barrett for editorial assistance, and Grant Dyer for discussions on cultural anthropology; and most of all to my colleague and friend Tracey Brown who spent a great deal of her valuable time giving this piece some sort of coherence. Finally, as it is traditional to cite inspirations, I should say that my interest in the subject was originally stimulated by the terrible yet exhilarating events of Hungary in 1956. I hope that spirit of real independence can one day return.

1

The New Eastern Europe – Problem or Opportunity?

From Victim to Problem?

> Let us imagine that someone had predicted ten years ago the collapse of Europe's communist regimes. He would have been dismissed as an optimistic fool. Suppose he had then gone on to say that after a hard struggle to reform their economies, the former communist economies would find their goods banned by a European Community that claimed to be operating a single market? He would have been dismissed this time as a Soviet agent trying to fob off dissidents with horror stories. Unfortunately horror stories have a habit of coming true.[1]

Thus the distinguished economist Samuel Brittan commented on the European Union's exclusion of goods from the new democracies of the former communist bloc in 1993. And well he might. For all the Western homilies about free trade, 40–50 per cent of all East European industrial products could not be freely imported through being deemed 'sensitive' goods. All agricultural produce is effectively excluded through being subject to the tariffs and quotas of the Common Agricultural Policy. With the main things East Europeans can produce at competitive prices excluded by protectionism, it is hardly surprising that the EU was able to record a record trade surplus with the region of some £4 billion in 1993 alone. Even if the agreement to drop tariffs on steel and textiles by 1998 is implemented, there is not even a rhetorical commitment to open up agricultural markets.

In making his discomfort plain, Brittan provided a rare moment of reflection on the region's change in status and treatment. If most would agree that there has been no real transformation in economic fortunes, there has certainly been a revolution in perceptions of the old Soviet European empire. As Brittan indicates, the former communist bloc, and what to do with it, has now become something of an embarrassment. This is especially the case because of the ideological place that the region held in Western post-war self-presentation. Even for the hard-headed Henry Kissinger, 'It is hardly to the credit of the West that after talking for a generation about freedom for Eastern Europe, so little is done to vindicate it.'[2] Having held up the liberation of Soviet controlled Eastern Europe as a defining objective for so long, confronting its apparently disappointing results has not proven an attractive proposition. There is now little desire to focus on the aspirations of the peoples of Eastern Europe. If anything, as we shall later point out, it is more common to denounce them, or only cynically profess surprise at their naivete in having believed Western promises throughout the post-war years.

More practically, discomfort is evident around the question of EU membership – perhaps the central question in the new relations between East and West. Membership would effectively integrate this 'other Europe', and represent the last act of the process of change begun by communist collapse in 1989 and 1990. Yet, it is a matter which most European leaders would like postponed to the indefinite future. Despite the irony of this being virtually the only part of the continent where any real enthusiasm remains for European institutions, their applications have been put on hold until into the new millennium – even then there is no question of membership for all the states of the area. In the meantime, six (Poland, Slovakia, Romania, Bulgaria, the Czech Republic and Hungary) have signed agreements which put them first in a hypothetical queue for membership. Slovenia and the Baltic states hope to join the line soon.

Insofar as faster integration has been proposed, by the United Kingdom for example, it is primarily as a means of putting pressure on Germany. In their rhetorical war with Europe, the British hope to expose the hollow claims of the 'European super state' to fulfil its promises to the East, and thereby gain political space. But the British are no more serious about extending Europe eastwards than their European rivals. It may be a nice idea, but any firm commitment remains a subject best avoided. *The Times* complained that 'If there is any issue crying out for a political leader to cut through quite genuine but soluble problems and to sell the case for knitting Europe back together, surely this is it.' Instead, as they point out, the real state of play is exemplified by the visit to Bonn last year of British civil servants to debate these problems: '... they were astonished to be told Germany did not wish to provoke any public discussion for at least a couple of years'.[3]

But this is no uniquely German evasion. It is an attitude summed up by the British Queen during her first visit to the region in March

1996. 'We welcome your *aspirations* to join these institutions' (emphasis added), she told a banquet in Warsaw.[4] 'Thanks, but no thanks' is the message here – 'we are flattered that you consider our institutions so attractive, but let's be realistic'. Into 1997, and the managing, rather than embracing of the East is still evident. The March 1997 discussions in the Dutch town of Apeldoorn were ostensibly concerned with the grand task of EU enlargement – to include perhaps ten more countries by early in the next century. But membership was dangled principally as a carrot to discipline outsiders, rather than seriously set about the incorporation of European equals. An EU spokesperson explained that 'It is seen as a way to encourage everyone ... to feel part of the European club.'[5] As the Queen was keen to encourage aspirations, so the EU is happy to make the East *feel potentially*, but not actually *be* European. The unseemly squabbles among those waiting in the EU ante-room – the Apeldoorn meeting was overshadowed by rows between Greece and Turkey – are hardly surprising given the ways in which potential membership is so cynically being used as an instrument of European foreign policy. The reality is that even Germany's formal commitment to the earliest possible entry for their selected 'Central' European friends, Poland, Hungary and the Czech Republic, has been replaced with emphasis instead on consolidating monetary and political integration among existing member states.

Continued exclusion from the EU is not simply a problem of fulfilling the technical prerequisites for membership, as suggested by the British intellectual Perry Anderson among others, in his interesting contribution on the subject (his assertion that Western leaders have been committed to granting entry by a popular media consensus, is also questionable).[6] Certainly with the most immediate Western barrier confronting the East, the continued exclusion of goods from the East, the assumption that their removal would exacerbate economic crisis is unsustainable. As Richard Portes, one of the most astute economic analysts of the region concludes, 'The question then arises why policy makers have continued restricting access for products from the CEECs [Central and East European countries]. The evidence in this volume shows that it is virtually impossible to find significant negative effects of opening trade with the CEECs.'[7]

As for the larger question of integration into the EU, it is not difficult to indicate a financial strain that would be put upon the EU as it currently stands by integrating Eastern Europe. German economist Helmut Leipold, for example, explains how EU meetings would become very difficult as the minimum duration of each meeting would stretch to six hours, new translators would have to be employed, and the weighting of votes between member states would become complicated. But the question which arises here is why Leipold feels it necessary to start counting up the costs and difficulties for a project of enlargement which he does not see as viable. The distinct impression is one of hiding behind technical problems. Given the discrepancies between the productivity levels of member states, the project of monetary union is hardly less daunting, and yet here the EU shows a determination not to allow such difficulties to stand in their way.

There is surely more to the question of enlargement to the East than only technical difficulties. So many of the arguments against admission are merely circular. Leipold himself points out for example that 'The demand to make the accession of reform countries conditional on the reduction of economic disparities', hardly makes sense, 'since it is unimpeded access to the Single Market itself which enables effective trade and prosperity creation effects'.[8] Comparison with the EC expansion to the South in the 1970s is here useful. As the renowned British commentator on Central Europe, Timothy Garton Ash points out, 'Almost every argument that was made in the 1970s for admitting the fledgling democracies Spain, Portugal and Greece into the EC could be made in the 1990s for, at the very least, Poland, Hungary and the Czech Republic.'[9] 'Where there's a will, there's a way', but it seems that expansion to the East involves rather more than just economic factors. There are significant ideological and political issues at stake – as much of the rest of Anderson's article rightly suggests. It is not just that these societies are less wealthy, they are surely quite different to our own, according to current European thinking.

The hotly debated question of Nato membership indicates that institutionally integrating the East is not merely a technical problem. The current Western enthusiasm to integrate at least some East European states into the alliance, stands in apparently stark contrast to equivocation over EU expansion to the East. Membership for Poland, the Czech Republic and Hungary is expected to be confirmed in mid-1997, in time for the fiftieth anniversary of the alliance. Curiously, however, the significant cost (into the billions of pounds) of such an enterprise has not been raised as an obstacle. The United States, in particular, is apparently so determined to ensure the security of the new democracies that Nato expansion has been announced as the defining foreign policy objective of Clinton's second term. Indeed, the whole discussion of Nato expansion appears to turn the clock back regarding the problems of East and West in Europe. Once again it would seem that it is Russia which stands as the barrier confronting Eastern Europe, and the West which is doing its best to rescue its Eastern neighbours. Western determination to integrate Eastern Europe militarily could even be seen to be the first step toward their fuller economic and political integration, and the final, if belated, reunification of the continent.

So why is it considered so important for East European countries to join a military alliance organised exclusively to combat communism? Communism no longer exists, and even if some sort of Russian threat could be seen to have become a replacement, who can seriously argue that the Russian military is about to invade Eastern Europe? Hypothetically supposing there were an intention to do so, these are the armed forces, we should remember, which proved incapable of defeating, often even engaging, a small force of Chechen rebels.

From an East European perspective, it is clear that Nato membership is indeed viewed as a first step toward wider integration – establishing a foot in the door to the more important Western institutions, especially the EU. They are not faced with foreseeable military threat, and their scramble to gain admittance to the alliance only makes sense in the context of continued exclusion from the West. For Eastern Europe, it is a substitute for wider integration and investment. This is the spirit of Lech Walesa's joke that if he couldn't have American generals on Polish soil, a General Motors plant flying the stars and stripes would do. Denied access to Europe, costly and purposeless membership of Nato will have to do for the new democracies of Eastern Europe. For Russia too, this issue is not essentially concerned with military affairs. Expressing opposition to expansion is an all too rare opportunity for Russia to pose as a great power, as it appears to be these two 'superpowers' who are once again determining the fate of Europe. Russian opposition to expansion, and their ominous talk of the revival of Cold War tensions was entirely rhetorical however. Behind the scenes, American Secretary of State Madeline Albright was already talking of United States–Russian cooperation, even a joint military brigade, before any public agreement over the 'row'. The real issue for Yeltsin was using their rhetorical opposition to Nato expansion as a means of extracting concessions from the West, specifically entry to the exclusive G7, now 'G7 plus one', group of major powers.

The apparent contrast between Western reluctance to even discuss the question of EU expansion to the East, and firm resolve to integrate some East European states militarily, is not as contradictory as it might first appear. The German enthusiasm for Nato expansion which began around 1993 and the more recent United States conversion to the cause are, as with Russia and Eastern Europe, not about military affairs in themselves. They are certainly not driven by a determination to heal European divisions, and constitute the first step toward the end of East and West in Europe. Without the Cold War, Nato lacks purpose or direction, as indeed do the principal Western powers which make up the alliance. Politicising the expansion of Nato has given a Clinton administration, now reliant upon the international arena for moral authority, much needed coherence. Setting the task of expansion to the East also casts Germany as the central shaping factor of Nato in Europe. More broadly, promoting this issue is an attempt to recreate old certainties in international affairs, and at least take some of the more uncomfortable questions posed by the end of the Cold War off the agenda. In this it has been largely successful. While that discussion continues to be shaped by negotiations over expansion, no one asks what Nato actually is, why the United States is still organising European affairs, or indeed, why the end of the Cold War has not led to the proper reunification of Europe, only attempts to relive the East–West battles of the past?

Significantly, the voices of Eastern Europe have rarely been heard in the West during a debate which is ostensibly solely concerned with their futures. The real stuff of this exercise are high profile summits organised around the United States. Overall it is evident that 'liberated' Eastern Europe has not been welcomed with open arms by the West. It remains excluded economically and politically. Partial military integration has become a poor substitute and, more importantly, a means for the West of sustaining in a modified form the old status quo. All in all, the new Eastern Europe has been treated less like an opportunity than a problem.

Cold War Sympathy

Back in the Cold War, when Eastern Europe was dominated by the USSR, matters were very different. Then, it was said, the West would have liked nothing better than for the region to free itself of Russian control, and be greeted with open arms by their fellow Europeans. Eastern Europe was not a problem, but a victim.

It is now difficult to recall that in the post-war years, these were the peoples who stood as the symbol of Western freedom against the totalitarian menace. At the height of the Cold War back in 1959, the United States held its Captive Nations Week for the states of East Central Europe apparently held hostage by Soviet power. Through the 1960s and 1970s, they continued to represent opposition to the denial of democracy said to be at the very heart of the Western political project. After all, these were peoples who had voted with their feet in flocking to the West before the Berlin Wall descended, and were now prevented from rejoining their compatriots in the West only by force of arms.

The United States President Gerald Ford made it clear in the early 1970s that they remained at the top of the Western agenda. 'We still weep for the Polish workers of Poznan ...' he declared, 'We are still outraged over the bloodbath 17 years ago in Hungary ... Our hearts go out to the people of Czechoslovakia ....'[10] In the 1980s, the East's victim status became, if anything, more pronounced. The images of Solidarity's battle for freedom rarely left our television screens. Even Western conservatism had apparently found its militant cause, as the Polish trade union's symbol was reproduced on T-shirts and badges, and Margaret Thatcher announced her sympathies. So too Ronald Reagan, who encouraged all Americans to place a lit candle for Poland in their window after Solidarity's demise in 1981.

These words were rarely backed by action, despite the frequent declarations of solidarity – there was not even the tokenistic boycotting of the Olympic Games that marked the Soviet invasion of Afghanistan. Words in fact were at the heart of the West's campaign, with the funding of Radio Free Europe to broadcast its message of the virtues of Western society to Russia and the satellites. Nevertheless, although we might view Reagan's tears over Solidarity a little cynically, there was no question that they would be welcomed with open arms should they manage to liberate themselves – even if it would have to be achieved without the assistance of Nato and the West.

The suggestion frequently encountered today, that East Europeans have a predisposition to non-democratic government, was markedly absent until the end of the communist bloc. Defiant uprisings in the face of Russian armour – most notably in Hungary and Czechoslovakia – surely demonstrated their refusal to resign themselves to the absence of liberty. Perhaps, unlike others outside the 'free world', the peoples of Eastern Europe had a unique affinity with the West. As one academic describing *The Dynamics of Communism* in 1961 explained, 'The peoples of Eastern Europe, in contrast to those of Russia and Asia, were therefore well aware of alternatives to authoritarian government.'[11] As for the source of any historical backwardness, according to a popular text of the period, its origins lay in 'Colonial rule over Eastern Europe for most of the last two hundred years ....'[12] Even if it was behind the West economically, it was still seen to have more in common with the First, rather than the Third World. As the author continues, while it may be '... poorer than Western Europe', it was certainly 'far wealthier ... than most of Africa, Asia and Latin America'.

There was no question, therefore, '...that the aspirations of East Europeans, are, of course, the same as those of people anywhere ...'.[13] They were 'one of us', or at least potentially so. As late as 1991, the EC's official publicity on the new Eastern Europe quoted above declared that 'Under communism, the desire of the peoples of Eastern Europe to return to fundamental principles of freedom and democracy was always present, rising irrepressibly to the surface at regular intervals.'[14] No wonder that the existence of communism in Eastern Europe was not publicly regarded as 'organic' – something naturally rooted in the character of society and its peoples. It had been introduced from the outside at a moment of weakness following the devastation wrought by the Second World War, according to the declared view of the time.

This sympathetic perspective was then dramatically confirmed in the heady events of the late 1980s. In 1989 and 1990, they tore down the artificial barrier separating East and West with their bare hands. In one fell swoop, 40 years of history were apparently erased and many anticipated the rapid erosion of the East–West divide. After all, quite apart from anything else, 'The "East" and the "West" have much more in common now than they have had at any time since the Second World War...' as one economist explained.[15] Consequently, for the European intellectual Claudio Magris summarising that consensus, 'It would be unthinkable to construct a Europe from which they will be excluded.' Further, 'After the great events of 1989, at least we now know that there is no "Other Europe" and that the lands of Central and Eastern Europe share our destiny.'[16] In a similar spirit, *The Economist* pointed out that, 'The division of Europe between East and West was a product of Soviet power. It cannot survive its extinction.'[17] Europe could now be united, and the notion of an 'Eastern Europe', long understood to be a term exclusively identified with the Cold War Soviet capture of traditional Central Europe, could be confined to the proverbial 'dustbin of history'.

The Reappearance of Divisions

After the heady euphoria of the revolutions, 1990 was indeed the year of hope and optimism. The influential United States economist Jeffrey Sachs looked forward to an Eastern Europe '... very much in the style of the United States and even more closely in the style of Western Europe'.[18] Eastern Europe remained at the centre of Western attentions, partly, as the Slovene academic Slavoj Zizek pointed out, because events there suggested 'the reinvention of democracy'.[19] Otherwise flagging principles of the West were reinvigorated by the fact that East Europeans were apparently prepared to risk their lives for Western democracy, according to Zizek. This proved to be only a passing phase however.

Remarkably quickly, there were ominous suggestions that not all of the region might be able to enjoy immediate benefits, and that divisions would not be overcome as easily as expected. Some were apparently more 'Eastern' than others. According to the renowned journalistic commentator on the region Misha Glenny, already, 'By the Summer of 1990 the West appeared to have divided Eastern Europe in two.'[20] Not all the peoples of the region were the same according to a rapidly developing Western consensus. For the Conservative Minister Nicholas Ridley for example, there was an important distinction to be made between those who had indicated sufficient '... determination to join the free world', namely Poland, Hungary, Czechoslovakia and East Germany, and the rest, who apparently lacked such resolve.[21] This was reflected in the packages of financial support which individual Western countries and European institutions drew up; they generally favoured this new 'Central Europe' of Hungary, Poland and Czechoslovakia (East Germany of course, ceased to exist).

Timothy Garton Ash, among others, celebrated the apparent recognition that integration was at least a possibility for some. The ground had really shifted quite considerably in the direction of establishing limits rather than greater opportunities, however, not least in the fact that integration now appeared conditional upon conduct – in particular the approach taken toward market reform. Out of this, a new threefold division has emerged between an 'East Central' Europe, 'the Balkans' and 'Eastern Europe' proper (Belarus, Ukraine and Russia). Significantly here, the measure is not so much geographical, as the extent to which they have conformed to externally imposed standards. Thus 'East Central' Europe according to a standard academic explanation is such because these are '... countries that have made a decisive break with their communist past, taken concerted steps towards the establishment of a democratic political system, embarked on privatisation and the construction of a market economy ...'.[22]

Democracy and the market exist in all these societies – to an extent in a more unregulated and therefore perhaps fuller sense than in the West. Nevertheless, a peculiar 'how much like us are they?' test has been used to redraw the map of Europe. Maybe this was good news for those who made the grade and managed to slip into 'East Central' Europe, but it has disturbing implications for the rest, those deemed to have indicated insufficient enthusiasm for 'the free world'. More broadly, qualifying the potential for integration was evidently part of an increasingly bleak outlook regarding the region as a whole.

By the end of 1991, the general consensus had become blatantly pessimistic. The development of war in Yugoslavia created near panic in the West, and was seen to anticipate a wider emergence of submerged ethnic conflict. In some senses, this was a remarkable turnaround. Retrospectively blaming this about turn on media punditry, the editor of the *Atlantic Monthly* describes the shift from the end of the Cold War when, '... the world was said to be flowering with hundreds of democracies. A year or two later, the world was degenerating into hideous ethnic feuds.'[23] Whatever the cause of this anticipation of conflict in the East, however, Yugoslavia was not seen as a one off, but a sign of things to come.

Quite apart from the outbreak of war on European soil for the first time in 40 years, it began to appear unlikely that the new democracies would be able to catch up economically in the near future – if at all. A prosperity divide was going to replace the political divide of the Cold War. As a journalistic report in that year remarked, the EU was already '... a rich man's club, against whose frosty window panes the Easterners will press their noses for a long time ...'.[24] After all, most of the countries on the prosperous half of the divide were deep in recession, so prospects were surely even gloomier for their poorer neighbours to the East. In a few short years the division appeared complete, as the *Times Atlas of European History* now explains. According to this representative account,

> The immediate euphoria following the fall of the Berlin wall had evaporated by 1993. Europe once more seemed divided in two: an Eastern zone of instability and poverty beset by ethnic tensions and open warfare, and a Western area, above all the EU, prosperous, if still prone to regionalist movements.[25]

Clearly it was not simply a question of a prosperity divide according to the new consensus that evolved in Western analysis. There was perhaps an even more profound problem of political culture that stood in the way of transformation. Despite having apparently demonstrated their desire for democracy by overthrowing the old regimes, consolidating these gains was considered an altogether more difficult task. This would require more than the politics of rejection – saying no to foreign domination. Democracy would have to be fought for, and built. Already in early 1992, a briefing for schools on the subject by *The Economist* asserted that '... removing communism will not alone bring democracy'.[26] Where the end of dictatorship in Spain and Portugal in the 1970s brought its more or less straightforward return, matters were apparently not so simple when it came to the East.

To an extent, this related to economic problems; without prosperity a healthy society would struggle to establish itself. More importantly, however, the legacy of an undemocratic past would weigh down the present, and maybe the future. This past now figures prominently in understanding the region. The prominent historian and high profile writer on Central Europe, Tony Judt, for example, thus sees that the experience of Nazism and communism combined to eradicate the basis for law and rights. His pessimism is based on history rather than the present. From this, he foresees a further revival of nationalism. More broadly, the sense that supposedly native traditions of intolerance and resentment would persist, and even intensify, has itself intensified. Such a vision of the East's future was posed with growing conviction in works such as those of Jowitt. It is manifest in the peculiar framework through which developments in the region have subsequently been understood. The extent of 'transition' to the Western model has become the measure of progress, spawning a new academic industry to replace the old 'Kremlinology' of the past. 'Transitology' now involves a veritable army of analysts measuring the extent of 'transition' in the various societies of the former communist bloc, even though it still remains unclear what they are in transit to, and how it will be clear that they have finally arrived. But if it is unclear when transition has been accomplished, it would certainly appear that to be deemed 'in transition' is a dubious distinction indeed. No wonder the most self-confident politician in the region, the Czech leader Vaclav Klaus, categorically insists that his own country has long since made it.

It is also important to understand that a significant undercurrent of pessimism with regard to the prospects for the region was there from the very beginning. Witness the 22 May 1989 cover of *New Republic*, and that of the 25 November *The Economist* for example. The former headlined with 'Can the East Europeans get the hang of it?', while *The Economist* simply begged the question 'Gatecrashers Europe?' Interestingly in both, East Europeans are portrayed as exotic and rather surly peasant types; in other words, 'gatecrashers' who looked distinctly unlikely to 'get the hang of it'. In a similar spirit, a reporter who visited the region in mid-1989 noted that 'The bleakest new thought this survey writer brought back from Eastern Europe is that the main obstacle to freedom's return is neither political nor economic, but something deeper ... to persuade people to resume the responsibility for decision taking ....'[27] Away from public expressions of support (and surprise – most commentators refused to recognise their imminent collapse right up to the last moment), there was considerable unease at the implications of change. To this day, many in the United States see in the EU's reluctance to admit their Eastern neighbours, profound fears about migration and agricultural competition for example.

That commentators were already anticipating problems on the basis of the distinctive qualities of East Europeans is significant. It suggests a predisposition to problematise that is not simply given by a worrying set of issues posed by the peculiarities of the region itself. Long before so-called 'ethnic cleansing', or any other of the developments within the former Soviet bloc still said to account for Western pessimism were even on the horizon, a significant minority were already foretelling disaster. A highly defensive sensitivity to intractable cultural barriers was discernible even in 1989. It is perhaps not too speculative to suggest that this outlook among Western observers was already in place before they turned to the East, and therefore that its source lay within the West itself. Given the disjuncture between perception and reality here, it would not be illogical to suppose that the presentiment of disaster in the East and the consequent impulse to keep it at arm's length was determined by a consciousness already shaped by negative experiences closer to home in the West itself. Despite any predisposition, however, the formalising of the increasing qualifications attached to Cold War promises are nevertheless very important, particularly as it was through this process that a new perspective on the region emerged.

However we understand the reaction, East–West European unification was already written off by 1992. 'In the intervening three years, the assumption that the East European countries would promptly become West European countries has also vanished', explained an American analyst.[28] To reiterate, this was not merely a matter of suggesting that real democracy had not been established – nor even that it might take longer than expected. There was a hardening conviction that the region would never be a normal part of the continent, and perhaps remain somehow 'Eastern'. With remarkable speed, the earlier assumption at the heart of European politics – that division was a temporary condition born of an unfortunate post-war settlement – was abandoned. In its place arose a new certainty; that the two halves of the continent are quite distinct, and will always be so. In line with this new pessimism, the whole experience of the last few years, and indeed the previous period, has come in for reappraisal. There have been a number of important areas in which a redefinition began to take place; the problem of expectations, a nostalgia for the old regimes, the real nature of the revolutions, and the very meaning of democracy itself.

Redefining the Problems – 'Expectations' and Nostalgia

The relative failure of rapid transformation has been scantily dealt with in the literature as an economic question. There have been few attempts to locate the relative paucity of investment in the region – in many respects the key question – in a global perspective. It has become more common to suggest that it was foolish to have ever imagined that East could become like West. This view was articulated by Vladimir Tismaneanu, one of the principal United States based academic writers on the region. For him, 'The East European dilemma is aggravated by unrealistic expectations about what it means to adopt Western values.'[29] So too for the renowned foreign policy guru Zbigniew Brzezinski. The very first lesson of the transformation process for him, 'Is that expectations on both sides – in the old communist states and in the West – were much too high, and rather naive.'[30] Others are more reluctant to state this case so forthrightly. After all, it openly suggests that the prosperity of Western society is more of a dream, an advertisement, than a reality that can be realised. This is understandably not a message with which many commentators feel comfortable, and therefore few will state so openly as the brash Brzezinski. Nevertheless, it is a widely shared assumption that the apparent crisis of the East is the fault of having expected too much from those societies.

This sense of regret for the loss of old arrangements is strengthened by the changing reflections on the communist period itself. Here too, a substantial revision of the public consensus on Eastern Europe is evident. There is a tangible sense of nostalgia for the period of Soviet domination. Such a perspective was anticipated by the thorny problems apparently thrown up by the events of the late 1980s. The key question, that of German reunification, led Margaret Thatcher to famously declare herself happier with the Berlin Wall staying put. However distasteful, even an arch anti-communist like the former British Prime Minister was all too aware that Soviet control had at least removed the historically troublesome German question from the European agenda. Interestingly, her fears that Germany would arise once again were placated only by reassurance that acquiring the problem of the East would be more of a burden than an opportunity. At a famous consultation with historians at Chequers, Thatcher was told by the former Oxford historian Norman Stone '... that East Germany was not an accretion of strength, but, rather, 12 enormous Liverpools, handed over in a tatty cardboard box, with a great red ribbon round it, marked "From Russia with love"'.[31]

The apparent unleashing of nationalist tensions throughout the region led many others to suggest that, for all its faults, perhaps communism had at least kept a lid on historic problems with which Europe would prefer not to deal. As American academic Daniel Nelson put it, 'For all that was reprehensible about Soviet control ...', it at least 'dampened the antagonisms that have bedevilled Eastern Europe'.[32] For the historian Philip Longworth meanwhile, 'If one regards Soviet communism as a disease, then it seems that Eastern Europe may have had a predisposition to the infection.'[33] In other words, communism was 'meant to be' in Eastern Europe, rather than the accidental by-product of the rapid advance of the Russian army at the end of the war.

As with decrying 'unrealistic' expectations, these open declarations of nostalgia for authoritarian rule among Western commentators are also problematic, challenging as they do unequivocal identification with democracy. But such views are not unrepresentative, even if they are stated more plainly than most would prefer. This consensus can be seen in the general response to the success of nominally socialist parties that emerged in various Central and East European countries in the mid-1990s (a development already reversed in the November 1996 elections in Romania and Bulgaria). Support for these parties was automatically and sympathetically diagnosed as an understandable reaction to the damaging rigours of the free market. Western commentators thus implicitly share the feeling that perhaps things were better under the communists, as they do not ask whether voting for so-called 'socialist' parties might not be what it seems. The pervasive sense that the market is bringing ruin to the new Eastern Europe implicitly casts the Stalinist era as a period of relative calm and stability by comparison.

Real 'Revolutions'?

A third significant area of reappraisal, although rather more complex and important, concerns the nature of the change process itself.

Recent books on this subject question whether very much at all really changed in the late 1980s. With a particular focus on events in Romania and Hungary, some authors now suggest that the end of communism was more a change of appearance than of substance – at least in relation to some specific events, if not in characterising the experience as a whole. It is now commonly acknowledged that the old elites remain in power, a fact which in itself implies that the transformations of the late 1980s were far from thoroughgoing. For some writers therefore, particularly those of a conservative and cynical disposition, the 'revolutions' of 1989 and 1990 now stand in inverted commas, denoting their lack of authenticity. As Tad Szulc states with disdain, '... communism collapsed from internal rot .... It was not defeated by freedom loving masses as legend makers here and there would have us believe.'[34]

If we carefully examine the actual events of '1989 and all that', it is indeed difficult to conclude that these were revolutions in any meaningful sense of the term. There was not even the appearance of social change in cases such as Hungary or Bulgaria. Insofar as a general picture emerges from the various national episodes that made up '1989 and all that', it is that the real transfer of power took place behind closed doors, as the old communists repositioned themselves to take over in a manufactured democracy. This was the signal sent out by Gorbachev in the late 1980s; that unless they acted fast to abolish their old roles and reinvented themselves in democratic clothes, they would be left to their own fate. There would be no support for unreconstructed Stalinists from the new Soviet leaders. And without a Soviet guarantee, the East European nomenclature lacked legitimacy, and therefore had little choice but to follow their lead in attempting reform.

Even where there was an appearance of dramatic change, as with the gun battles on the streets of Bucharest, this was only a rearguard action by a section of the secret police. The old apparatchiks displaced were generally a minority who had failed to realise what was going on, or were for some other reason incapable of making the necessary adjustments. Their more astute and ambitious colleagues meanwhile had been gearing themselves up for change throughout the 1980s; sending their sons and daughters to business schools in the United States, and using their official contacts with the West to sound out potential trading partners. The old elite was uncommitted to a system which was clearly unsustainable from the mid-1980s at the latest. In 1986 Hungary's leading reform communist Imre Pozsgay, for example, submitted a report, 'Turning Point and Reform', which called for the full implementation of the profit motive, law, rights and an independent judiciary. More far reaching proposals for pluralism and neutrality followed. In mid-1987 Mieczyslaw Rakowski, the Deputy Prime Minister in Poland, gave Jaruzelski a secret report noting that the Soviets could no longer be counted on for support, and that their best chance for survival lay in regrouping in a democracy. Of course, most significantly, Gorbachev came to power in Russia and embarked on a survival strategy of reforming communism in order to retain authority. Those elites in Eastern Europe who had not independently realised that things had to change, were forced by Gorbachev to commit themselves to a strategy of relocating their roles in a capitalist democracy – in effect to attempt a transition from a Stalinist bureaucracy to a capitalist class. The sooner this was embarked upon, the better the chance of survival, and, from Gorbachev's point of view, the greater chance of retaining friends for Russia in high places in their former satellites.

Having committed themselves to such a transformation, the isolated and unpopular elites then proceeded to build links with potential reformers as Pozsgay did in 1987. Invariably this was through 'round table' talks following a declaration that the old party had changed its ways. Mladenov in Bulgaria for example, once he had removed President Zhivkov, announced the country was to become a modern democratic pluralist state and would hold elections after round table talks. The old apparatus was announced as a 'modern party of the European left'. Opposition forces were drawn into a process of managed reform. This was far from unproblematic. However, this was not due to the power of revolutionary forces, or even popular pressure. If anything, the problem was the lack of any opposition to integrate. Critical currents throughout the region had become increasingly marginal and demoralised since the traumas of Hungary in 1956 and Czechoslovakia in 1968. More generally, these were highly individualised and atomised societies where the struggle for personal and family survival mitigated against any form of real collectivity. The opposition in Czechoslovakia for example, had to be virtually created out of nothing after demonstrations stimulated by false reports (widely considered to have been started by the KGB) that students had been killed in demonstrations on 17 November. Far from facing revolutionary opposition, in the late 1980s the bureaucracy was trying to identify and elevate potential partners in a joint project to 'rejoin Europe'.

Even in the one place where there was organised opposition, Poland, where Solidarity might have been expected to render elite strategies difficult, Jaruzelski retained the initiative in the late 1980s. Economically, much of the old elite turned itself into a new capitalist class through control of the privatisation process. Politically, through the round table talks in the winter of 1988–89, they integrated (and split) the former opposition. It took place behind closed doors, reflecting the fact that the transition and the new political formations never contained any popular input. Nor did this elite bargain go unnoticed by the population at large. Considerable bitterness was created in Poland and elsewhere by the retention of power by the core, and sometimes even the heads of the old elite.

This is not to argue that all elites, certainly not all the top leaders, pushed for transformation. Generally it was those more confident of their ability to dissolve and reconstitute themselves, like the Hungarian nomenclature, who willingly embarked upon such a course. Others, like Zhivkov in Bulgaria and Jakes in Czechoslovakia, who doubted their ability to survive in a new environment, resisted change. They had to be pressured by Gorbachev, and eventually sacrificed 'for the greater good' of the old elite as a whole. Under these circumstances, it fell to those who were lesser known, or less compromised to push through with the survival strategy. Overall, this was a process of managed change from above, not revolution from below. It was an 'elite bargain' as it has been dubbed by some experts, in this respect akin to the successful self-abolition of apartheid in order to preserve their essential domination of society embarked upon by the South African elite from the late 1980s. More cynically we might describe a process of 'rats jumping a sinking ship'.

To an extent, the greater receptivity to seeing the process of change more critically is the product of the greater pessimism that developed in the early 1990s. Some certainly looked back in the light of subsequent developments. That reappraisal was coloured by new fears is evident from suggestions that not only was there no real change, but that it was driven by 'tribal loyalties' rather than a desire for freedom. For Michael Walzer of the radical American magazine *Dissent* for example: 'It is now apparent that the popular energies mobilised against totalitarian rule ... were fuelled in good part by "tribal" loyalties and passions.'[35] The preoccupation with ethnic nationalism which emerged in the wake of the Yugoslav war, led to new interpretations of the 'so-called revolutions'. Given that there was little popular energy mobilised against totalitarian rule, it is difficult to know why it has become 'apparent' to Michael Walzer that 'tribal loyalties' lay behind these events. It would appear to be a retrospective interpretation made in the light of the discourse of 'tribal loyalties' which subsequently developed.

At the same time, it is important to realise that the debate over the events of 1989 is not clear cut. It is undoubtedly the case that a rubbishing of those events is more evident than at the time. On the other hand, many still, at least publicly, insist that these were real revolutions. Indeed, events are reinterpreted in the other direction by some, in the sense that they have been made even more revolutionary than anyone ever suggested. The Polish sociologist Piotr Sztompka, for example, continues to make extraordinary claims for the events of that year. According to him, these were '... drastic, dramatic changes of regime ...' which 'occurred due to the extreme mobilisation of the masses and huge social movements ...'.[36] He produces no evidence to substantiate this remarkable assertion.

The argument for revolutions is based more on word play than evidence. Sztompka asserts for example that 'the breakdowns of the communist regimes are revolutions'. But of course a breakdown is not the same as a revolution; this is why they are quite distinct words, with very different meanings. To conflate the two is a sleight of hand. 'Did it fall' or 'was it pushed', is not the same question, and has very different consequences. While any revolution coincides with a social crisis, this is not to say they are the same thing. In this case we are not so much talking about a revolution where power was wrenched from their grasp, as a process where the elite abandoned its former role in society.

Given the overwhelming material that now supports this analysis of events, it is remarkable that Sztompka and others insist on referring not only to 'revolutions' but explicitly to mass participation. More qualified judgments argue that what began as a process of reform from above, then got out of hand and became a revolution. Without doubt, the elite even in such a passive climate, could not and did not retain control throughout. It was always risky, but there was little choice given the economic and moral collapse of these societies. Nevertheless, losing control does not a revolution make. The mass of the populations did not generally even have a walk-on part. In countries like Hungary and Bulgaria, the elite abdicated without any popular protest (and it was the actions of the Hungarian elite which precipitated the crisis in East Germany by allowing safe passage to Austria). Where there were demonstrations, as in Czechoslovakia, they were passive and apolitical – certainly not revolutionary. The marginal individuals who found themselves 'representing' these protests, such as Charter 77, were quickly voted out of office after the transition – reflecting the fact that they were thrust to the fore more by accident than design and had no basis for sustaining themselves. They were not the leaders of a revolutionary movement; Vaclav Havel had long since renounced the quest for power as playing the same game as the bureaucratic enemy, and self-consciously pursued an anti-political programme.

Ultimately the case for there having been revolutions in Eastern Europe derives from redefining the meaning of 'revolution'. In this respect it is hardly surprising that there has been an academic debate on the 'meaning' of revolutions occasioned by the events of the late 1980s. The general impulse here is to ever widen the scope of what can be considered a 'revolution'. This is reflected in the popular description of a 'velvet revolution' to describe the abandonment of power by the Stalinists in Czechoslovakia. We can only presume that a new term is needed to describe events precisely because this was not a revolution at all. We should add that this redefinition cannot be considered a useful refinement of the term that captures the particularities of that process. 'Velvet revolution' is no more meaningful than, and might as well be called, 'nice revolution'. Above all it gives us no sense of the way in which the decisive aspects of that experience took place behind closed doors, not on the streets.

Is it merely being pedantic, even unsympathetic, to challenge this process of generously widening the scope of 'revolution' so as to include what happened in Eastern Europe? First, it is important to recall the consequences. The notion of a 'revolution' becomes meaningless and all sense of proportion is lost. Where does a real attempt at the seizing of state power and self-regulation of society such as happened in Hungary in 1956 stand in this light? Are we to conclude that that experience is to be equated with the elite manoeuvrings that took place in Bulgaria, Hungary, Poland and the rest in 1989? Even more importantly, we need to retain a sense of perspective because it allows us to ask the question why there is such a determination to assert that they were revolutions when it is not warranted by the facts. No doubt some were excited by that experience and through sympathy with the peoples of Eastern Europe feel it is right that their contribution be recognised. Understandable enthusiasm might then account for playing up a role for 'the people' that is not warranted by the actually negligible part that they played: confusing the undoubtedly historic significance of these events with a revolution. However, it is clear that writers such as Sztompka have little identification with 'the people', or indeed any sense of excitement about that experience in fact, quite the opposite.

Reading between the lines of this literature, the insistence on revolutions appears to be posited in order to back up an argument that the problem now is the cultural habits of the people in the region, a people with a '... general lack of discipline and diligence' (among many other personal failings) according to Sztompka.[37] In order to blame the problems of society on the shortcomings of its inhabitants, it must be 'insisted' that they have played a central part in developments since the end of communism. If we recognise the people to have been marginalised from events since the very beginning, they can hardly be held responsible for anything that followed.

All those who insist on the absence of 'civil society' must continue to pay lip service to the notion that 'people's power' drove the process of transformation. Without this misreading, the targeting of East Europeans' alleged lack of 'the art of association' becomes more difficult. If it is recognised that the peoples of the region have been innocent bystanders, it can hardly be argued that their failings are at the heart of the problem now. While there is rewriting of the past to argue that nothing really happened, therefore, at least publicly, there has to remain an insistence on there having been 'revolutions' in 1989. Considerable scepticism is therefore quite appropriate whenever it is insisted that it was revolutions that swept through the region in the late 1980s. What might appear a more positive, if naive, endorsement of the capacity of ordinary people to bring about change, is perhaps even more cynical than Szulc's contemptuous dismissal of 'freedom loving masses'. The flattering of the people's role back in 1989 is part and parcel of the process of rewriting the original aspirations involved in ending the division of Europe. Arguing that they were central to the process of change makes them responsible for the decidedly disappointing outcome. Cultural barriers of the people replace the real barriers maintained by 'Fortress Europe'.

These events have therefore been rewritten in both directions – both being shaped not so much by new evidence, as differing intellectual priorities. The real issue that underlies these differences is the stake in promoting the most important redefined objective for Eastern Europe, that they need 'civil society' not 'mere' democracy.

From Democracy to 'Civil Society'

The most important example of redefining the issues is the shift in the measure, indeed the definition, of democracy. Back in the 1980s, the overriding objective was simply restoring freedom of expression and political pluralism – the opportunity to vote for the party of your choice. This is now the case throughout the region, and certainly at a time when politics in the West has narrowed to the contestation of the centre ground, and parties have become virtually indistinguishable, at least formally in Eastern Europe, there remain a variety of political options on offer to the electorate. Where 'left' and 'right' have become largely meaningless in the West as all have merged in the centre, in some countries of the East there remain parties representing, on paper at least, competing visions of the future; communist, social democratic, liberal and conservative. Certainly in comparison to Western contests such as the recent Presidential elections in the United States, the turnout generally remains high, as does the occasional show of enthusiasm for the outcome – as demonstrated in the defeat of Iliescu with the November 1996 elections in Romania for example. What is more, mass protest in the likes of Serbia and Bulgaria in early 1997 appears capable of bringing about a change of government in a way which is now unimaginable in the West. As has been indicated, however, this is no longer considered sufficient to qualify the polities in the region as truly democratic. Instead, the goal is now one of establishing 'civil society', a phrase which has become a mantra for academics, policy makers and activists alike.

Precisely what constitutes 'civil society' is difficult to say. It has undergone a series of transformations in meaning since its formative modern use by the Scottish Enlightenment thinker Adam Ferguson to delineate the rise of bourgeois society. In some respects we can say, however, that it is only a repackaging of the goal of democracy. As the sociologist Krishan Kumar points out in his interesting survey of the history of the term, 'Civil society simply becomes all that is desired in the making of a democratic society ....'[38] In the context of the terms; contemporary revival in Western proscriptions for the East however, it goes further and specifically highlights the cultural 'habits of the heart' and 'art of association' (demonstrated by the strength of civic institutions) now deemed necessary to qualify non Western societies as truly democratic. A society that lacks these 'arts' and 'habits' is not truly civil. Significantly here, the question immediately posed is: who is to say when Eastern Europe has established 'civil society'? How do we quantify this 'art'? There can be little doubt when elections are taking place – it is a clear measure of the existence of democracy. The shift to establishing 'civil society' before the existence of democracy is acknowledged, is a redefinition whose principal consequence is making the fulfilment of democracy a more elusive, even potentially impossible goal.

What is especially ironic is that it was precisely East Europeans themselves who not only reinvented the term in the 1970s and 1980s, but also put it into practice – certainly in its previous, more particular meaning as civil movements outside of the state. The experience of defeat at the hands of the Soviet Union, most importantly in the crushing of the Hungarian revolution in 1956, led to the demoralisation of opposition and resistance throughout the region. In particular, it was no longer seen to be realistic to fight for power. The quest for power, and even the pursuit of politics, was consciously eschewed. Instead, the best that could be achieved was to ignore the state, and limit opposition to the withdrawal of consent. Most importantly through the actions of Solidarity in Poland, 'civil society' was reborn as an alliance of trade unionists and intellectuals carving out a separate sphere of activity which bypassed the state. Interestingly now, with the further redefinition of the term, 'civil society' has been turned back on those who reinvented it, and put it into practice, and the demand is made that they conform to its vagaries.

George Soros, the Hungarian born multimillionaire who has been at the forefront of westernisation, sees 'civil society', or as he prefers it, the 'open society' (from his mentor the philosopher Karl Popper), as something which 'sets free the critical powers of man'. But it is no surprise that arguably the most combative and independent politician in the region decisively rejects the term as he does also the dubious notion of 'transition'. The no nonsense Vaclav Klaus has made it plain that 'If necessary, I will fight with all my might to preserve the term "democratic society".... For me the term "democratic society" is enough.'[39] He rightly senses in the term 'civil society' a means of presenting new obstacles in the path of an acknowledgement that his country is as much a democracy as any other.

A more substantive criticism of the concept is that it is based upon a profound misreading of the problem with formal democracy. In the process of highlighting the limits to the transformation, both advocates and opponents of the revolutions argument conflate the establishment of formal democracy with the widespread redistribution of power, using the failure of the latter to argue the inadequacy of the former. As a result we are supposed to work to a standard of democracy in the East which is far more ambitious than that of the West, where formal democratic institutions have not transformed social inequalities. Insofar as formal democracy masks social inequality, both East and West, it is a worthy subject of criticism. However, in the context of the moral authority awarded to the West by suggesting that others are more inept and do not warrant the meritorious status of a recognised democracy, the people of the region themselves are being identified as a problem. The masses may not have been politically motivated and organised to make a revolution, but it does not mean they are incapable of carrying out the basic tasks of formal democracy.

Formal democracy does not preclude – indeed as we can see from the Western experience it accompanies – the concentration of social power in the hands of an elite.

A Problem not an Opportunity

No one seriously advocates a return to the old arrangements; a return to communism is obviously not on. In its absence, however, 'post-communist' Europe is seen to be far more of a burden than an opportunity. Without the containment of Soviet domination, all manner of potential problems are seen to threaten. Curiously, the various forces deemed to constitute a problem are rarely substantiated. Keitha Sapsin Fine's ominous portrayal of a region crying out for the 'tolerance training' of Western NGOs is based upon a 'new racism' which she somehow detects. The evidence? There are '... a growing number of active groups of neofascists and skin heads', the author tells us. The only specific fact is that there are '... at least a dozen (fascist) magazines across the region'. We are not told anything about the circulation of these magazines, still less about their popularity or how these 'new racists' are going to establish serious influence within Eastern Europe.

Apparently unconsciously sensing the weakness of a suggestion based on no evidence, Fine then plumps for telling us that they are especially sinister regardless of size. Having mentioned alleged East–West fascist cooperation, the author then tells us that 'The groups differ from western gangs by their instrumental use of violence and the breadth of their intentions ....'[40] From what she draws this conclusion is a mystery. Similarly, a special fifth anniversary supplement by the *Guardian* concluded with the threat of fascism. According to the paper's Richard Gott: '... the age old alternative of clerical fascism – the solution of the inter-war years – is still one of the dangerous possibilities that hang over several of the "liberated" countries of Eastern Europe'.[41] Given the absence of fascist movements in evidence, the journalist's dramatic prognosis was based upon disappointment with illiberal feelings indicated by Czech hostility to wealthy Germans. The implication is that they have 'liberated' only a deeper intolerance and immoderation within the people themselves. This is the thinking behind the title of a British book on the alleged rise of the far right in East European politics. *Free to Hate* by Paul Hockenos implies that 'liberation' should perhaps also stand in inverted commas.[42] Post-communist freedom of movement and expression has only allowed more sinister forces to emerge, is the often unspoken assumption behind such analyses.

An influential formulation in this line of thinking, and the one that informs the extensive interference in support of minority rights in the region by European institutions, is the idea that state oppression of minorities will spiral out of control. For *The Economist,* 'The real worry about East European security is more subtle. It is that nationalist tensions, tightened up either by conflicts with neighbours, or with smaller groups within countries ... could cause a gradual shift of attitudes towards paranoid nationalists.'[43] The scenario is neither subtle, nor has it turned out to be true. Mechanical formulations whereby East European societies will automatically set about the oppression of minorities, which in turn helps consolidate anti-democratic politics have not transpired.

We have indeed travelled a long way from the 'victim' status of the region during the Cold War. Far from being welcomed with open arms as might have been expected according to the declarations of Western politicians, Eastern Europe is now regarded as a problem – and one that refuses to go away. In seeking an explanation for this unexpected state of affairs, the gaze has turned on the apparent peculiarities of Russia and Eastern Europe themselves. Explaining why so little investment has materialised – why total private foreign investment for the area only totalled $10 billion as of 1993 (a figure dwarfed by investment for single countries in Latin America and Asia), or the effect of renewed German domination of the area, has generated little interest. Nor for that matter has there been any questioning of the woeful inadequacy of Western predictions and assumptions about the region. The lack of any correlation between the fortunes of different countries and whether they pursued a 'fast track' or more cautious approach has been conveniently forgotten, as has the widespread assumption that a pogrom of former communists would overshadow political developments (ironically, it has been Germany that has pursued high profile show trials of old Stalinists, for reasons that will be indicated later).

Instead, attention has fixed narrowly upon identifying internal barriers to transformation. 'What is it about this place that stops us investing in it?' is the question asked, rather than the perhaps more logical, 'Why is the world economy so sluggish that it has not been able to take advantage of such an open field?' Ultimately, an insistence that we look for answers by inspecting the character of 'Eastern-ness' can only result in condemnations of the people themselves – just as if we were to try and explain the stagnation of African society outside the context of its subordinate relationship to the world economy, we would be forced to conclude that there is something amiss with the African character.

2

The People as Problem

A Lack of Qualities

More and more, attention has focused on the supposed peculiarities of the region itself in understanding the relative failure of market relations, and the persistence of a divided continent. Much has been made of the legacy of communist rule; a dilapidated infrastructure, grossly inefficient industry and outdated attitudes. With the former problems of industrial inefficiency seeming apparently irresolvable, the focus shifted to an inspection of the qualities, or rather disappointing absence of qualities, among the peoples of this perplexing part of the world. For the historian John Lukacs for example, '... national conditions and, yes national character remain as important as before ...'.[1] Aspects of this 'national character' which are singled out are invariably negative – principally a dangerous nationalism which demands restraint by the West. Part of Jowitt's Leninist legacy is a 'lack of individually self reliant behaviour'.[2] Those seen in the past as victims, are now conceived of in far less flattering terms. Longworth diagnoses a people 'susceptible to rumours' with a 'disinclination to compromise and tendencies to romanticism and romantic excess'.[3] Altogether, they seem less like us than ever before.

This sweeping stereotyping transcends the political spectrum. In the liberal *Guardian* newspaper, Jonathan Eyal tells us that, 'moderation and consistency were never great Balkan virtues'.[4] Meanwhile the paper's David Hearst, after explaining that 'Northern Ireland is a model of cerebral calm by comparison', expressed surprise that 'You can have quite rational conversations with Serbs.'[5] We can imagine the furore were such remarks to be made about numerous other ethnic groups. With regard to those in 'the Balkans', however, especially the Serbs, it is acceptable to suggest them to be so degraded that it needs pointing out that some retain the ability to hold 'a rational conversation'. The conservative *Sunday Telegraph* meanwhile casts its net even wider. 'There are still two Europes ...' one of which is inhabited by 'a conservative, even curmudgeonly people, relishing authoritarianism and censorship ...', according to their correspondent.[6] Peoples in the other, Western, Europe meanwhile, must be blessed with more attractive qualities – setting the standard against which these negative judgments can be made.

It is striking how casually such unsubstantiated prejudice trips off the tongue. Charles Gati tells us in the world's leading foreign policy journal that '... some of the people of East Central Europe are susceptible to nationalist passions and the authoritarian impulse, but then again many are not'.[7] Gati does not bother to tell us how to tell the difference. Presumably it is of no great moment; normal reasoning probably will not get you very far in this peculiar part of the world! Jowitt, meanwhile, descends into socio-babble. These peoples never developed a 'culture of impersonal measured action', instead, they are only '... familiar with sharp disjunctions between periods of intense action and passivity ...'. They, presumably all the millions of citizens in the former Soviet bloc, would find the '... Protestant liberal capitalist way of life boring, demeaning, and, in good part, unintelligible'.[8] At the same time of course, we are all, perhaps even the poor deficient peoples of Central and Eastern Europe, supposed to find his own talk of 'sharp disjunctions between periods of intense action and passivity' and the like perfectly comprehensible!

Not surprisingly, given such unique proclivities, it is difficult to anticipate behaviour in the usual fashion. 'The Balkans' epitomises the supposed unpredictability, indeed, positive irrationality of the region. There, human behaviour apparently follows little recognisable pattern. 'For much of what is happening there is simply no rational explanation ...' suggests one academic in a typical intellectual contribution on 'The Mystery of Nationalism' in the former Yugoslavia.[9] Keitha Sapsin Fine in her article (mis)titled 'Understanding Conflict During the Transitions', speaks of 'spontaneous combustions' which are 'irrational' and 'defy our attempts at explanation'.[10] Meanwhile, United States news coverage raised even more squarely the question of exactly who is being irrational. 'Once aroused, tribal nationalism rarely defers to reason', declared one writer for *US News and World Report* about the break up of Czechoslovakia. Apparently unaware that the majority of the population were against the division, let alone spilling blood over it – as far as Fouad Ajami was concerned, these were peoples doing 'battle with phantoms and shadows'.[11]

'Demonising' the Serbs?

It is the Serbs of the former Yugoslavia for whom the most vitriolic attacks are reserved, particularly the Bosnian Serbs. The presentation of the Serbs, particularly in Britain and the United States, has been frequently little short of hysterical. According to a resident scholar at the American Enterprise Institute, the Serbs are the '... new barbarians ... motivated by nothing more complicated than primitive ethnic fanaticism'.[12] Nothing more, just fanaticism. In British newspapers like the *Independent*, the Serbs were portrayed as monkeys in cartoons reminiscent of the crudest racial propaganda.[13]

Even with large scale military conflict long over, the presentation of the Serbs in the West has hardly become more balanced. The demonstrators who protested against Milosovic's annulment of local elections in late 1996 were roundly denounced as little better than Milosovic himself. They too, as Serbs, were infected with the same disease according to journalistic reports: the disease of intolerant nationalism. For Chris Hedges of the *New York Times*, for example, it is '... virulent Serbian nationalism that has increasingly coloured the anti government protests'. He complained that journalists such as himself are turned away by protesting students 'as "liars" or "American scum"'. He does not entertain the possibility that Serbs might have legitimate grievances against the reporting of Serbs by Western journalists. Instead, there must be something wrong with Serbian society, and presumably its peoples. He claims that this is '... a society that considers racist remarks to be acceptable and has learned to express itself in the language of hate'.[14] His own language meanwhile is presumably that of international brotherhood and understanding! When it comes to Serbia, the ideological shortcomings of opposition forces are subject to a scrutiny that would appear peculiar in other circumstances. This is leaving aside the fact that the protest movement centred on Belgrade is nothing but diffuse and difficult to characterise in any sort of clear ideological terms.

Attempts have been made to substantiate Serbian 'evil' through history. *Serbia's Secret War* by Philip J. Cohen, for example, is concerned with 'proving' extensive Serbian cooperation with the Nazis.[15] In this revision of history, Serbs are singled out as particular collaborators of the German war machine, despite the widespread acknowledgement that others, like France or Serbia's Croatian neighbour, were far more more directly involved in collaboration – in these cases through the puppet Vichy and Ustashe regimes. Ironically, Cohen's book is subtitled 'Propaganda and the Deceit of

History', which seems a more appropriate title for his own venture, than accurately capturing the wartime relationship between Serbia and Germany. Certainly there is little place here for the mass murders of Serbs carried out by the Wehrmacht, such as those at Kraljevo, Cacak and Pancevo. Others are attempting to indict the Serbs by delving further back into history. Michael A. Sells' recent work argues that the 'roots' of Serbian 'ethnic cleansing' are to be found in the nineteenth century revival of Serb nationalist culture.[16]

For the majority of opinion, however, this hostility is not something which might be described as prejudicial. It continues to be seen as a legitimate response to their singularly brutal behaviour as the driving force behind the whole Yugoslav tragedy. But it is important to understand that the perception of, and action that was then taken against, the Serbs was based upon a very particular, invariably one sided interpretation of the facts.

The stories which circulated were not treated with the sort of caution one would expect. In other conflicts, such as that between Iran and Iraq, claims made by one side or another about numbers of casualties or alleged atrocities are treated as 'claims' and nothing more, without independent corroboration. In any war it is clearly in the interest of all parties to blacken the enemy's name: the propaganda war in modern times is as important as the real war, and truth remains the first casualty. Peculiarly however in the Yugoslav conflict, there was no such caution. Claims such as that of the Bosnian Muslims that some half a million were killed in Bosnia, making it a latter day 'holocaust', have been assumed to be true by Western media and government alike. Similarly, the Bosnian government claim that 250,000 were killed in Sarajevo was accepted, even though the government itself later revised this figure down to 145,000 – itself a highly questionable statistic.

Despite authoritative evidence from George Kenny, former senior diplomat on the American Yugoslavia desk, for example, that the true figures are nowhere near these levels, these Bosnian Muslim claims became fact. Of course, whatever the numbers of dead, this still represents a terrible tragedy. But while contesting casualty levels might seem an inappropriate, even distasteful exercise, it is vital when we consider that if the Muslim claim stands, the Serbs are by clear implication the reincarnation of Nazism, rather than only one of several combatants in a civil war. What is more, the Bosnian experience of that war becomes comparable with the extermination of European Jewry.

The presentation of the Serbs as uniquely responsible rests upon a series of high profile media stories. These were decisive in swinging public opinion – to such an extent that new terms such as 'ethnic cleansing' used to describe Serbian motives entered common parlance. They were also important in determining Western military intervention, and the later prosecution of Serbs for 'war crimes'. The emotive picture of an emaciated Muslim behind barbed wire at Trnopolje camp in August 1992, for example, not only swung Western public opinion against the Serbs, but cast the die for United States intervention and the passing of UN resolutions 770/771, which in turn led to the creation of the War Crimes Tribunal. Other events too, like the Sarajevo marketplace bombs assumed to be the work of the Serbs, and the alleged mass killings of some 8000 Muslims at Srebrenica, were important in setting the world against these 'new barbarians'.

There are entirely plausible alternative accounts of these events which tell a very different story to that of Serbian evil and Croat/Muslim good. Contrary to the impression created by the sensationalist picture of Fikret Alic in Trnopolje, for example, this was not a 'concentration camp' at all – a fact which helps explain why it was not systematically secured against escape. Trnopolje would more accurately be described as a holding camp, with a mixture of those present voluntarily (Muslims from Serb controlled areas afraid of Serbian irregulars); those in transit to other camps – like Fikret Alic; and prisoners of war awaiting exchange for Serbs held by the enemy. It was certainly not a pleasant place to be, but crucially, given the consequences of such a portrayal, Trnopolje was not a 'concentration camp'.

There is a great deal of important information about the war which has been ignored. A suppressed UN report into the February 1994 marketplace bomb in Sarajevo indicated that it was the Muslims, not the Serbs, who were responsible (noted by only a handful of media sources). Nor is the existence of 'mass graves' at Srebrenica by any means clear. Even one of the founders of the Muslim SDA has contested the alleged figure of 8000 dead, and indicated that many of the supposed victims are alive and well – a fact which would help account for the fact that nothing like this number of corpses have been found. More generally, it would not be an exaggeration to say that there is a different story to be told, more importantly, heard, about virtually every high profile incident attributing exclusive blame to the Serbs during the war in the former Yugoslavia.

This is not to suggest that terrible acts were not committed by Serbs, still less to justify their actions. It is to point out that the West's determinedly anti-Serbian stance was not simply a reaction to events themselves. There was (and remains) an entirely different story to be told for those who wished to listen. It is perhaps hardly surprising that all sides in the war spread black propaganda to discredit their opponents. What is more surprising, and indeed reprehensible, is that the Western media chose to report and dramatise only those that cast the Serbs as the villains of the piece. On the other hand, there was little attention paid to suffering on the Serbian side. There was no mention of the Serbs killed in the suburbs of Sarajevo, only the mainly Bosnian Muslims killed within the city itself for example. The mass expulsion of the Krajina Serbs was not only virtually ignored, but aerial photographs of alleged 'mass graves' were circulated (and faithfully reproduced by newspapers) to grab the headlines, and distract attention from the mass offensive against the Serbs in the Krajina region. In fact any important event which did not paint the Serbs as villains, such as the Croatian siege of Mostar (and indeed their continued aggravation of relations within that city), proved of little interest to Western journalists and policy makers.

The 'understanding' of the war created as a consequence of media reporting is strange indeed. The sort of ignorance unchecked, if not actually created by the character of the coverage on the Yugoslav war, is the still common idea that the war in Bosnia was one of conquest from outside. In fact, there was no such thing as a 'Bosnian', only the Bosnian Muslims, Bosnian Croats and Bosnian Serbs. The vast majority of the savage fighting, including that of the Serbs, was carried out by natives of the region (although that native Bosnian Serb population is probably now only half its pre-war total). Certainly it was not the 'invasion' from Serbia now established in Western mythology. More broadly, the disintegration of the Yugoslav Federation has been attributed with varying degrees of explicitness to an alleged Serbian 'master plan' for expansion and racial purity. Unlike most conflicts, the war that followed the secession of Slovenia from Yugoslavia has not been analysed as the complex process of action, unintended consequence and reaction that characterises every such confrontation. Never mind that this conflict was not simply Muslim–Croat resistance to Serbian domination, but at various times, Muslim versus Croat, Muslim versus Muslim, and Serb versus Serb. Without anyone having unearthed any Serbian blueprint for dominating the Balkans, we are to believe that nothing more be known than the malevolent intentions of those unfortunate enough to be born to that congenitally violent 'race'. Curiously, in the process, Serbia, a poor and comparatively powerless state on the fringes of Europe, has been attributed with the capacity to shape the destiny of the continent.

The very notion of objective reporting, and indeed the role of the journalist, was redefined through the experience of the Yugoslav war. Incredibly, for supposedly objective reporters of the news, some journalists made it quite plain that the whole Yugoslav tragedy was for them a moral campaign. Codifying this approach, BBC journalist Martin Bell recently called for the public acknowledgement that war reporting should not be 'merely' objective, largely as a result of his experiences denouncing the Serbs. 'I do not believe we should stand neutrally between good and evil', he declared.[17] He calls instead for a 'journalism of attachment'. The consequences were graphically demonstrated by his recent article about the 'largely benign' influence of television as a 'powerful weapon of modern warfare'. The article was illustrated by the well known picture of Trnopolje mentioned above, and the famous image was captioned as a 'true face[s] of the Bosnian war'.[18] As I have already indicated, this picture is extremely misleading. It indicates the profound dangers of this sort of 'attached' journalism, not least for those such as the Serbs who find themselves on the wrong end of Bell's 'benign weapon'. Presumably sharing his decision on who is good, and who evil, and that it is his place to make our minds up for us, other journalists have supported his 'journalism of attachment' nevertheless.

The 'attached' journalism evident in the portrayal of the Yugoslav civil war was often little more than propaganda intended to make clear that Serbia was to blame. Any sense of proportion, or even journalistic integrity, was lost. In this climate of 'who could go furthest in their denunciation', even liberal newspapers like the *Independent* and the *Guardian* could print condemnations of Serbs which in a different context, they themselves would condemn as racist. A rare exception to the rule of journalistic bias, Matthew Parris, writing in *The Times*, is hardly exaggerating when he points out that 'The entire Serbian people have been demonised, their name associated with unparalleled wickedness. Public discussion has bowed to an unspoken imperative to present the conflict in simple terms.'[19]

A Serbian Exception to the Rule?

No doubt such scholars and journalists, even if acknowledging the disfigured character of Serbian portrayal, would protest that this sort of depiction is reserved for the Serbs, a breed apart from other more rational East Europeans. However, a strong case can be made for suggesting that the Serbs are understood to be only the most uncivilised of a generally uncivilised lot – a sort of ideal type of East European backwardness. Certainly the other protagonists in the Yugoslav civil war are not genuinely regarded as inhabiting a different moral universe from their Serbian enemies: even the Bosnian Muslims, designated favourites of the West, are not immune. Slavoj Zizek, highlighting the assertion of *Time* magazine that 'Western weaponry would probably not be useful to Bosnians without special training ...', complains of the 'blatant racism' which says that Bosnian Muslims cannot handle Western weaponry.[20]

For some of the Westerners on the front line, there seems little doubt that the various protagonists are all as repugnant, and presumably inferior, as each other. Colonel Gregory Fontenot, a commander of the Nato IFOR forces in the former Yugoslavia, expressed in the *Wall Street Journal* (rather too frankly for some), what others have learned to keep to themselves. The Bosnian Croats were 'racist motherfuckers', Fontenot the peace keeper exclaimed. 'They don't think I trust them – and they're right ... . These are people who kill women and children and attack their neighbours. They're offended by me? Hell, I'm offended that I had to come here because of all their fighting.'[21] For Fontenot, it is perhaps only an altruistic 'white man's burden' that forces the United States military to try and impose order on these 'racist' savages. His own racial contempt of course does not require such attention.

Similarly, Major General Lewis MacKenzie, former UN commander in Bosnia, could only describe the protagonists to a congressional committee in Washington as '... like having three serial killers; one had killed 15 (Serbia), one had killed 10 (Croatia) and the third had killed five (Bosnia)'.[22] There is here no sympathy for those caught up in a conflict not of their making. Clearly, MacKenzie believes it to have arisen from the pathological tendencies of these nations of 'serial killers'. As for the response, according to another officer, the trick is not to 'descend to their level'. Instead, you 'get even' as Brigadier Duncan puts it: '... if someone pushes you over the edge, then you shoot people'.[23] And shoot people the British did, although significantly, not even bothering to confirm exactly how many.

There is here a picture of a sliding scale of inhumanity: in MacKenzie's case from those that butcher five, through to those that can only be satisfied by larger numbers. This is perhaps why their deaths seem of so little moment to the British army. But it is not a picture confined to the protagonists of the war in the former Yugoslavia, nor to being painted by the Western peace keepers. Such distinctions are in fact crucial to the picture of the region as a whole. In a sense it is widely assumed that to venture East is to encounter backwardness. Insofar as there is little evidence of such trends, the assumption is that it will only take the right rabble rousing demagogue to bring them to the surface. It is but one step in this reasoning to suggest that the further East one ventures, the more backward it becomes. That this is little more than a vague prejudice is illustrated by the fact that in practice there is no precise geographical delineation here however. While in general, the disease is sensed to be less acute the nearer we approach civilisation in the West, this need not be the case – further indicating that we are dealing with essentially the same affliction – with some cases being more far gone than others.

This prejudice need not necessarily be expressed in precise geographical terms, as is illustrated by the treatment of the new republic of Slovakia. Although a country whose capital is a mere 60 kilometres from the Viennese heart of Europe, it has found itself victim to the language and treatment more generally reserved for Balkan neighbours. Criticised since independence as a bastion of intolerance, by the end of 1995 Slovakia was more or less officially confirmed as being on the wrong side of the new European divide. The Slovak Republic was singled out for its allegedly anti-democratic trends by the US State Department's 1996 human rights report. More ominously, at the EU's December 1995 summit in Spain, German Chancellor Helmut Kohl omitted Slovakia from the list of early entrants to the Union – despite the country's membership of the Visegrad group of advanced democracies.

Typically, this was blamed on the conduct of the Slovaks themselves, in particular the conduct of their Prime Minister Vladimir Meciar, a man apparently so repellent that Kohl continues to refuse to even speak to him (although for example, the Turkish war against the Kurds seems not to have prevented German courting of Turkey and its politicians). 'Thanks to Mr Meciar's pugnacious style of rule, Slovak hopes of making the EU grade alongside their neighbours appear blown', explained Ian Traynor of the *Guardian*.[24] He omitted to explain why the anti-European antics of his own country's leadership did not similarly disqualify it from 'making the grade'.

A similar double standard exists on the key policy issue said to be disqualifying Slovakia from integration into the West: their treatment of the country's Hungarian minority. This is not a question of state oppression, but the reluctance of the regime to implement a minority language law guaranteeing the status of Hungarian, particularly in education. While Bratislava's hesitance was typically singled out by the US Deputy Secretary of State in March 1997 for particular criticism, there was no question of raising the issue of equal status for minority languages in the countries of the West. Arabs in France for example, are not even afforded the status of a minority, only 'immigrants'.

Meanwhile, the pressure on Slovakia is unrelenting. In what was remarkably the most senior official visit to Slovakia to date by a German, Bundestag chairwoman Rita Suessmuth concluded a two day visit in February 1997. She took the opportunity to lecture the Slovaks that their 'deficit in democracy' must be overcome, and steps taken to demonstrate 'sincerity' in meeting international standards. She threatened the consequences, generously stating that she 'doesn't want an isolated Slovakia'. Given that the country has already been isolated by German pressure, it was difficult to see exactly how they were to escape marginalisation through overcoming their 'deficit in democracy'. There is certainly little question of any such deficit being the business of Slovaks themselves, as the country is effectively being destabilised through intense international pressure.

Within the distinctions then, it remains a question of degree. There is no real qualitative difference between any peoples of the region in the eyes of the West, only degrees of susceptibility to the 'authoritarian impulse'. As we have mentioned, even the Czechs, allegedly the closest to ourselves, and affectionately regarded as a true outpost of Western standards by some, remain potential converts to clerical fascism as far as Richard Gott was concerned. For Tad Szulc, they have a 'police state in their national mentality'. While perhaps thicker than most, nevertheless, the Czech veneer of civilisation remains just that.

From 'People' to 'Mob'

Experts have their own preferences as to where to draw the line. For some, it is the Balkans as a whole which is the source of the problem. Others make distinctions between the various societies said to constitute this mountain range which has come to denote a regional culture. 'The Balkans', however, is generally regarded as the real 'East' to be distinguished from the more civilised 'East Central' or simply 'Central' European belt of Poland, Hungary and the Czech Republic. Others are far less generous, however. Some even place Austria as a non-democratic culture which does not really belong in the West.

East Europeans are a problem people. This understanding has informed much of the original demand that 'civil society' be established in addition to, or perhaps in place of, democracy. The rule of the people was regarded with suspicion precisely because these are not people to be trusted – despite the rhetoric of the Cold War about 'freedom loving' peoples. According to Tismaneanu, for example, writing on the dangers of premature trust in democratic practices, '... in all these countries, the xenophobic rhetoric of charlatans, rabble rousers and crackpots lends itself to stir responsive chords among more than fringe political groups'.[25] He is quite clear as to why the building of civic culture is so imperative. For him, '... those nations have to build their civil societies in order to avoid the calamitous slide from oligarchic tyranny to the tyranny of the mob'. Significantly here, 'the people' have become 'the mob', against whom civil society must be erected. Regulation and order need to be brought to the indeterminate and dangerous masses. Tismaneanu backs up his point with Dahrendorf's *Reflections on the Revolution in Europe*: '... "we the people" is a nice slogan, but as a constitutional maxim it is a mirror image of the total state that has been dislodged. If the monopoly of the party is replaced merely by the victory of the masses, all will be lost before long, for the masses have no permanence ... . The key question is how to fill the gap between the state and the people ... [to] create social sources of power.'[26]

Certainly for these two writers (and I would argue it is a widely shared assumption), 'civil society' is still deemed necessary in order to prevent the atavistic instincts of East Europeans being able to dominate society. It is an approach which found its most grotesque expression in the so-called elections in Bosnia organised by the Organisation for Security and Co-operation in Europe (OSCE). There it was decided that the democratic wishes of Bosnian Serbs to vote for the party of their choice was unacceptable. The OSCE not only banned the elected Bosnian Serb leader, Radovan Karadzic from standing in the elections, it proscribed even the mention of his name at election rallies, or the use of his photo on election posters. East European people, especially Bosnian Serbs, are clearly not to be trusted – even the sight of their leader may have unfortunate consequences. Instead 'civil society', in this case a United States security organisation, is deemed necessary to come between the people and their own worst instincts.

If Eastern Europe more broadly remains the region of 'diversity' coined by Joseph Rothschild in his famous book, it is then perhaps only between 'the backward and very backward' as the British world historian Calvorecessi has put it.[27] But where does this disdain for the region and its peoples come from? To an extent, we can regard it as the reappearance of prejudices put into temporary storage by the exigencies of the Cold War. Now that it is no longer necessary to shed crocodile tears for the victims of Soviet 'totalitarianism', the contempt for the countries of the region which marked the interwar period in particular, has come to the surface once again.

Old Prejudices Reborn?

In this section the question to be raised is whether the views of Eastern Europe are shaped primarily by wider concerns within European society which really have little to do with the realities of life in the East. We should begin by recognising that expressions of disdain, even contempt about Eastern Europe, do not come from nowhere, and nor are they without precedent. The conception of East Europe as backward and intolerant has its own (entirely neglected) history. Take a famous example – Bram Stoker's novel *Dracula* (an image of Transylvania that rankles with Romanians to this day). On the first page, the hero Jonathan Harker recalls in his diary that the '... impression I had was that we were leaving the West and entering the East', as he left Budapest station (from which he 'feared to go very far').[28] As he journeys to his appointment with the Count, he is particularly horrified by the Slovaks – '... the strangest figures we saw ... who are more barbarian than the rest, with their big cowboy hats, great baggy dirty-white trousers, white linen shirts, and enormous heavy leather belts, nearly a foot wide, all studded over with brass nails'.[29] Stranger than their attire perhaps, is that these barbaric Slovaks make constant appearances in Transylvania; they are not geographically confined to their land further West. The apparent scattering of races confirms Stoker's picture of Eastern confusion and indeterminacy. There are no recognisable rules or patterns, only a strange backwardness in this particular Western portrayal of the mysterious European East.

Stoker's portrayal of the East is not exceptional, but fits into a wider pattern. Fascination and patronage of exotic but feisty peoples, expressed today in the treatment of the Bosnian Muslims, and, at the same time, revulsion at a supposedly unique backwardness embodied today by the demonised Serbs, is not a new development. Such was suggested by Anatol Lieven, an expert on the Baltics. 'For a hundred years or more, Western journalists had swung between two contradictory stereotypes of East European nations', he explains, either 'gallant little freedom loving peoples, fighting against wicked empires for the sake of independence and liberal democracy' or 'horrid little anti semitic peasants, trying to involve us in their vicious tribal squabbles'.[30] Clearly it was the image of 'freedom loving peoples' that prevailed during the Cold War, and the latter prejudice which has come to the fore since its end.

A distinction Lieven does not draw to our attention is that these stereotypes were in the past expressed in more openly racial terms.

The British geographer Mackinder, for example, made famous by his declaration that he who controlled the heart of Europe (or rather, Eurasia) held the key to the future, was one of the first to draw English attentions to the potential significance of the region. He most certainly did not do so on the grounds that they were our equals. Central Asia was a disaster zone according to Mackinder, where, echoing the early revulsion expressed by Stoker, he deplored '... that mixture of races which has made the near East a plague to humanity'.[31] They were a disease which threatened to infect Europe as a whole and the semi-European East was the potential means of transmission. For the Frenchman Count Gobineau, in many ways the founder of modern racism with his *Essay on the Inequality of Man*, meanwhile, 'The Russians, Poles and Serbians ... even though they are far nearer to us than the negroes, are only civilised on the surface; the higher classes alone participate in our ideas, owing to the continuous admixture of English, French and German blood.'[32]

Classically, Eastern Europe was conceived of as the meeting point of Europe and Asia. It did not qualify as a fully civilised region, yet it was viewed as representing some degree of civilisation in its conflict with the 'Asian hordes'. With the emerging centrality of racial consciousness in modern Europe, degrees of civilisation were explained in terms of race, and the distinction between Eastern and Western Europe was therefore implicitly a racial one. However, the problem for racial thinking was that these semi-Europeans were white. They came to be viewed as forming an alien frontier – defenders of Western civilisation, and yet never wholly part of it. This in turn produced consternation, East and West, as to where the line could be drawn. The desire to alienate the region was compromised by the proximity, both geographically and racially, of the people. As a result, even though the more explicitly racial character of characterisation is more pronounced than today, from the beginning, the insistence on the difference and inferiority of East Europeans was expressed in more cultural than openly racial terms than was the case with other 'non Europeans'. Culture, and the related concept of 'ethnicity' which developed after the Second World War, offered a more differentiated means of making distinctions, without compromising racial thinking, and yet also able to absorb the ambiguities of the relationship with the East.

For Gobineau (and many others to this day), the ambiguity of the relationship could be dealt with by claiming that it was only the Eastern elite who managed to remain relatively immune from Asian despotism and savagery. Although there were, in his time more than recently, great distinctions to be made between the conditions of the elites and masses in the region, Gobineau's comments do not represent an observation of that difference. Rather, he and others sought to preserve the integrity of racial thinking from the contempt with which people uncomfortably similar to themselves were held. Through exempting the Eastern elites, he was able to maintain a racial invective against the East without implicitly undermining the racial superiority of the West. At this time, a racial distinction between elites and masses was commonly accepted within the West. The distinction has endured and is still particularly evident in the discourse on civil society in the East. But this too has been metamorphosed into a cultural rather than racial separation, as elites in all parts of Europe came under pressure from a mass challenge to superiority.

The precariousness of its status has stimulated a desire for acceptance in Eastern Europe by their 'betters'. Inevitably this meant that there has been a native resonance for the definitions of the East that were being constantly pronounced by the West. Years of attempting to elaborate on the alien frontier have seen their reflection in the discord between Eastern countries themselves as to where the line of civilisation could be drawn. Similarly, the Western elevation of Eastern elites has seen its parallels in the self-justifications of those elites. In Gobineau's time, the Eastern elites were happy to emphasise their exoneration from the more extreme expressions of Western scorn. Today, those who dominate society in the region are equally anxious to point out their familiarity with the values of civil society by berating their mass populations for not sharing them. The result of this discourse, in different forms over the years, has been to create a heightened sense of difference within the region and to exacerbate its tensions, as will be shown later.

Today, as racial thinking has become compromised through other experiences, virtually all expressions of superiority are through the language of culture rather than race. It is the now more dynamic and sensitive rubric of 'ethnicity' through which all that was discussed in the past through the category of race, is now discussed. 'Race' meanwhile has been left as a discredited and largely empty idea associated only with eccentric theories of biological difference.

In many ways, the experience of trying to negotiate the alien frontier of the East prepared a language and pioneered notions of difference and ethnicity, into which racial thinking would later retreat when more widely discredited.

A 'Squabbling Mixture of Races'

Given this sense of difference, these peoples were easily targeted for the apparent degeneration of Europe from the First World War.

Perhaps it was because we had made the mistake of drawing in these peoples to Europe proper (through granting their independence, and involving them in the new balance of power) that the return of any sort of equilibrium seemed so elusive. Interwar hostility to Eastern Europe was very much related to the problems that this 'squabbling' 'mixture of races' might cause for European order. Thus the (then Manchester) *Guardian* warning against the post-First World War dismemberment of the European empires which independence for Eastern Europe would involve, bemoaned that 'These small Slavonic nationalities seem to have a wonderful capacity for fighting each other.'[33]

Such prejudices were forcibly expressed by Robert Lansing, Secretary of State to Woodrow Wilson, architect of the new European order based on self-determination and equality. They are of significance in indicating that even the more integrationist impulse in the Western approach was not necessarily founded on a greater sense of equality. For Lansing, as events unfolded after the First World War, '... the more convinced I am of the danger of putting such ideas into the minds of certain races'.[34] These misgivings about the granting of independence to certain East European races were put to one side only by an appreciation of the utility of a string of independent states loyal to the West in containing the twin threats of Germany and Bolshevik Russia. Whatever was thought of these new (semi) Europeans, they might profitably be turned against the key threats to the major Western powers. Their nationalism also might at least make these entities more durable than the Ottoman and Austrian empires from which they were made. Such was the logic behind Western endorsement for their independence after the First World War.

Barely disguised hostility, if anything, intensified through the interwar years as the sense of folly at creating these 'artificial' nations grew with the persistence of divisions in Europe more widely. An increasingly divided Europe was at least partly blamed on its newest members. Into the 1930s, and with European tensions again intensifying, the states of Eastern Europe appeared only as an obstacle, rather than a potential solution – as they had figured immediately after the First World War. Ironically, the very integration of the peoples of the 'successor states' into the new European order only confirmed their unfitness to be considered equal. In this context, contempt for the peoples of the successor states became more explicit. Montagu Norman, interwar Bank of England chief, complained that '... it is the misfortune of Poland that she is populated by Poles'.[35]

The British Minister in Prague considered Czechoslovakia to be '... an injustice ... it is a fictitious country founded on several injustices ...'. He went on to make clear what he thought of not only the Czechs ('arrant pigs ... suffering from persecution mania'), but all the Slavs who had so foolishly been integrated into Europe. He asked:

Can we get back to the state of affairs in which the Slovaks return to their natural job of scrubbing windows, the Romanians are confined to the exercise of their only national industry (according to Lord D'Abernon's statement in an official memorandum that is fornication), the Poles are restricted to piano playing and the white slave traffic, and the Serbs are controlled in their great national activity – organising political murders on foreign territory?[36]

In a similar spirit, eminent Oxford historians, reflecting on the causes of the new war in 1940, bemoaned one of the '... great misfortunes of Europe that the little peoples who divide the Teutonic from the Russian mass have never shown any gift for combination'.[37] The increasingly dominant conclusion drawn from this perception of Eastern inferiority in the interwar years was that without external regulation these supposed pillars of the post-war order would only disintegrate. Already in 1924, one writer for *Foreign Affairs* argued, '... if left to themselves they will relapse into despotism or anarchy and barbarism'.[38]

Despite the more expressly racial understanding demonstrated in this sort of writing, there is some continuity between these interwar prejudices, and those to which we have become accustomed today. It would help to account for the fact that the idea of an 'Eastern' Europe has not died with the Soviet empire which was its supposed creator. As Wolff puts it in his portrait of *Inventing Eastern Europe*, 'The shadow persists, because the idea of Eastern Europe remains, even without the iron curtain. This is not only because the intellectual structures of half a century are slow to efface themselves, but above all because that idea of Eastern Europe is much older than the Cold War.'[39]

In this light we can make better sense of the general feeling of indifference, even relief, at the Soviet takeover of the region after the Second World War. Especially before a paranoid sense of alarm overtook Western perceptions with the Czech coup of 1948, much influential opinion was not unduly concerned at the prospect of the Soviet Union taking on responsibility for this 'irksome fringe of the continent' as they saw it. Witness the Yalta agreements, at which

Churchill infamously scribbled on a napkin for Stalin the names of all those Eastern countries where he had no objection to Soviet domination. To a large degree there was a perception that Stalin was removing a troublesome thorn in the side of the West – one that had perhaps 'dragged us into' world conflict one too many times. More than this, might not these peoples, so different to ourselves as they were now felt to be, perhaps be more suited to the rigours of Stalinism? The Slavs (and non Slavs, as long as they were of the 'East'!) were assumed to be suited to a less demanding, more uncomplicated means of running society.

Today, now that the 'containment' provided by Soviet control has gone, the sense that a new form of regulation is required has reappeared in Western discourse. Without it, 'the East' constitutes a hazard – in one of the most popular foci of Western alarmism – a health hazard.

The East as Contagion

It would be mistaken to imagine that nothing has changed, and that we can explain hostility to the region as only the return of old prejudices. The threatening 'otherness' of Eastern Europe today is expressed in new ways. There is a discernible medical emphasis, more particularly a suggestion of disease, in several of the principal themes through which the region is understood. For the Polish writer Adam Michnik, for example, a disease is ravaging the Balkans where, '... an epidemic of a new, terrible and dangerous disease is spreading. It is worse than the plague and worse than AIDS ... ethnic cleansing'.[40] In response to such thinking, one academic complains for example about how United States foreign policy toward the former Yugoslavia in particular is organised around the containment of the 'virus of nationalism'.[41] The notion of 'ethnic cleansing' is perhaps questionable enough. On the one hand, it denotes an allegedly new practice – hence the need for a new term. On the other, it suggests clear continuity with Nazism. Even leaving this contradiction aside, however, that it can be described as a disease suggests that we are being told about the sort of people who inhabit this region, not simply provided with a useful term to aid our understanding of what is actually going on.

'Post-communism', a popular term to describe the new democracies, is said to be a 'condition'. Again the choice of terms is significant. The post-Franco period in Spain was not described as a 'condition', for example, perhaps because there was no such thing as 'post-

Franco-ism'. Expressions of social science when it comes to the East imply a psychological, even biological emphasis which would not be taken seriously in other arenas. This has even led to a viewing of what is happening in the region through the prism of this naturalised biological emphasis.

The conception of 'the East' as metaphorically diseased, has disposed analysts to exaggerate all manner of real medical conditions, to the extent that they may even infect the West. The World Health Organisation launched a campaign in March 1996 to stop what it regards as a frightening return of diseases such as syphilis, cholera and diphtheria in Russia and Eastern Europe. Significantly, this was described in newspaper reports as posing a threat of 'Cross-border contagion', where for example, 'Prostitutes from Eastern Europe are moving West, spreading risk of sexually transmitted diseases.'[42] A year into the WHO's campaign, and the scale of the alleged problem in 'the East' is now even more dramatically described. Nor, despite no discernible impact on the West of this 'epidemic', have the attempts to suggest that it constitutes a threat abated. 'UK faces disease invasion from East' cried the headline reporting the WHO's latest figures. And the evidence for this 'invasion'? According to the UK Public Health Laboratory Service, '... one in five cases of syphilis in Britain between 1994–1996 *could* [my emphasis] be linked to travel to or from eastern Europe or Russia'.[43]

There is a clear identification of the East with disease both literally and metaphorically. The response is not idle concern or sympathy, but the problem of 'contagion' infecting the West. That such scenarios are highly fanciful – sexual diseases are not unique to Eastern prostitutes, and nor are these prostitutes likely to be moving en masse to infect the West – seems of little concern to Western commentators. There appears to be a determination to indicate a problem – in the case of the Public Health Laboratory Service through highlighting only the one-fifth of syphilis cases which 'could be linked' with the East.

Too Many People?

A new vocabulary posits the East as uniquely diseased both literally and metaphorically. Most dramatically a contagion looms. This is nowhere more lucidly expressed than in relation to the potential for the physical movement of people themselves. More than any other single factor it was through the anxiety of immigration that change in the East was viewed. Castles and Miller's book on international migration for example, notes that 'By 1990, a new spectre haunted Europe: that of an influx from the East ... . In Western Europe there was speculation about mass immigration on a scale not seen since the collapse of the Roman empire ....'[44]

To an extent, the very 'revolutions' themselves were the product of concern about immigration. The reunification of Germany, the most important event of that experience, was announced so quickly in order to prevent the mass emigration of East Germans. Certainly, fear of numbers has informed the general anxiety that emerged so rapidly after the 'revolutions'. As Castles and Miller continue, 'The spectre of uncontrolled mass immigration from Eastern Europe became a public issue in the West ... . For West European leaders, the initial euphoria prompted by the destruction of the barriers to movement was quickly succeeded by a nostalgia for the case of migration control of an earlier epoch.' As a consequence, 'Before long, Italy deployed troops to prevent an influx of Albanian asylum seekers, while Austria used its army to keep out Romanian gypsies.'[45] The 'captive' peoples of the East became a military problem in a matter of years. The fourth Conference of European ministers in 1991 was unexpectedly overwhelmed by concern about the prospect of mass migration from the East in the wake of Albanians arriving in Italy. Earlier in the year, the Council of Europe convened a conference on migration where, as the Council itself described, 'West European countries were disturbed – in some cases, terrified – by the prospect of migration from countries of the former Eastern bloc.'[46]

It was for this reason that, as *New Republic* explained, 'For most Germans alarmed at the prospect of mass migration by unemployed Slavs, the region is a source of anxiety rather than a potential sphere of influence.'[47] Similar demographic reasoning meant that Poland was especially frightening. One expert noted the irony that '... despite its leading role in the process of dismantling communism, [Poland] was treated with even greater reluctance due both to the larger size of its population and to the sizeable legal and illegal emigration in previous decades'.[48] Albanians were even more unfortunate. While the first emigrants to Italy in 1991 were welcomed, the second wave were rounded up like cattle in a football stadium, and deported – but not without a final twist to the sorry tale. As Albanian artist Edi Rama points out, in a final insult to add to injury, they were told their specially laid on transport was taking them to Northern Italy. 'In fact, the proposed chartered flights that were supposed to bring us North brought us back East to the same prison we were born into, and where, it seems, we are destined to die.'[49]

The irony that East Europeans are kept out by the West, as effectively as they were kept in by the old regimes has been lost on most commentators (at the time of writing, my Russian house guest, lucky enough to obtain a visa, has had to register with the British police – and pay £34 for the privilege). Just as remarkable is the lack of comment on just how misplaced the fears about mass immigration from the East turned out to be. There has been no mass influx (the immigration remained a specifically German 'problem'), yet few have highlighted this fact – even to draw a public sigh of relief that these peoples did not arrive on our doorsteps. It is particularly clear in retrospect that the sense of demographic threat was evidently not simply based on real analysis or experience. The scale of reaction cannot be accounted for simply by the real potential for mass population movement from East to West.

Fears were partly the product of being confronted with Cold War rhetoric encouraging Eastern freedom, at a time when there was no longer a Soviet Union intact to ensure this propaganda remained just that. This was the 'free world' as opposed to the closed one of the enemy. As a consequence of this propaganda stance, Germany was formally obliged to accept 'ethnic Germans' and allow others freedom of movement. In addition to the fear generated by outdated rhetoric, there was also the continued prejudice of an 'unstable East' prone to self-destruction which might propel victims westwards – something which only happened as a consequence of the internationalisation of the Yugoslav war, not more generally as a result of congenital instability.

The fear of foreign numbers is an expression of Western anxieties, not Eastern realities, even if the most central European focus has now shifted to keeping out immigrants from North Africa (significantly this is also 'ideologised' into a potential 'fundamentalist' invasion). Although now more amorphous, concern about the potential movement of peoples remains considerable in the literature on Eastern Europe. Writing on the supposed upsurge of nationalism, one recent contribution explains, 'Continuing the theme of menace, always a vital promoter of nationalism, is my second common stimulus to nationalist upsurge: demographic flux.'[50] Despite writing in 1995, by which time even the most alarmist analysts have had to cool off on ethnic warfare scenarios for lack of evidence, this writer foresees the prospect of population displacement as minorities are attacked. This proposition remains a staple of writers on the subject. It indicates an already existing disposition to read events through the prism of demographic concern with 'flux'.

Criminal Fears

One reason why these numbers are so frightening relates to another great Western obsession of the 1990s, crime. Through this focus, indeterminate fears of migration are given more specific expression and legitimacy. Migrating East Europeans are potential criminals in the suspicious environment of post-Cold War Europe. A meeting of 100 international police officers and justice officials were told that 'In five years there is no doubt the major threat confronting the inner cities of the UK will be from Central and Eastern European and Russian crime.'[51] No wonder, given such official signals, that the Austrian right winger Jorg Haider could tell another meeting of police officers that the Poles are the car thieves, Yugoslavs the burglars, and the Russians specialise in blackmail and mugging.[52] In a further twist to the tale, fears of Eastern tribes have been blended into the crime wave scenario by some observers. Thus Simon Sebag Montefiore writes in the London *Evening Standard* of '... a new and barbaric species of trader: the ethnic mobs, the Chechens, Kazakhs, the Georgians, the Armenians, the Odessa Jews, who descended on Western businessmen with a ruthless savagery new even to the Thiefs in Power'.[53] Criminal activity, particularly by these ubiquitous 'mafias', is even seen to be a large part of the explanation for the failure of reform – especially in Russia. Hence, 'Crime Block Change in the East ... paralysing economic reform' as a typical newspaper story explains, disregarding the fact that 'crime', even so loosely defined, can only be a symptom, not a cause of economic failure.[54] More recently, the whole experience of Albanian collapse in 1997 has been interpreted predominantly by the Italians as a problem of criminality. Albanian refugees fleeing chaos back home are apparently all intent on linking up with, and reviving the fortunes of, a flagging Italian mafia.

These are not just isolated prejudices, but are a part of reality – particularly for East Europeans themselves if they try to travel freely as they were told they would be able to once Soviet control was removed. Instead of free movement, however, as Wolff describes, 'In the 1990s Italians are worriedly deporting Albanian refugees: Albanesi, no grazie reads the graffiti on the wall. Germans are greeting visitors from Poland with thuggish violence and neo-Nazi demonstrations, while tourists from Eastern Europe are being arbitrarily stopped and searched in Paris shops, under suspicion of shoplifting.'[55] Such treatment is of course reserved for those lucky enough to get a visa to visit the West in the first place.

Quarantine the East

If the East is accepted as a diseased part of the world, it is hardly surprising that many now consider it a menace which might spread further afield. To Daniel Nelson's disappointment, 'Unfortunately, the skills, strength, and cohesion do not exist.' In his security jargon then, '... the entire Eastern half of Europe is a threat rich environment'.[56] *Conflict and Chaos in Eastern Europe*, the title of a recent book on nationalisms in the region, already conveys a lurid and alarming picture before the book is opened.[57] Inside, we find a portrayal of the region as ethnically baffling, and the assumption that this ethnic mix leads inexorably to conflict. Nelson and Hupchick are not alone: there has been a veritable industry of books warning of this menace on our doorsteps. *Nations in Turmoil*, by Janusz Bugajski, sees a 'potential drift toward dictatorship', and looks forward to enhanced roles for security bodies like the Organisation for Security and Cooperation in Europe to contain the threat.[58]

At its most extreme, this security perspective comes down to keeping instability contained to the region. There is little point in involving ourselves in their squabbles – it is congenital, and therefore incurable. The more reform based perspective demands we at least attempt a cure – reflecting greater confidence in the West's capacity to bring order and reason. It is still driven by fear, however, summed up by the phrase that 'If we do not Brusselize them, they will Balkanize us.' In this spirit Jacques Attali, former head of the European Bank for Reconstruction and Development, asked, 'Will Balkan tribalism spread to the West?' imploring that 'We have only a limited period of time to stop the slide towards tribalism before it engulfs Eastern Europe and quite possibly takes us with it.'[59] We might ask what is the mechanism whereby Western Europe is to be engulfed in 'ethnic cleansing'. Apparently it is enough to believe that a disease exists, and that therefore it can spread like any other.

It is evident that this dark vision of an amorphous Eastern threat is pervasive among both those who seek more interference, and those who suggest we give up on Europe's Eastern half. It is also apparent that the threat of the East is not confined to the spectre of ethnic nationalism. Particularly regarding the former Soviet Union, the unsubstantiated threat of fascism, or that of a takeover by the military, appears to play a similar role.

Not all commentators and politicians express an alarmist view of the East. A handful of academics have gone so far as to suggest that prejudice, far from being an innate characteristic of the peoples in the region, is something which characterises Western thinking on the subject. The British sociologist Tom Nairn, for example, in an article attacking the 'Demonising of Nationalism' in the East, contests that 'The creaky old ideological vehicles trundled out to cope with the post Soviet and Balkan upheavals explain nothing whatsoever about their subjects' with their 'gore laden pictures of ethnic anarchy ...'. It is the West that has the problem, he continues, as '... the shocked, semi hysterical response of the West to the Eastern rebirth has plunged it into the style of unreason once supposed typical of rabid chauvinists and wild eyed patriot poets'.[60] For Slavoj Zizek, even the actions of the Serbs '... are totally rational within the goals that they want to attain. The only exception, the only truly irrational factor in it, is the West babbling about ethnic passions.'[61] These remain honourable exceptions to a far more uncritical rule however.

There is again something of a consensus that these are problem societies – with problem people. The sense that the region might fully overcome its marginal 'Eastern' status has long since been abandoned. Turning now to these categories, it is important to establish that 'East' and 'West' have little real geographical meaning, but are instead means of codifying who is 'one of us' and who is not.

3

Moral Geography

'The East' as Metaphor

The apparent persistence of a distinct, often threatening, Eastern political culture raises the question of what it is that makes it 'Eastern'. As I have indicated, the traditional post-war view was that it was only domination by the USSR that conferred (temporary) Eastern status. As one academic reminded us in 1991, 'The great events in Eastern Europe in 1989–90 abolished the Soviet empire in Europe and in so doing abolished Eastern Europe itself, which had existed as a separate, and separated region only by virtue of its conquest and subsequent communisation by the Soviet Union at the end of World War Two.'[1]

However, Eastern Europe has clearly not been abolished along with the Soviet empire: if anything it seems more enduring than ever before. Certainly, according to official categorisation, it is now even larger than during the Cold War. According to the new United Nations definitions, Eastern Europe has gained the Western parts of the former Soviet Union (Belarus, Moldova, Russia and Ukraine), and thereby more than doubled in population size. There appears to be more to being 'Eastern' than a temporary status conferred by Soviet domination.

There have been many terms and definitions used to describe the countries of present day Central and Eastern Europe. Beyond the most common 'Eastern', pre-war definitions included a 'political shatter belt', the 'Eastern march lands of Europe', an 'Isthmian Triangle' and a 'shatter zone'. More contemporarily, there is the idea of a 'shadowland'. Meanwhile for Lech Walesa, they are a 'grey buffer zone' left behind by the West, while for the historian Ivan Berend, 'ferryboat countries' between East and West. Invariably they are something 'in between'. Wolff sees this as a status 'in between' European civilisation and Asian barbarism; a half way house established in the imagination of Enlightenment thinkers. In more modern thinking, the region has figured as a land 'in between' the giants of Germany and Russia. With the demise of Russian power, however, the region is perhaps not so much 'in between', as simply 'out there'.

Whatever the term, however, they are all more than simply directions enabling us to locate it on a map. These ostensibly geographical categories like 'Eastern' and indeed the more prosaic 'Other Europe' or 'shadowlands', certainly 'shatter zone', are neither neutral, nor self-evident. In one way or another, they tell us not only *where it is*, but something about *what it is*. Some are overtly pejorative. Rebecca West, in the early 1940s, explained how the French used the epithet 'Balkan' as a term of abuse. 'Balkan! Balkan!' screams the French woman alerting us to barbarism in her midst.[2] Others warn us of the region's explosiveness – its tendency to 'shatter' and implicitly fling its debris further afield, into the rest of Europe. A more important theme, which will be discussed later, is that of a 'shadowland' where the past stalks the present. Equally important today is the wider notion of 'Eastern' denoting a threatening intolerance. As John Feffer notes in his *Eastern Europe After the Revolutions*, '"Eastern" has never possessed a precise geographic meaning. It has always been more a cultural designation used to refer to sections of Europe not considered 100% European ...'.[3]

So important is this association that it overshadows much of political life and foreign policy in the region. All the regimes of the former communist bloc try to escape inclusion within this unenviable category of 'the East'. All consequently try and advance claims for their Western, non Eastern status. They rightly sense in the term a negative implication of backwardness, and the marginalisation that follows. The buzzword in capitals like Bucharest is 'image', which means trying to convince the outside world that their inclusion in 'the East', 'Balkans' or whatever, is mistaken. In the Romanian case it involved hiring the services of the British advertising house Saatchi and Saatchi in the early 1990s to shake off this misconception, and establish the country as a legitimate part of Europe proper.

Given the implications of this moral geography, it is not surprising that a substantial literature has been generated around the question of where boundaries should be drawn (although there is not, as already suggested, a large literature questioning the reality of these divisions). According to the outstanding British historian Robin Okey, a German writer claimed in 1989 '... that a bibliography of the symposia, books and periodicals published on the topic since the first edition three years earlier could itself fill a whole volume'.[4] Most contested of all definitions is the notion of a 'Central Europe' – a sort of half way house between semi-civilisation and civilisation proper.

Being 'Central European' suggests being different, but not in such an overtly inferior manner. 'Central Europe', which as Tony Judt notes, was rediscovered by Western intellectuals only in the 1970s, provides a means of establishing distance from 'the East'. For some admirers, it has even '... become the idealised Europe of our cultural nostalgia', as Judt describes.[5]

It is far better therefore to be designated 'Central', rather than 'Eastern'. 'Central European-ness' is a discussion of who is less unlike us than those in 'the East' proper. Who 'deserves' this description is by no means clear. Okey cites a German geographer who demonstrated in 1954 that twelve eminent French, British and German maps of 'Central Europe' share in common only most of Czechoslovakia and various fragments of the country's neighbours. There is clearly scant literal sense that can be made of the concept. This is even more the case with the other terms used to describe the area; those such as 'shadowland' do not even pretend to tell us where it is, even though the expression retains the geographical element in the 'land' which follows the 'shadow'. That these shifting definitional sands have little to do with geography is indicated by the recent fortunes of Greece.

Greece now appears to have become a part of the East, or at least the Balkans. It has been quickly forgotten that it stood as a pillar of the West during the Cold War. Greece is now covered by specialist magazines on the East European region such as *Transition*. This is not because it has slipped anchor, and drifted away from Brussels, certainly not in the literal sense. It is perhaps more because Greece was unenthusiastic about the sanctions imposed on neighbouring Yugoslavia. This was seen as siding with the Serbs in many quarters, and suggested it was politically no longer truly Western. Athens' contestation of the status of Macedonia was taken by the West to further indicate the country's roots in 'the Balkans'. Apparently petty nationalistic aggression over the name to be given to a former Yugoslav province on the Greek border was interpreted as evidence of an 'Eastern', perhaps 'Orthodox' mentality which dominates Greek affairs. The country was publicly censured, and has found itself treated quite differently. That countries like France and the United States display equal hypersensitivity as this to issues of sovereignty and otherwise trivial cultural symbols was ignored. Certainly France has not found itself isolated and written off because of national quotas on the amount of French music to be played, nor the United States castigated for its obsession with the Stars and Stripes. Greece, however, now finds itself dismissed as backward, and therefore worthy of inclusion in 'the Balkans' rather than 'the West'.

It is then not a matter of geography, but a question of who is 'one of us', and who is not – the judges being the principal international powers. It is a socio-psychological judgment masquerading as geographical reality. This moral geography leads to all manner of peculiarities. The Poles do not exist according to the logic of their joke that they are a country which is 'East of the West', and 'West of the East'. Look at a map, is Finland not Eastern if the others are? We have an 'East Central' Europe according to many, so why not a 'West Central'? If, as many claim, Hungary, Poland and the Czech lands – even a Baltic state like Lithuania – constitute 'Central Europe', while Russia and the Balkans are not really European at all, we then have, as Okey suggests, 'a continent with a West and a centre, but no East'.[6] Of course, we might then say it is Russia which constitutes the East. But as so many, for example the author Milan Kundera, do not recognise Russia as ever having been a part of European civilisation, we are left with Okey's 'East-less' continent. Certainly, this 'centre' would appear to have no real meaning. If we were to judge by a common understanding of Europe, as stretching from the Atlantic to the Urals, then the centre would be somewhere in the Ukraine – an idea for which there are few takers, apart perhaps from Ukrainians themselves! And what of 'Europe' itself, which is after all, as Pocock has explained, only '... an unenclosed sub-continent on a continuous land-mass stretching to the Bering Straits'?[7]

Certainly, it would appear that these divisions have little to do with Russia or the former Soviet Union. In fact, as Wolff explains, Russia is more victim than villain with regard to imposing divisions in Europe. 'Russia may resign its military domination of Eastern Europe,' he explains, 'but it cannot banish the idea of Eastern Europe, for it did not invent or impose that idea.' As he continues, 'Russia was subjected to the same process of discovery, alignment, condescension, and intellectual mastery, was located and identified by the same formulas: between Europe and Asia, between civilisation and barbarism.'[8] Russia has perhaps an even more complicated history of inclusion, and then exclusion from the Western camp. We can shed further light on these distinctions and, more importantly, the impulse behind their casting, and by whom, if we draw out the changing definitions of Europe through the ages. What becomes clear is that changing definitions, in particular the narrowing of 'Europe' to 'the West', is not a product of unique developments in 'the East'. It is a function of changes in the West.

Changing Definitions Through Time

The boundaries between East and West are not fixed. Nor is the meaning, and indeed who precisely is included within these divisions. In this section, I indicate some of the ways in which perceptions have changed; specifically, that a systematic sense of divisions within Europe, and even between Europe and the rest of the world, are relatively recent. For example, the idea of 'Europe' which began with, and was therefore defined by, Athenian democracy is an invention of the nineteenth century. The radical banker and historian George Grote first posited the idea that the cradle of European civilisation lay in Greek democracy, rather than the establishment of Christianity towards the end of the Roman empire. Laying claim to a democratic tradition rooted in the past is often unlikely to be the product of new historical evidence. More plausibly, it tells us that democracy has become problematic in the present, and is therefore in need of reinforcement – in this case through marshalling an historical 'tradition'.

Many writers on the region suggest that the seed of East Europe's distinctiveness was sown many centuries ago. For the historian Ivan Berend, for example, in explaining the historical evolution of Eastern Europe as a region, it '... was already displaying specific traits as early as the very beginnings of mediaeval European development, in the fifth to eighth Centuries'.[9] Assuming the 'traits' singled out by Berend were indeed present, we then have to assume that they retained their influence – essentially impervious to historical development. Even a radical critic of the projection back into history of spurious European traditions such as Gerard Delanty, in his *Inventing Europe*, appears to accept that 'traits', or in his case 'consciousness', could have been cast in pre-modern times, to then remain intact throughout the ages, and somehow account for divisions in the present. Discussing the now popular theme that the constituent nationalities of the former Yugoslav federation were somehow doomed to inevitable confrontation, he contends, 'Thus it came about that the consciousness of the Croats and Slovenes was formed by Latin culture and Roman Catholicism. ... The Serbs, in contrast, remained more firmly in the Eastern tradition.'[10]

But what can these historically ever present features be? What is the 'Eastern tradition'? It is difficult to identify any clear elements of continuity. It is perhaps for this reason that efforts to substantiate an historically determined division have centred on the vague question of culture and values. It is implied that there has always been a different way of life between East and West, between the full, and half European. This perhaps is what we can trace back to the Middle Ages and beyond, and thereby give substance through history to a division between real Europeans, and those caught in a nether world between the European and Asian. For the British world historian Arnold Toynbee for example, Russia is excluded from Europe by history because Byzantine Christianity created a different civilisation from a West based upon the Roman inheritance.

A Religious Divide?

For Samuel Huntington, the contemporary guru of the centrality of cultural difference with his theory of a 'clash of civilisations', religion is the key. And religion provides the most common means of historically distinguishing between the real Europeans, and the 'impostors'. The renowned British theorist of nationalism Anthony Smith, in discussing the absence of a real European identity, asks whether religion might do the trick. 'Might this not provide a test of European inclusion and exclusion? There is a clear sense, going back at least to the Crusades and probably even to Charles Martel, in which Europeans see themselves as not Muslims or as not Jews.'[11] The idea here is that identification with Christianity is the beginning of a European identity. But what did these so called 'Europeans' from the time of Charles Martel see themselves as? Surely this is relevant to any discussion of 'identity'?

When Christianity was in the ascendant, it completely dominated thinking about the (European) world. It was an expanding doctrine that for its believers, like the Crusaders, was destined to dominate the globe. Certainly at this time, there was no potential for necessarily secular distinctions (as 'East' and 'West' are) to be drawn between different parts of the world. If the whole world was to be one under God, even the basic idea of civilisation permanently struggling against barbarism, to be discussed in the next chapter, had limited purchase. Hay, in his classical study of the idea of Europe explains how any issues of division were secondary: 'The concepts of civilisation and barbarism were in every sense subsidiary to the developing sense of unity based on the church.' While it may have been 'Christians against the rest ... this was by no means a simply territorial antithesis as Christianity was not tied to any narrow man made frontiers'.[12]

Then, as now, the very idea of hard and fast divisions only makes sense once limits have been reached. To take a more contemporary example, it is significant that it was not thought necessary to precisely define the borders that separated the states which made up Tito's Yugoslavia. As the former Yugoslav ambassador to the EC describes, 'They were assumed to be so united in their purpose that the question of officially determining boundaries and fixing them by law never really occurred to the new authorities.'[13] It was only with the contestation of the federation that boundaries became important. Returning to the subject of 'Europeans', it was only once Christianity had evidently been geographically confined, was there even the possibility of a sense of differences being consolidated. Then, and only then, might there be the idea of 'Christian peoples' of one sort or another, and 'others' who were not. Partly as a consequence Hay continues, '... the name of the continent was more or less devoid of content ...', and therefore any notion of a further sub-division of the continent into East and West was precluded.[14] Even the Crusades did not consolidate a sense of civilizational difference. As he further explains; '... the crusades, one might have thought would stimulate a revival of the Greek notion that there was natural hostility between East and West [but it could] hardly flourish in an atmosphere where the global mission of Christianity was still regarded as the prime issue'.[15] As it was expected to cover the whole earth, divisions were not an issue. These were servants of God, not 'Europeans'.

In contrast to the commonly expressed view that modern conceptual boundaries have deep historical roots, logic suggests that there has been no continuous sense of difference between 'Europe' and the rest, or 'East' and 'West'. In general, such a reflex is stimulated in response to a crisis of purpose. Just as during times of optimism geographical domination is confused with its ideological forms – that the 'white man rules the world' for example, so the loss of expansionist nerve is confused with, represented as, a geographical limitation. To contend otherwise is to project back into the past very modern conceptions which have only meaning in the context of modern conditions. It requires accepting the irrationality expressed by the Romanian Grigore Gafencu, in his address to the Royal Institute of International Affairs in the late 1940s. There, in staking a claim for the extension of the notion of Europe further East, he argued that, 'In its modern sense "Europe" existed before the politicians discovered it. And the peoples of Eastern Europe, even before they knew its name, were already fighting in defence of certain values which linked them to a world in which they felt at one.'[16] More well known, but no less nonsensical, is the declaration of T.S. Eliot that 'We are all, so far as we inherit the civilisation of Europe, still citizens of the Roman empire.'[17] No 'European', from East or West, could have fought for something of which they knew nothing, any more than we 'proper' Europeans are 'citizens of the Roman empire'. Yet this is the logic of an historically determined division of Europe.

An alternative explanation for the 'roots' of this division has to be found. And if we cannot find evidence of any real division, as in religion for example, we need to examine why and when the perception of such a division arose. It is clear from the work of Dennis Hay and, more recently, the excellent historical presentation of Pim den Boer, that definitions are very recent, and cannot be imposed back through history. What is more, we can even historically locate the point at which writers first began to project back into history the idea that Europe is divided into two identifiable halves.

Tracing the Division

That there was little sense of Eurasian division before the nineteenth century is made clear by den Boer. There are writings from the classical Greek Hippocrates which suggest some sense of geographical division between Europe and Asia, but they are partial and insignificant. Later, with the Romans, '... there was no question of a notion of European identity, a feeling of oneness shared by all Europeans'.[18] Under Charlemagne, for some the father of 'Europe', the notion was deployed in relation to the external threat of the Moors. But it was vague, and not coterminous even with Christendom. The oldest known separate map of Europe – from the twelfth century – includes roughly the Carolingian empire of Charlemagne – excluding Spain, Britain, Scandinavia, and the whole area to the East of the Adriatic from Vienna down to Greece and Macedonia. Europe was not yet even united in Christianity, let alone some set of wider beliefs from which areas like present day 'Eastern' Europe might be excluded.

It is only with the Ottoman challenge, coupled with the social and religious crises of the fourteenth and fifteenth centuries, that Europe became the Christian continent, and therefore distinct limits were drawn. Under these circumstances, '... the Eastern boundary of this Europe had been shifted a considerable degree West'.[19] Significantly, however, this unity was more apparent than real. Christian Europe was moving into the schisms of those centuries, and the heresies of the sixteenth. Only once 'Christendom' was evidently confined to Europe after denominational fracturing, was there even the possibility of any real demarcation. This could not be an automatic process, however. The notions of East and West are non religious concepts, and therefore could not arise from a pre-modern religious outlook on the world.

Only in later thinkers, like the great Italian Machiavelli, can we begin to detect the notion of a Europe based on secular characteristics (although, as den Boer points out, there is still no sense of proper division even in Machiavelli). At a more systematic level, the idea of Europe, the prerequisite for that of East and West, did not acquire real meaning until the age of the Enlightenment in the eighteenth century. Until this time, any geographical distinction had little significance. Matters such as whether Russia was a part of Europe, were of no consequence so long as Europe was only a name on a map. It began to have direct relevance only with the emergence of Europe as the symbol of a way of life in the Enlightenment.

To an extent, Enlightenment humanism involved looking down upon those parts of the world which remained outside, and in that sense perhaps provided the language for the casting of divisions. However, this new found sense of superiority for European civilisation did not necessitate the absolutising of boundaries. Reflecting the confident humanism of the age, Europe saw itself leading the way, certainly, but not inhabiting a separate moral universe from those to the East and South. Thus '... this feeling (of superiority) did not stand in the way of an increasing interest in areas outside Europe. This seeming contradiction is understandable if one realises that the concept of civilisation should not be conceived as fixed, but rather as a process directed towards an ideal state.'[20] If Europe had the fortune to lead the way toward enlightenment and progress, it was perhaps for more or less accidental reasons of climate or topography, as far as the leading thinkers of the age were concerned. It certainly was not the fixed delineation imagined by many contemporary writers. In this context, the Enlightenment vision did not preclude the genuine admiration of those outside Europe; 'Indeed non European peoples were frequently held up as being exemplary.'[21]

The notion of Europe became an increasingly secular one. By around 1700, Europe had become a standard framework for political thinking. Through the eighteenth century, it became increasingly associated with a balance of power, and also with superiority over other continents. By end of the eighteenth century, Europe was no longer coterminous with Christendom. Instead, emergent '... feelings of superiority were based on a conglomeration of ideas proceeding from the Enlightenment which, in turn came to be associated with the notion of civilisation'.[22] However, as has been indicated, 'civilisation' was less a place than a process. Notions of division were not projected back through history during the Enlightenment, in the manner that historians now are so keen to do.

It was only the break with tradition in the revolutionary years from 1789 to 1848 that saw the attempt to assert a 'Western tradition' of some sort. Then, as den Boer explains, 'The concept of Europe was not only historicized, but also politicised.'[23] After the revolutionary upheavals at the beginning of the century, there originated the notion of '... the *history* of European culture as an idea in itself ...'.[24] It was once the limits of this civilisation were experienced, that its existence was projected back and cast in stone. Den Boer explains this process well, and is worth quoting at length;

> At the beginning of the nineteenth century the idea of Europe was projected back much further in history. A search was instigated for the roots of European civilisation. Europe, which in the Middle Ages had in fact hardly existed as a geographical expression, became an accepted historical category. The historical writings of the Nineteenth century romantics made it appear that in the Middle Ages there had been a conscious idea of Europe: 'The notion gained ground that out of the ruins of the Roman empire (the Latin element), the Barbarian peoples (the Germanic element), led by the Christian church, had been amalgamated to form the true European civilisation.'[25]

It is once 'Europe' becomes contested that it becomes fixed as an historically meaningful category. From the late eighteenth century there were now competing 'Europes' – both radical and conservative: one developed by the Holy Alliance, and one by the liberals. Interestingly, it is the liberal version of Europe which insists upon a division of the continent, as we can see in the 'Europe of diversity' developed by Francois Guizot. The conservative version was hardly likely to draw such a division as it would most likely exclude Russia, the pivot of the Holy Alliance. As den Boer again explains, 'It is notable that liberal authors were already making a distinction between West and East European powers. One of them even speaks of a division of Europe into "deux zones de sociabilite", a Western one which is liberal and an Eastern one which is conservative.'[26] East and West came to represent progressive and reactionary political organisation; constitutional and absolutist forms of government; for or against revolution; for the future, or restoring the past.

However, even then, the political distinction was not always expressed in the more contemporary division between East and West. As Okey points out, public perceptions were still influenced until the early nineteenth century by a North–South axis as they had been for thinkers in the Renaissance. Russia was seen as a Northern power under Tsar Alexander I for example. According to Okey, the modern distinction was not codified until the interwar period. For, while 'The term "Eastern", even "oriental", had often been attached by English and French writers to places in the Balkans, Romania, Transylvania or the Russo-Polish borderlands ... Its increasing application to an entire regional state system, observed by Lheritier in 1935, broadened the area of its use and inevitably had a distancing effect.'[27] Another Frenchman too, the geographer Emmanuel Martonne, noted a 'cultural descent' in the interwar years, as one moved eastwards.[28]

Why? The disintegration of the interwar system was most graphic in Central and Eastern Europe. As a consequence, it was increasingly written off. This was the meaning of the developing sensibility regarding 'the East'. And at the same time, this geographical expression had also become a means of expressing specific intentions on the part of the key powers. Thus, 'In the 1930s Western statesmen referred to Poland and the Danube basin countries as Eastern Europe or Central Europe. Their usage depended upon their purposes. If they wanted to include these territories in their own sphere of influence they referred to Central Europe; if they wanted to exclude them, they referred to Eastern Europe.'[29] In other words, the region was defined through its relations with the West. As Hobsbawm puts it, it was a 'second colonial zone'.[30]

Arbitrary Divisions

For the renowned British 'East Europeanist' Seton Watson, 'It is clear that the main strands in European culture have come through Christendom, from Hellas, Rome, Persia and the Germanic North as well as from Christianity itself.' This gives us a 'resultant compound'.[31] It is actually anything but clear – not least in the fact that Seton Watson's definition places Persia in Europe. It is a pick and mix process. Abandoning religion for the moment, Anthony Smith asks what makes real Europeans. His requirement for entry is that '... at one time or another all Europe's communities have participated in at least some of these traditions and heritages ... . They include traditions like Roman law, political democracy, parliamentary institutions and Judeo Christian ethics, and cultural heritages like Renaissance humanism, rationalism and empiricism, and romanticism and classicism.'[32] Inclusion or exclusion on the basis of historical traditions is therefore an essentially arbitrary process. These 'traditions' are very recent. Perry Anderson notes that 'Cultural borders are no more clearly marked than geographical: Muslim Albania or Bosnia lie a thousand miles West of Christian Georgia or Armenia, where the Ancients set the dividing line between Europe and Asia.'[33]

Any attempt to define who merits inclusion and exclusion from Europe only highlights the impossibility of doing so. To attempt the appropriation of human achievement for the cause of 'Europe' might boost authority, but it does not stand up to scrutiny – particularly at a time when there is such anxiety about all forms of identity. We are left with essentially arbitrary cultural exclusion. Smith himself asks, 'If religion is a real criterion of identity, should not Poland, rather than Greece, be a member of the new Europe? And what of the other great division – between Catholic and Protestant?'[34]

The often absurd consequence of claiming contemporary authority on the basis of a particularist reading of the past is illustrated by an American author. He writes of 'Our Greco–Roman mental and intellectual traditions' which are apparently 'under growing challenge from non Western ideas'.[35] Is William Woodruff's thinking 'Greco–Roman' in a way that a Serb's is 'Byzantine' or 'Orthodox'? Where does the more limited impact of the Enlightenment on certain Central European countries leave the United States – a country which barely existed at the time? If we are to exclude countries in this way, we could equally put forward an argument that the contribution of Scandinavia, for example, was insufficient to qualify as a true part of Europe. Maybe as so many developments took place first in France, Britain and Germany, only they constitute Europe proper?

The more immediate and practical the focus of this mistaken approach, the more it becomes unsustainable. The clash between 'traditions' rendered meaningful by academic writers and the inevitably more confused contemporary reality is stark. Returning to the vexed question of differing traditions in the former Yugoslavia and their supposed basis in religion, we should recall that this was a largely secular society. As the satirist P.J. O'Rourke archly put it, '... Serbs and Croats are so much alike that the only way they can tell each other apart is by religion. And most of them aren't religious. So the difference between Serbs and Croats is that the Serbs don't go to Eastern Orthodox services and the Croats don't attend Mass. And the difference between Serbs and Muslims is that five times a day the Muslims don't pray to Mecca.'[36]

Contrary to commonly held perceptions of Eastern and Western 'civilisation', the achievements of humanity cannot be isolated so rigidly. We should recall that the idea of a war between civilisation and barbarism is the language through which Hitler pursued his murderous campaign against the Soviet Union. It is a dichotomy which has some meaning in relation to understanding the development of civilisation in ancient times. It has only only the most reactionary and self-serving purpose in the twentieth century.

The notion that humanity can be meaningfully divided into cultural or 'civilisational' blocs is, however, a popular idea of our (pessimistic) times. It is expressed most extravagantly by the notion of a 'clash of civilisations' developed by the American political scientist Samuel Huntington.[37] It is worth making something of a detour to further challenge the assumptions behind such thinking by emphasising how such divisions meant little even as far back as the very beginnings of civilisation. A more general look at human history is also useful in challenging the corollary of the 'backward East', that the West is the very embodiment of human achievement – the sole repository of reason, individuality and creativity. On this basis we can then more specifically question the notion of a confrontation between 'civilisation' and 'barbarism' – a notion that continues to underpin the culturalist understanding of the world, especially relations between the 'West and the rest'. Such a perspective also I would add has particular relevance to the notion of Eastern Europe as the ground upon which Eastern barbarism and Western civilisation met. Mackinder's presentation of Eastern Europe in relation to a Eurasian 'heartland' cast the region as being defined, or rather distorted as a hybrid product of successive waves of Asian invaders. It is to the broader patterns of history that we now turn, not in a fruitless search for meaning or identity, but to emphasise the artificiality of imposing divisions, and the mistaken methodology which such an enterprise involves.

4

The Myth of Distinct Historical Civilisations

A False Method

The divisions of East and West figure prominently in a wider approach to the world and its history which sees cultural divisions as decisive. It is an outlook which has made a significant comeback in the post-Cold War period – both at the national and international levels. Mirroring the domestic 'culture wars' declared by the likes of United States right winger Pat Buchanan, the wider global picture is again seen to be shaped by confrontations between competing cultures, or as they are traditionally known at this level, 'civilisations'. This, an approach which as the sociologist Samir Amin has noted, is bound up with a traditionally colonial outlook, is again setting the agenda.[1] It is now Samuel Huntington's 'Clash of Civilisations' thesis which is the starting point for understanding the post-Cold War world. While these dark vistas are the hallmark of an eccentric, although influential right, the assumptions behind them – that we can meaningfully speak of distinct and separate cultures or civilisations – are widely shared.

Most Western societies are now deemed 'multicultural': composed of separate cultures living side by side with varying degrees of cooperation or conflict. It is a notion of 'separate development' which needs to be intellectually challenged if we are to more fully understand the irrationality of the East–West divide. The contemporary view of Eastern Europe is shaped by the vision of clashing civilisations. It is clearly important to Huntington – the 'Eastern boundary of Western civilization' is the only such division in his book which merits a map of its own. This line, forged for Huntington in the fourth century has been intact for at least five hundred years, and provides the answer to how we set the limits – how we 'bound the West', as he puts it. As this outlook depends upon a particular, and particularist reading of human history, it is to that which I now turn.

The civilisational and cultural approaches rely upon a fixed and static view of human development. In insisting upon the centrality of cultural distinction, it must deny the complex interaction which is the story of our past. This interaction is not simply a question of 'cross fertilisation', where one culture borrows from and lends to another, yet remains essentially the same. From a very early stage, the real 'cultural' achievements; agriculture, writing, scientific innovation became the common property – to varying degrees – of mankind as a whole. Exceptions only proved the general rule of an inexorable drive toward the common pool of human achievement that is 'civilisation'. Speaking of Eurasian history in particular, the historian Marshall Hodgson explained that:

> ... it becomes clear that these interrelations were not purely external, accidental cultural borrowings and influences among independent societies. They reflect a sequence of events and cultural patterns shading into each other on all cultural levels. The four nuclear regions are imperfect historical abstractions. All regions formed together a single great historical complex of cultural developments.[2]

Thus for Hodgson, it is the 'interrelations of societies in history' that are of moment. The divisions through which we compartmentalise our history are not real, but only a rough tool with which to try and fix patterns and trends in our minds. In reality, a quite different picture emerges.

It is when we turn to the study of history that the inadequacies of cultural essentialism are most apparent. At its most extreme, it involves the creation of entirely fictitious cultures, as with the 'Magian' culture made up by the famous British world historian and one of the pioneers of the 'civilisational' approach, Arnold Toynbee.[3] More generally, evidence that characteristics were rarely unique to, and therefore could not be said to define separate cultures, is invariably ignored, as we can see in the countless historical errors of the most infamous member of this school of history, the German Oswald Spengler, author of *The Decline of the West*. In his excellent critique of such civilisational understanding of history, another British historian R.G. Collingwood notes that, 'The reason why Spengler denies these obvious facts is because he cannot grasp the true dynamic relation between opposites; his philosophical error leads him into the purely historical blunder of thinking that one culture, instead of stimulating another by its very opposition, can only crush it or be crushed by it.'[4]

It is precisely because of this fluid and dynamic reality that, as Collingwood continues, there is '... no static entity called a culture, there is only perpetual development'.[5] History is process, and to deny this is to deny history itself. The denial of this fluidity may make the job of the historian easier, but it takes us nowhere. Rightly angered by the stupidity of culturalist history, Collingwood insists of Spengler's approach, that 'His atomistic view of cultures ... cuts out the real problem of history, the problem of interrelating the various cultures, which is the problem that requires profound and penetrating thought, and leaves only the problem of comparing them, a far easier task for those shallow minds that can accept it.'[6] He concludes that without the process, development and interaction which constitutes human history, '... we are not talking about history but about the labels we choose to stick upon the corpse of history'.[7]

The Complexity of History

A far more complex pattern than the neat but meaningless boxes imposed by Spengler, Huntington and their ilk, is evident from a look back at the course of human history. Making sense of it is no easy task. As the authoritative Australian historian Gordon Childe pointed out, particularly in pre-modern human history, 'The picture presented is frankly chaotic; it is hard to recognise in it any unifying pattern, any directional trends.'[8] Insofar as we can establish it, useful classification is not so much geographical, as historical. Mankind has moved through broadly defined successive stages, related to the tools and materials through which he is able to transform his environment, and thus himself. Hence we have the stone, bronze, copper and iron ages for example. At each point, the locus of achievement, the area which most successfully manages to fuse and deploy innovation, changes – although the same areas often managed to sustain their edge for significant periods in these slow moving times. But it is not necessarily most useful to focus upon the particularities of the region where innovation first developed. In many respects this was merely accidental – the availability of metals, or often, in the first instance, a favourable climate: the suitability of Europe to sedentary agriculture (and correspondingly, the Asian steppe to nomadic 'barbarism'); and at an earlier stage, the particular challenges and opportunities offered by the fertile crescent. It is those developments which proved to be of universal application which are of enduring significance. Thus for Childe, the history of science can be understood as the diffusion of useful ideas beyond the environment that originally inspired them.

Given the relatively stagnant character of pre-capitalist social formations, it is interesting to note how early this process of diffusion can be identified. Childe notes, for example, how even before 3000 BC, the achievements of fertile crescent civilisation had spread to the Aegean, Turkestan and India. He suggests that by the Second Millennium we can meaningfully speak of a pool of civilisation where the kings of Babylon, Assyria, Mittanni, Halti and Egypt interchanged ambassadors, wives, presents, deities, physicians and soothsayers. After recovery from the early dark age around 1000 BC, from 500 BC a continuous civilisation of literate urban societies can be identified running throughout Eurasia. Childe illustrates how times had now changed, pointing out that:

> The several portions of this zone were integrated and interconnected to a degree never before attained. An educated Persian or Greek, however vague and inaccurate his knowledge of its extremities, could feel himself an inhabitant of a humanly populated world – an oikoumene, as the Greeks called it – four times as large as an Egyptian or Babylonian would have dreamed of a thousand years earlier.[9]

Later, in '... the three centuries beginning in 330 BC the frontiers of civilisation were enlarged to now include a continuous zone of literate states from the Atlantic to the Pacific'.[10] A high point is then reached in the Roman empire which, as Childe suggests, brought together a unique pool of human experience and achievement. But, as the very expanse of the empire suggests, to imagine its impact can be restricted to Rome itself would be absurd. The effects of Roman 'pooling of civilisation' were obviously felt far beyond the confines of their capital – indeed around the world as it was then known; through Europe, Asia and Africa. By AD 250 Rome, and with it the ancient world, had disintegrated. Nevertheless, the general historical pattern which emerges is that while culture becomes more diversified, at the same time, '... cultures are tending to merge into culture'. Superficial variety, different types of water so to speak, should not obscure the fact that increasingly they '... all flow into the same river'.[11]

Of course, within this general pattern there were varying degrees of inclusion and marginalisation from this stream of civilisation. Besides the localised centres of bronze working in Mexico and Peru, civilisation did not reach the New World, Oceania or Africa South of the Sahara until late historical times. Within the zone of civilisation, perhaps most isolated was China, standing as it did beyond the Himalayas – impenetrable even to the energies of Alexander the Great. Yet even here, we can identify elements of continuity with the experience of the Afro Eurasian world. As Hodgson points out, the Mongol armies conquered much of China, as they were also victorious in Germany, Iran and on the Indus. Buddhism from India profoundly affected the life of both China and Japan. As is well known, many Chinese inventions such as gunpowder, the compass, paper and printing made their way through the Middle East to India and Europe.

Again, however, it is worth emphasising the unity of the whole, rather than the sum of parts. It is important not simply to list these neglected Eastern contributions to civilisation in the spirit of suggesting their inclusion in an account book of separate 'cultural' borrowings and bestowals. Against the one sided Western emphasis on 'their own' achievements, we should not be equally one sided in response, and highlight uniquely 'Chinese' elements. Here, Hodgson is again useful.

> When we look at human history as a whole, it will not do simply to give more attention to 'Eastern' societies – either for their own interest or as influencing or contributing to Europe. We must learn to recognise the Occident as one of a number of societies involved in wider historical processes to some degree transcending or even independent of any given society. Though the Occident was relatively isolated, the effect even on the Occident of its involvement in these wider processes cannot be reduced to the sum of influences or borrowings from this or that society.[12]

There is one civilisation, not many, and it is unbecoming of human achievement to quarrel over whose was the greater contribution – even if it were historically meaningful to speak of such a thing.

Which Lines to Draw?

Another question that needs to be asked of the 'civilisationalists' about the uneven development of humanity, is why they choose to emphasise only differences along selective lines. Why civilisational or cultural divisions? Or, to put it another way, why is it assumed that 'cultures' are somehow homogeneous in a way in which other historical abstractions are not? Why 'Islam' for example? By the sixteenth century at the latest, Islam in Eastern Europe, the Middle

East proper and in India, were following quite different trajectories. So why use religion as a means of classification, when it is evident that religion is subordinate; clearly shaped by more decisive factors such as nation, class and capital? Defining the East by its adherence to Orthodox Christianity is equally meaningless. For Hodgson such an approach makes little sense, as '... there is no point where the sort of differences that existed between the great regions could be decisively distinguished from the sort of differences that existed between particular nations'.[13]

Defining 'culture areas', as they are known in cultural anthropology, is an essentially arbitrary affair – as arbitrary as attempting to establish who is historically European in the manner we have already discussed. Melville Herskovits, for example, a student of the influential Franz Boas at Columbia University, developed the concept of culture areas in his study of Africa.[14] In defining what he calls the East African Cattle Area, Herskovits admits to all sorts of problems in cataloguing traits. The idea that it could be defined by wife beating was made difficult by its existence also in the Congo area (and many other places!). Attempts to define culture just produced longer lists of material, psychological and communicative traits that the anthropologist was told to account for in defining his or her culture areas. Usually, however, they tried to latch on to one, such as religion or music. In Herskovits' case it was cattle farming in the East of Africa; the Congo area included 'the extensive use of the banana'! In such a scenario, Eastern Europe would presumably be characterised by the consumption of fatty food and excessive alcohol abuse. Although absurd, it only highlights the necessarily arbitrary creation of divisions based on 'culture'.

Simply because the civilisational divisions are the broadest, does not mean they are any more meaningful. Divisions are an important theme of history, but the decisive ones at any one time vary considerably. Certainly in early history, as Hodgson indicates, drawing retrospective civilisational lines obscures more than it reveals. At a banal level, differences are manifold. But with no clear prioritising principle, an instinct of superiority suggests they simply be drawn where prejudice most suggests a people are unable to cope with modernity. In this respect, the modern 'industry' of 'conflict prevention' is reduced to examining the ability of inferior cultures to deal with differences.

Civilisation versus Barbarism?

Perhaps the most important division within civilisational discourse, especially between 'East' and 'West', is that between the 'civilised' and 'barbarian'. Despite the formal equality now relativistically afforded to different 'civilisations', it is evident that they are implicitly morally unequal. That the formulation of 'the West' manages to monopolise much of human achievement, including the faculties of reason and rationality, suggests that others are not so blessed in this regard. Others in the East lack these universally lauded qualities, and are therefore less than civilised. If the contemporary language of moral superiority is now generally tempered – although not, as pointed out, with the 'barbarous' Serbs – the content is similar. The principle division in the post-Cold War world is effectively that between the 'civilised' and 'barbarian', or as it is now often put, the 'intolerant', and the West. But what is the real meaning of this dichotomy? Did it have any – at least historically?

The challenge of 'barbarism', insofar as we can now speak of it as a valid historical category (it has been so compromised by pejorative, moral use that it is now difficult to use), can be understood as when:

> ... the natural oscillation of warrior shepherds between winter and summer pastures became exaggerated into paroxysms of war and conquest, which sent tribes of Indo-Aryan, Turkish, and Mongolian nomads careering out of the steppe against the sedentary societies bordering it.[15]

With the development of settled agricultural society and animal domestication, those still bound to a nomadic existence now represented themselves as the limits and boundaries of a growing civilisation. As was suggested in my comments regarding method, it is a process of encroachment and inter-relation. In this sense we can say that the barbarian is a product of civilisation. As the famous historian of the frontier, Owen Lattimore, describing East Asian horse nomadry put it,

> The barbarian terror that harried the northern frontiers of civilisation did not erupt from a distant, dark and bloody ground that had nothing to do with civilisation; it was an activity of people who were the kind of people they were because their whole evolution had been in contact with, and had been moulded by, the advance of civilisation.[16]

This is not to minimise the differences between the two. Jones is perhaps right in suggesting that early on, the most distinctive attribute of the civilised as opposed to the barbarian, was literacy. His relativistic emphasis goes too far however, when he then says that '... the principal difference between it and "barbarism" may simply have been its self awareness, i.e. its consciousness of being different and its ability to express this'.[17] To minimise the significance of self-consciousness is surely mistaken: it is a key to humanity. Nevertheless, at the same time, it is right to emphasise similarity as well as difference – particularly as history has demonstrated that barbarism was to be subsumed into civilisation. This is especially important when considering the issue of the 'civilisational fault lines' so beloved by those suggesting the inevitability of cultural conflict replacing the political conflict of the Cold War. For the likes of Huntington, these meeting points of 'clashing civilisation' are the focus of conflict and the shape of things to come. In reality, however, even much further back in history, these 'fault lines' were more apparent than real.

What of these historical borderlands where separate worlds come into head on collision? As one would logically imagine, the borderlands were precisely where these 'worlds' more obviously merged into one – forming something hybrid. Jones describes a process whereby:

> Civilisation diminished as it approached the barbarian realms; and barbarians became less barbarous as a result of prolonged association with civilised folk. Indeed so strong was the cultural drift on the frontier that the walls raised against the barbarians may have served as much to keep civilised men within as to keep barbarians out.[18]

These were indeterminate zones of contact, rather than clear 'fault lines'. The fixing of frontiers is in fact very much a modern development. Thus John Hale, in his rich history of Enlightenment Europe, notes that:

> Even in the West, where political nations rubbed up against one another, the unbending term 'frontier' was seldom used; the words 'confines', 'border', 'boundaries' were preferred since their vagueness allowed some elasticity for future conquests or territorial trade offs.[19]

Such indeterminacy should hardly come as a surprise – the assumption that meeting points between different peoples involves perpetual strife is simply untrue. Throughout history, the routine of daily existence has required cooperation and coexistence – regardless of origin or 'culture'. Thus we can see, for example, that national prejudices against minorities are often strongest in areas where the majority population has no contact or experience of these 'others'. Whatever their prejudices, the locals have to do business with whomever, and whatever it takes to survive.

This is not to deny that there have been what we might term real clashes between civilisation and barbarism. Hodgson identifies three confrontational periods of exceptional intensity, the last of which was the expansion of Genghis Khan across Eurasia in the twelfth and thirteenth centuries. Significantly, barbarism had a diminishing impact on civilisation. The fragile 'oases of civilisation' of the early river valley societies were almost overwhelmed in the first wave, forces were evenly balanced in the second period; '... whereas the "last massed fury" of barbarism under Genghis Khan was more a desperate gesture of self defence against the steady encroachment of civilised society on the steppe, than a potentially lethal blow to civilisation as a whole'.[20] As we approach the modern era, civilisation has triumphed. 'The barbarian challenge to civilisation, represented by the Central Asian nomads or in the West, by the semi-pastoral peoples who invaded and occupied the Roman empire, gradually ended; and by the Sixteenth and Seventeenth centuries historical barbarism had succumbed ...' as Jones puts it. More elegantly, and in a manner appropriate to his confident age, the great historian of Roman eclipse, Edward Gibbon, declared: 'The reign of independent barbarism is now contracted to a narrow span; and the remnant of Calmucks or Uzbecks, whose forces may be almost numbered, cannot seriously excite the apprehensions of the great republic of Europe.'[21]

Of course, the real end of any contest between civilisation and barbarism is not the same as the end of its expression. Long after these polarities had any historical meaning, they continued to be invested with significance. In fact, its usage intensifies as this vernacular becomes a moralised means of suggesting superiority, and legitimising domination. This language, and more broadly the whole notion of a morally and geographically divided humanity, becomes bound up with the project of colonial expansion, and perhaps less famously, the internal challenge to the 'cultured' elite, by the masses.[22]

The regionally compartmentalised conception of history – and the present – also endures. As Hodgson notes, 'Western scholars, at least since the Nineteenth century, have tried to find ways of seeing this Afro-Eurasian zone of civilisation as composed of distinct historical worlds, which can be fully understood in themselves, apart from all others.' In seeking an explanation, he suggests that:

Their motives for this have been complex, but one convenient result of such a division would be to leave Europe, or even Western

Europe, an independent division of the whole world, with a history that need not be integrated with that of the rest of mankind save on the terms posed by European history itself.[23]

The dichotomy between civilisation and barbarism continued then long after it had any historical meaning. Ironically, the potential for the barbarian to become civilised was also precluded to an extent that was unclear even in ancient times, and certainly in the age of progress with which the modern era began.

In the first instance, as we shall now indicate, this new view of an East which had apparently set itself apart is the product of the rapid progress made by the West from the eighteenth century onwards. Still at this time, however, there remained the possibility that they might catch up, and become like ourselves. The need to elevate 'the West', and set a distinct limit to its expanse at 'the East', is an expression of the increasing difficulties experienced by great powers once confident of their ability to transform the world in their own image, not be confined to only one part. First, however, more needs to be said on the question of the roots of division lying in the Enlightenment. While it is acknowledged by some modern thinkers that the East is very much a product of developments in the West, it is invariably only to say that the fault lies with the emergence of a confident humanism in the Enlightenment of the seventeenth century.

5

Defined by Western Development

An 'Other'?

We have already critically highlighted the traditionally conservative views that 'we are descended from the Romans' so to speak; that correspondingly, Eastern Europe is not; and that this somehow accounts for the division of East and West. Before looking at the real forces of Western development and perception that really sent 'the East' to the fringes of Europe, it is worth mentioning the more contemporary approach of 'the other'. This 'otherness' methodology correctly highlights intellectual developments in the West rather than the given backwardness of the East. But it is important to point out that this approach still shares much in common with the ahistoricism of the very traditional Eurocentrism which these writers are so keen to attack. The idea that 'others' will always be created; that it is not the product of a specific social system, and the problems it has in reproducing itself, is debilitating. It suggests a timeless, almost natural process based on human suspicion and group mentality. Its one sided emphasis upon only intellectual expressions of prejudice outside any social context, also highlights the need to examine the real processes of material, not just ideological development, if we are to put the creation of the East in proper context.

It is conceded in some contemporary writing that divisions such as that between the civilised and barbarian, East and West, are not simply given – certainly they are not straightforward expressions of geographical realities or inherent cultural abilities. They are historical creations. As with the notion of nationalism, it is also sensed that these are modern ideas bound up with our own modern era. In recent writing, it is with the Enlightenment that the creation of systematic division between the civilised West and uncivilised East becomes important. In *Inventing Eastern Europe* for example, Larry Wolff recently argued that the notion of Eastern Europe was an intellectual invention of the Enlightenment. Here he is applying the argument and conclusions of the 'Other' school pioneered by Edward Said's classic *Orientalism*, which surveyed the increasingly separate and inferior presentation of the East beyond Europe in the works of Western thought and literature.[1] Typically in these works, a wealth of artistic, geographical and intellectual expressions are marshalled to substantiate the argument that the original contempt shown by Enlightenment thinkers for the rest of the world set the pattern for prejudice that was to reproduce itself throughout the following ages.

But in the process, any sense of the relative importance, impact and significance of a notion of inferiority is lost. All becomes blurred into one unfortunate tale of misunderstanding and malice. The original critical insights provided by Said's work should not blind us to the significant shortcomings of what has now become very much the mainstream approach. Methodologically, as with the more traditional ahistoricism, 'the other' approach focuses too much on apparent continuity in expressions of prejudice against the 'Orient'. As with the older school which projected these ideas back into the Middle Ages and beyond, formal continuity is emphasised to the neglect of the different meanings that different social circumstances gave to apparently similar expressions of disdain for 'others'. While we can find instances where the term 'Europa' for example, was used from early on – in fact, right back to the ancient Greeks – the notion that there was a conscious idea of Europe in the Middle Ages is nonsense. National identity, let alone a wider European identity was virtually non existent. As already pointed out, there were no 'Europeans' at this time in any meaningful sense, and therefore no 'others' to the East – 'non Europeans' morally excluded from a consolidated sense of superiority. Only in retrospect can such a consciousness be imposed. Such an idea was primarily an invention of nineteenth century romantics who sought to give historical substance to the idea of 'Europe'.

There is no continuous sense of difference between 'Europe and the rest'; between 'East' and 'West'. To contend otherwise is to project back into the past very modern conceptions which have meaning only in the context of contemporary conditions. Fundamentally, the systematic dissemination of ideas was not possible. With no society in the modern sense of the term, it was a time of localised myths and mythology. Generalised ideological notions are bound up with the more intense social development that came with the capitalist epoch.

Blaming the Enlightenment

A more specific objection to the ostensibly more critical approach to history of 'the other' school is the way in which it is invariably the Enlightenment that is singled out for criticism. Authors point to the contradiction that the age of reason was also that of the distinctly unreasonable deprecation of 'others'. Reflecting the now popular consensus that reason and rationality lead only to destruction – that there is a straight line from the arrogance of instrumental rationality to the gas chambers of the Holocaust – the age of humanism which created the possibility of decisively overcoming irrational prejudice, is held responsible for contemporary hostilities. Why is this objectionable? Because in denigrating the Enlightenment, they are at the same time attacking reason. Not only is it general human qualities which are then blamed for the creation of problems such as the East–West dichotomy, but specifically those which are most positive and potentially liberating. But can we make a connection between Enlightenment humanism's view of 'others' and those of today?

'The Europeans have sailed around the world and for them it is a sphere. Whatever has not fallen under their sway is either not worth the trouble or is destined to fall under it.' Thus Hegel, the high priest of the age of optimism in the nineteenth century, brought out the spirit of the earlier Enlightenment. In so doing, he expressed a confidence which seems sheer arrogance to our generation. It is true that 'The optimism of the Enlightenment inevitably proclaimed the definite leadership of Europe and the spontaneity and rapidity of its development in comparison with the other peoples of the earth', as the Spanish historian of ideas Luis del Corral suggested in relation to Hegel's assertion.[2] Such a statement could be easily interpreted as the sort of racial and cultural denigration characteristic of colonial attitudes, and no doubt would be by contemporary sensibilities, as yet another example of 'other' creation. But we must be careful to ask what is the meaning, and more importantly, the spirit, of Hegel's proclamation. It is not a condemnation of 'others', so much as confidence in the possibilities of man and his inexorable progress. It is a celebration of the ground breaking progress established by European man that had left the stagnant East behind. Hegel is not essentially concerned with regional differences, certainly not suggesting they are intrinsic or natural. He is interested in man and his self-realisation. In this regard, a sense of superiority is not necessarily a bad thing: it depends upon what it is expressed against. A sense of superiority over nature, or the past, is a celebration of worthwhile human achievement.

I have indicated that the sixteenth century Europe of the Enlightenment was not concerned with geographical divisions. As John Hale tells us, the term 'frontier' was seldom used, vaguer terms were preferred, allowing for future trade offs. This was a time of the expansion of horizons and borders, not their consolidation. Thus within Europe during the sixteenth century, '... neither atlases nor maps showed a bias towards the West. Devoid of indications of national frontiers until late in the century, they were not devised to be read politically.'[3] This was the age of the perfectibility of man in general, where Prometheus stood as the symbol of limitless potential. Mankind was consequently divided into periods of accomplishment, rather than fixed areas. Voltaire, for example, had four such periods of cultural achievement: Athens, Rome, Florence and the France of Louis XIV.

Admiration for the East

For the Enlightenment mind, barriers were man-made and to be overcome. The West was certainly leading the way, but it was envisaged others would follow. Importantly for thinkers such as Turgot, it was circumstances that left them behind, not any innate incapacity. Consequently, the sense that (European) man had finally bettered the achievements of the ancients did not preclude fascination, and even admiration for 'others'. While such expressions obviously concerned 'the East' of the Orient rather than that within Europe (which had not as yet developed as a concept), they indicate to us that the attitude taken towards 'others' was distinctly more open. If the strange and foreign 'East' of the Orient could be admired, it was unlikely that those of the European East were deplored as they would be in contemporary thinking.

Alessandro Valignano, who saw the Japan of the late sixteenth century, '... recorded not just surprise but admiration, their politeness made them superior not only to other Eastern peoples but also to Europeans as well'.[4] While he was very struck by cultural differences, this clearly had no pejorative or moral meaning – it did not make them inferior. As China became known with the spread of trade and missionary work, the traveller Joseph Hall for example, in his *The Discovery of a New World* of 1608, could ask '... who ever expected such wit, such government in China? Such arts, such practice of all cunning [i.e. skill]? We thought learning had dwelled in our part of the world; they laugh at us for it, and may well, avouching that they of all the earth are two eyed men, the Egyptians the one eyed, and all the world else, stark blind.'[5] There are many more famous examples of this very different view of the Oriental East. Voltaire admired Confucius and India. He praised Mohammed to such an extent that

Parisian rumour had it that he would soon be moving to Constantinople himself. Importantly, as Maxime Rodinson has pointed out, nor did Enlightenment curiosity about the East yet descend into exoticism. In fact, 'The eighteenth century saw the Muslim East through fraternal and understanding eyes. The idea that all men were born with equal abilities, along with the prevailing optimism (the real religion of the age) now made it possible to seriously reconsider the earlier charges levelled against the Muslim world.'[6]

Enlightenment thinkers assumed that, ultimately, people of the East were essentially similar to themselves. The original humanist position did not insist that we were merely 'equal but different', but unequal (as yet), and the same. Maxime Rodinson, in his excellent, *Europe and the Mystique of Islam*, explains this well in the following quote.

In the eighteenth century, an unconscious sense of Eurocentrism was present but it was guided by the universalist ideology of the Enlightenment and therefore respected non-European civilisations and peoples. With good reason it discovered universal human traits in their historical development and their contemporary social structures. But with a kind of pre-critical naivete, eighteenth century scholars attributed to these civilisations the same underlying bases as European civilisation.[7]

This point is worth considerable emphasis. It meant that beneath expressions of hostility, the assumption that, even if avowed enemies, the view that we retained our essentially human character predominated. As Rodinson continues:

The Oriental may have been considered as a savage enemy, but during the Middle Ages, he was at least considered on the same level as his European counterpart. And, to the men of the Enlightenment, the ideologues of the French revolution, the Oriental was, for all his foreignness in appearance and dress, above all a man like anyone else. In the nineteenth century, however, he became something quite separate, sealed off in his own specificity, yet worthy of grudging admiration.[8]

What this begins to indicate is that the 'admiration' for the exotic so characteristic of contemporary attitudes is essentially anti-humanist. The stress on difference rather than essential human similarity betrays a retreat from this more unified picture of humanity.

This is not to suggest that this age was devoid of prejudice against the East. It is as easy to suggest admiration by reference to early travellers' impressions, as it is to imply that Western man has always hated the East. Nevertheless, a sensitive appraisal of such evidence indicates that the spirit of the Enlightenment was quite different to that of our own age, and this had a significant impact on their view of the world. Retarded evolution would eventually be overcome – there were no insuperable natural or cultural barriers. Expressed another way, 'civilisation' for French enlightenment thinkers was a *process* towards an ideal state. Their own society had made more progress along this road than others, but they believed and hoped that it was open to all.

By contrast, in the twentieth century, an important thinker like Weber posited rationalism as a very specifically Western trait. Generalising from historical enquiry into 'why the West was first', he begins to suggest there is something intrinsic to our world in a way which no Enlightenment thinker would have thought to do. Reflecting his own, and his age's disillusionment and disenchantment, Weber no longer saw man in general, but many men with different values and goals.

The Transformation of the West

We have to look beyond some sort of innate tendency for the West, or even human (un)reason, to always create 'others'. Before doing this, however, it should be registered that even in the nineteenth century, the 'cultural' differences between East and West were quantitative rather than qualitative in character. The empires of Central and Eastern Europe were affected by the Enlightenment and broader material progress. As the historian John Feffer points out, '... it is often surprising to be reminded that Luther nailed his 95 theses to the door of a church that would later stand in East Germany, that Copernicus studied and worked in Poland, that Kafka wrote ... in Germany ... that Bucharest was once known as little Paris ...'.[9] Historians such as Piotr Wandycz have pointed to this exclusion of the East from European history.[10] This is not to argue that the region was the centre of the cultural universe; rather, that differences were a question of degree. They varied from country to country, even between town and countryside, in the same way that the 'national contributions' – if we can speak of such a thing – varied also in what came to be 'the West'.

It was not the particular backwardness of the East, but rather the social and economic development of the West that was decisive.

Transformation of the West through the industrial and scientific revolutions also transformed their world view. Thus in Germany, '... economic progress led the German middle classes to elevate their differences with the Slavs in particular to an unbridgeable civilizational divide'.[11] With European development, especially through the nineteenth century, the Ottoman empire, a part of which later came to constitute the border of 'the East' of today, became not only 'the sick man of Europe' in Western eyes, but the embodiment of torpor and decay. The change here was not so much in the Ottoman empire. Certainly it had stagnated, but it was hardly unrecognisable. Rather, the change was relative to the new-found dynamism of the West.

It was the vantage point of the great powers that had really been transformed. They now looked down on those who had failed to reproduce their own astonishing rate of progress and innovation. Effectively, they naturalised the difference; seeing it as only the product of their own special qualities, rather than a particular set of circumstances which freed up a surplus to stimulate capital formation. Whatever the process involved, however, the whole world was now seen in a different light. Even grand old Austria, for the British statesman Disraeli, was now 'Europe's China' – in other words, synonymous with stagnation and the past. For the infamous Austrian statesman Metternich meanwhile, 'Asia began on the Landstrasse'. It was only beyond his own land that backwardness began – specifically on the road heading East.

Nor was it only the language of international relations that changed. The region now took on an entirely different appearance, as it seemed inexplicably left behind by rapid development in the West. Before that time, it was hardly exceptional. In Hungary, for example, it was only with the widespread diffusion of Enlightenment ideas of progress by the end of the eighteenth century that any differences could be judged. As the historian Andrew Janos, in one of the best historical studies of the region notes,

> ... differences between Hungary and the societies of the Occident had been noted by travellers ... neither Hungarians nor Westerners thought that Hungary was a bad country, or that the West was progressive by virtue of its material life. Rather they saw each other's countries as separate and mildly exotic parts of the world, different, but not inferior or superior to one another.[12]

In this respect it is difficult to know what to make of judgments such as that of the historian Daniel Chirot that, 'Eastern Europe was in some sense economically backward long before it was absorbed into the broader Western market'.[13] In what sense? Backward compared to what? It was only in relation to change in the West that backwardness became quantifiable. The title of his book, *The Origins of Backwardness in Eastern Europe*, however, suggests that the 'origins' of contemporary backwardness lie in, and indeed were predetermined by, a unique history. A great deal of significance is attached to the so-called 'second serfdom' for example, where backward relations prevailed in the countryside in particular areas of what later came to be known as 'Eastern Europe'.

It was by the new universal standards of progress of the eighteenth century, that Hungary now looked decidedly backward, more 'Asian' than 'European' – even when it was developing comparatively rapidly in relation to its own past. There were now different standards. The degree of change became the measure of society's worth. In this light, everything took on a different complexion. 'What is quite remarkable', Janos continues, 'is that despite such obvious signs of economic vigour and rising cash incomes, the first half of the 19th century is not remembered as a period of well being and material comfort ... but rather as an age of increasing pauperisation, differentiation and social malaise.'[14] With his visit to nineteenth century Britain, the famous Hungarian patriot Count Szechenyi experienced a shock, and thereafter saw his country as a backward wasteland. This stimulated a determination to catch up. In understanding the nineteenth century impulse to reform in Central Europe, the answer must therefore be '... sought in the broader context of a collective crisis of identity brought on by the technical advances of the Occident that culminated in the industrial revolution ... constantly rising standard of living against which the majority of mankind could measure its own misery'.[15] Conditions previously considered acceptable, exotic or not considered at all, now appeared intolerable by the new standards of modern Europe. While this did not automatically lead to a consolidated sense of superiority and inferiority, it certainly raised the question of why these societies seemed unable to replicate developments further West.

If parts of Central and Eastern Europe in the eighteenth century looked depressing to their elites, to the Western observer the region took on the appearance of a shocking backwardness rather than exotic charm. In the first instance, it was perceived to have declined by travellers and observers from the West. 'Nothing can be more melancholy', wrote Lady Montagu in 1717, 'than to travel through

Hungary, reflecting on the former flourishing state of that kingdom ... .'[16] As Okey points out, the subject of the condition of Poland in particular created a vast pamphlet literature, as intellectuals pondered the decline of the country. The Hungary which would not have looked so very different from Britain a century before, now looked 'grotesque' with its lack of modern centralisation, and relative absence of universalised language and behaviour. A country which still through the middle of the eighteenth century remained a mysterious land of natural wealth and beauty – to such an extent that it attracted nearly a million immigrants from overpopulated Alsace, Swabia and lower Austria – only became underdeveloped in changing Western perceptions from the last quarter of the century.[17]

Such views as these, while they became the dominant perspective on 'the East', remained of little significance however – as much as anything else, the area was of limited importance. Certainly for Britain, the region remained of marginal interest. More importantly, before the First World War, belief in the universalising capacity of Western development still suggested that 'the East' could catch up. While the idea of Western superiority became increasingly powerful, the prospect of joining the global elite continued to be held out as a possibility. Confidence in the ideas and principles upon which the success of Western industrialisation had been built, remained such that they, at least theoretically, were open for others to replicate. They remained universal rather than specifically Western, albeit that the idea of an Eastern contribution to civilisation had waned. The impulse to fix a definite boundary to these different worlds only arose once the sustainability of these achievements in the West was thrown into doubt. With the First World War, and the traumatic interwar years that followed, prophets of doom foresaw the 'decline of the West'. As with Weber, all was now concentrated on the apparently unique qualities of 'the West'. Where previously its power had been self-evident, and therefore in little need of justification, now it was ideologised. In the process, definite limits to where this new 'West' began and ended were drawn.

As one observer experienced it at the time: 'Prior to the world war, Europe formed a whole ... . Today Europe is dismembered ... the Eastern provinces of the old continent are getting far away; they are taking on an appearance of their own; for the moment at least they are in a state of regression.'[18] They are 'taking on an appearance of their own' in the context of a general European crisis – one which would require that the boundaries of 'the West' be fixed in order that something might be salvaged. As I shall explain at greater length in Chapter 4, 'the West' had to be played up ideologically to compensate for what was in the real world – from the First World War onwards – a flawed and even self-destructive character. This would require blaming much of European problems on 'the East'. In turn it would determine that 'the East' became more distant than ever. The conviction developed in Western minds that the East was uniquely stuck in the past. This strange idea that time functions differently in the East has returned with a vengeance, and it is this mysterious quality which so sets it apart, and to which we now turn. I shall suggest that the more significant preoccupation with the history of the East is rather among academics intent on sharing out the responsibility for the West's destructive influence in the twentieth century.

6

The Battle Over the Past

Overburdened with History

The question of 'history' in Eastern Europe has a significant history of its own. In the nineteenth century it was the lack of history that was criticised. For Hegel, 'the East' (the Orient) lacked a past. As for 'the East' with which we are concerned, after the failure of revolution in the nineteenth century, the subject of the 'non historic peoples' of Eastern Europe was raised by the likes of Frederick Engels. The failure of nationalities to free themselves from the domination of the old empires, and even help their oppressors suppress rebellion, led to discussion of their illegitimacy – their lack of any real historically validated existence.

In the twentieth century, however, the common view has been that the East is overburdened with history, rather than suffering from its absence – too much history, rather than too little. In the 1990s, this view has returned with a vengeance. It is now routine to understand the region as uniquely 'historical'; as a 'shadowland' where, '... palpable ghosts of the past compete with ill defined images of the future'.[1] These are haunted countries according to conventional academic wisdom. John Feffer for example believes, 'The 1956 revolution is just yesterday for many Hungarians, the 1795 partition that wiped their country from the map for 123 years is a matter of daily concern for many Poles, and the 1389 military defeat at Kosovo still stirs the heart of many Serbians.'[2] The author feels little need to justify such an astonishing statement – that 1795 or 1389 is a matter of daily concern. Nor does he specify exactly who it is that believes this to be the case. This is not only an academic preoccupation however. Richard Holbrooke, the architect of recent United States policy towards Bosnia, told the first ever session of the North Atlantic assembly held in a former Warsaw Pact state (Budapest 1995), that, '... they must be prepared for one final act of liberation, this time from the unresolved legacies of their own tragic, violent and angry past ... can this region free itself from history's ghosts and myths?'[3]

Philip Longworth's *The Making of Eastern Europe* systematises this approach. He begins with the most recent period of history, and then works his way toward the past. The unmistakable message is that the further back into history we go, the more we will understand 'the making of Eastern Europe' – we will discover when it was 'made', and by what. At the same time, it is an essentially arbitrary process as with where one draws the line between East and West.

While there are various differences among academics as to which aspect of the past determines the present, there remains a consensus that history is a living force. It has become a part of common sense on 'the East', as we can see with numerous recent pronouncements on the problems of contemporary Bulgaria. In an otherwise hard-headed analysis of the Bulgarian economy, Antony Robinson of the *Financial Times* explains that the reasons for the slow pace of change '... are rooted in the history and culture of a country liberated from nearly 500 years of Turkish rule a century ago with the help of a Russian tsar, Alexander II, and then converted into the most integrated of the Comecon and Warsaw Pact countries after 1945'.[4] So too for Robert D. Kaplan, the American cultural doom-monger, and author of *Balkan Ghosts: A Journey Through History*, Bulgaria is explicable through the culture of the past. Kaplan, however, sticks to the Ottoman period as he 'explains' the eruption of economic protest in late 1996. 'Bulgaria's disappointing experience with democracy', says Kaplan, 'clarifies the importance of geography and culture in East Europe's transitions.' How so? How is it 'clarified'? Because, 'As was the case between the world wars, those European countries with Ottoman legacies close to the Middle East have had an extremely difficult time adjusting to a free society.'[5]

Meanwhile, J.F. Brown, despite critically noting 'the cultural argument' of Jowitt, which says 'the communist system turned East Europeans into vegetables' (which he is against lest Bulgarians use it to excuse their contemporary failings), employs a similar method, only his period is an earlier one. 'Five hundred years of Ottoman rule has certainly left its impression on the Bulgarians ...', asserts Brown.[6] It remains unclear what this means, still less why he is so certain that this is the case. Conversations with Bulgarians suggest similar preoccupations to those of other people in the region: gaining access to the European Union; entrepreneurial opportunities; and the latest cultural products from the West. There is no reason to suppose that the Ottoman empire exerts any more of a real bearing upon Bulgarians, than the experience of domination under the British empire does on contemporary Americans. What is particularly remarkable is that 'history' accounts for whatever aspect of contemporary Bulgaria you choose: slow economic reform; the outbreak of protest; even the general mentality. Others go even further than Brown. Dennis Hupchick, for example, adopts the cultural argument with abandon. His *Culture and History* is advertised as a work which '... delves deeper to examine the more fundamental cultural and historical forces constantly at work, either consciously or subconsciously, among the inhabitants of the region'. He acknowledges the highly questionable assumptions behind this approach, however, adding that 'Some readers initially may react with a pang of skepticism to such a premise.'[7] He at least makes it clear that he is asking that we accept mass psychology as serious analysis. Few others make their method so plain. To explain contemporary developments as the product of history, would require that we see it as a living force, a thing, a transcendental 'geist'.

The assertion of the past's importance continues to be especially compelling for writers explaining the force of nationalism, especially what is termed 'ethnic nationalism'. More than any other force, it is these 'tribal' loyalties which are seen to transcend history. It was this assumption that informed fears about the region in the early 1990s. Because it is a force apparently able to survive regardless of historical experience and change, ethnic nationalism can apparently return from any attempt to overcome it. Even internationalist communism was unable to do anything to modify the power of savage ethnic identification, according to a key assumption of academic thinking. It only went into temporary slumber, to be awakened like an ugly sleeping beauty with the downfall of the old regime as suggested by the likes of the late Ernest Gellner. In fact, as we shall illustrate later, the phenomenon of 'nationalism' (a catch-all term for a whole variety of different trends) shows very clearly how even the most apparently timeless quality is continually reshaped and reformed. As the historian Thomas Simons Jr explains, nationalism is '... not a gift of East European history'.[8] On the contrary, 'It has never been a "given", it is always a contingent and specific phenomenon like all the rest, changing its form, weight, and its impact over time, and depending on circumstance.'[9]

Books on the history of other parts of the world are not so ready to amplify the impact of the past, certainly not to suggest that it has an increasing impact with its passage. The past is seen to have a much more limited role, second to the more powerful modern forces which render the past to be what it is – that which is no longer. Yet time appears to have a different, transcendental quality in 'the East'. As the eminent British East European expert Hugh Seton Watson put it back in 1948, 'In Eastern Europe, the 20th and 16th centuries still exist side by side.' This peculiarity is of great moment for Seton Watson. As he continues, 'The distortions resulting from this contrast have produced powerful explosive forces ....'[10] That 'explosions' have taken place in Eastern Europe is here removed from the context of having historically been the battleground for wider great power rivalries, and instead blamed on the refusal of the past to go away.

There is certainly less resonance for the idea that the past has a decisive bearing on the present in more dynamic societies than those of Eastern Europe. The success of United States society has determined a relative confidence about the future, and a corresponding conviction that, in Henry Ford's immortal words, 'history is bunk'. But with stagnation has come greater interest in historical myths to bolster identity in the present. Hardly a day passes in Britain without reference to the country's wartime experiences against Germany – from 'poppy days', to the presentation of the Tory war with the EU as a reliving of Britain's supposedly valiant and lone struggle against German domination in the 1940s. But history remains no more real than it is in the East. In both East and West it can be the form through which stagnation is vaguely sensed – that the past refuses to go away, rather than that transformation to the future is difficult. In a more specific sense, however, 'history' in Eastern Europe is weaker – because its myths are even less serviceable than those of the major powers in the West. Politicians there often have to go back way beyond the experience of the Second World War to find anything remotely heroic about the nation's past to suggest continuity as a resource for stability. And indeed, a host of unsavoury characters have been dragged up for precisely these purposes. In so doing, however, East European regimes only make plain the more limited possibilities of drawing on the past in the service of the present.

Condemning the Historical East

Using history in this teleological way has the appeal of simplicity. The temptation of history is that it appears to provide easy answers – they are as they are because of 'history'. But we must question the usefulness of this approach, which amounts to reading history backwards. It is tantamount to identifying a contemporary trend such as the de-industrialisation of Britain, and then looking for the explanation in earlier centuries – in the anti-entrepreneurial 'spirit' of the aristocracy for example. There is then no need to attempt the perhaps more difficult task of taking apart the present, because we have 'history' as an alternative. Insofar as we do, contemporary factors appear almost inconsequential compared to the power of what is historically determined. 'History' is more than a guide – the background noise, it becomes seen as a revealer of truth.

We could no doubt provide plenty of historical reasons for the backwardness of East Asia. Yet where would this lead us in relation to the recent success of South Korea, and now its industrial troubles? 'History' tells us nothing in and of itself. If it is overloaded it provides little more than dubious justification for the status quo ante. Speaking of communist historiography back in 1961, one historian pointed out that '... history and historical evidence carry a burden of meaning which is intrinsically beyond them ...'.[11] This surely can equally apply to the industry of historical accounts of East Europe. At the very least, they overreach themselves, giving too much importance to the past rather than the present. What is more, the flip side of their approach is to imply that the West embodies an ability to overcome the past, particularly its more negative features. Unlike 'over there' where the backwardness and ignorance of earlier centuries lives on, 'over here' such forces have been banished. In their place, reason, tolerance and creativity define a West oriented toward the future.

The flattery of the West which lies at the heart of the discourse on the historical East is revealed by a Russian writer (who presumably loathes her own country) back in 1991. For Tatyana Tolstaya, 'in the West the sense of history has weakened or completely vanished; the West does not live in history, it lives in civilisation ... . But in Russia there is practically no civilisation, and history lies in deep, untouched layers over the villages, over the small towns ....'[12] History here, as Pocock explains, is the '... memory of the past unprocessed, in the nature of raw sewage: unmediated, uninterpreted, uncriticised ... unimpeded in its capacity to drive humans to do unspeakable things'.[13] The non historical West is civilisation in this formulation; the East is sewage.

There are those who disagree with this condemnation of an East bewitched by the past. For example, Anne Applebaum, author of *Between East and West*, reflects a different current of thinking on the subject. She bemoans the absence of history, more particularly a lack of consciousness about it in the present. 'There is little evidence of obsession with the past, because the past is not remarked upon at all', she remarks.[14] And what is the purpose of this new insight? She berates the immorality of a new Eastern bourgeoisie for having forgotten the crimes committed by their forerunners in the Second World War and the communist period. She attacks other authors such as Rosenberg in her *Haunted Land* for excusing this failing in view of the fragility of society. More commonly, writers such as Noel Malcolm are keen to challenge the myth of the historical East because it lessens the extent to which Milosovic and the Serbs can be held responsible for the war in the former Yugoslavia.[15] However questionable the objectives of those arguing against the centrality of history, it is indeed the case that there is a clear contradiction between blaming history in general, and Eastern politicians in particular. Once again, as in the nineteenth century, the East is being accused of its lack – rather than over-abundance – of history; in particular their purported willingness to whitewash the embarrassments of recent history.

Now, as then, it is by no means clear why the East should be singled out in this regard. There is little evidence of the West seeking to dwell upon the far more numerous skeletons in its own cupboard – the decimation of Russia and Eastern Europe in the 1930s and 1940s to name but one. The clearly pejorative content of both propositions indicates that these sweeping generalisations are deployed in a utilitarian manner to suggest inadequacy on the part of the East. Whether this is achieved through insisting on an obsessive, or a criminally indifferent, attitude towards the past is perhaps less important in Western thinking than the consensus that something is amiss with the East. Significantly, contradictions between authors who diagnose too little, or too much history, obscure a fundamental agreement that the East has failed to negotiate the present – for reasons quite unique to itself.

It should be noted that there is also a more critical strand of thought developing on this question. There are now authors challenging the idea that the past can explain the present in this part of the world, and this disagreement is not simply put forward to suggest a failing of different order on their part. The American anthropologist John Bowen, for example, attacks 'The Myth of Global Ethnic Conflict', explaining that 'Contrary to the "explanations" of the war frequently offered by journalists, ordinary Serbs do not live in the fourteenth century, fuming over the Battle of Kosovo; nor is the current fighting merely a playing out of inevitable logic of the past, as some have written.'[16] The debate is moving on. But it is certainly not the case that even more critical authors no longer see special problems that are intrinsic to the region. Bowen, for example, identifies a lack of civil society as an alternative explanation.

Others, such as Lake and Rothschild at the University of California, have substituted fear of the future for the power of the past. 'Ethnic conflict is not caused directly by ... "ancient hatreds" and centuries-old feuds ... . Nor were ethnic passions, long bottled up by repressive communist regimes, simply uncorked by the end of the Cold War' they state, quite correctly. But instead, they argue that '... ethnic conflict is most often caused by collective fears of the future'.[17] As with Applebaum's inversion of the East being a uniquely historical proposition, this new argument ends up suggesting yet another way of suggesting a profound problem exists – so profound that it affects the whole outlook of society towards past, present and future. The latter emphasis is not derogatory, indeed it is sympathetic in its portrayal of a frightened people uncertain of what the future might hold. Nevertheless, it is an unwarranted generalisation, and one that again asserts special problems and the consequent necessity for unique solutions. Lake and Rothschild wrongly maintain that there is a special problem of ethnic conflict in the region. Significantly, theirs remains very much an argument for external interference in the region (through what they call 'confidence building measures'), only in this case to allay unproven fears about the future rather than the traditional thesis about the power of the past.

Many casually mention the significance of the battles of Mohacs or Kosovo as having some bearing on the contemporary politics of Hungary, Serbia and the region more widely. Maybe it is understandable for those who can see little future, that the past seems more alive and real than the present. It is surely mistaken, however, to impose this view on a whole society, or part of the world.

This morbid fascination with the past needs to be questioned. Why is the past so compelling that we are drawn to it as a source of truth? 'I imagine tens of thousands of old men and women whispering to their grandchildren ... repeating ancient stories ...' explains Michael Walzer, explaining why he is so certain that the revolutions of 1989 were driven by tribalism.[18] Why does he have these imaginings? The preoccupation with history as revealer of truth is perhaps really an expression of the author's own sense of pessimism. More generally the positing of a past, or indeed future, which bears down upon and paralyses the present indicates a wider disposition to insist that problems are intractable. In this discussion it is not only the cultural shortcomings of East Europeans today which stand in the way of progress. In this historical discussion, cultural inadequacy is projected back, and forward, and in the process becomes a transcendental power which precludes any attempt at change. The ghosts of the past may not haunt the imaginations of all the peoples of Eastern Europe, but they certainly overshadow Western perceptions of the region. Not only is it evident that the elevation of the past is intimately related to the exaggeration of problems and moral condemnation, but it also expresses a consciousness in Western thinking which is now closed to change.

Who Made Eastern Europe?

The role of the past in Eastern Europe is overplayed. It invariably involves moral condemnation, and tells us more about the general pessimism of Western thinking today than it does about contemporary Eastern realities. Nevertheless, it is the case that historical factors have given peculiar shape to the region. Eastern Europe's past has been a tormented one. More than this, many of the great tragedies of the modern age have taken place on her soil. As every schoolchild knows, the First World War began in Sarajevo, the Second with the dismemberment of Czechoslovakia, and then the blitzkrieg of Poland. Most ghastly of all, the extermination of European Jewry, and the systematic annihilation of Slavs carried out through the Nazi invasion of Russia, all centred on the lands to the East. The question of responsibility for this unfortunate history lies at the heart of the debate on the region's past.

In the book of the TV series *The Other Europe*, Jacques Rupnik rightly suggests that the '... debate about Central Europe hinges on the relative weight of indigenous factors and external forces'.[19] Is the 'tragedy of Central Europe' of its own making, or is it the responsibility of its far more powerful neighbours in the West? It seems that Rupnik, like so may others, prefers the former: that the fault lies with societies of the East. Hence while these external forces are mentioned in the form of 'benign neglect' by the great powers, far greater attention is given to factors supposedly unique to the region. Thus for Rupnik, any consideration of the determining forces of European history '... does not diminish the importance of domestic ingredients in the growth of authoritarianism and later totalitarianism'.[20] It comes to be seen as no accident that numerous regional conflicts and two world wars took place in this region: it has apparently invited such calamity. In effect, the victim is blamed for its own fate.

Philip Longworth has taken this viewpoint a stage further in arguing that '... there may well have been no war had the situation in East Europe in the thirties not invited Nazi aggression'.[21] The 'situation' he speaks of was perhaps not entirely the doing of Eastern Europe, but there seems little doubt for him that what he calls 'the region's singular political culture' played its part in 'inviting' aggression. Joseph Held in the *Columbia History of Eastern Europe* concurs. He tells us that while '... it is indisputable that external forces played a major role in the destabilisation of Eastern Europe in the inter war Europe ... the failure of the democratic experiments might be more reasonably attributed to internal factors in all the Eastern bloc countries' (except perhaps Czechoslovakia).[22] How might it be 'more reasonably attributed'? If such logic was deployed in relation to the extermination of European Jewry – that their culture or position in society had 'invited' extermination – outrage would be provoked. It is par for the course when it comes to Eastern Europe, however. Indeed as has already been noted, attempts to single out East European collaboration with the Nazis suggests an attempt to blame them for the terrible fate of the Jews, as well as their own.

In this scenario, the great powers have only walk on parts – sucked in involuntarily by the chaos created by native 'authoritarianism'. Instead of identifying the processes through which weak indigenous factors are driven and shaped by powerful external forces, Rupnik and others suggest them to be equivalents. In so doing, the weight of responsibility falls on the 'authoritarian' East, in a process that is analogous to drawing our attention to the provocative clothing and manner of a victim of rape. Both rapist and victim become part of the plot. We are left to draw the conclusion that had the victim not made him or herself available, the terrible act would not have occurred. In fact, the region figures so prominently only because of its weakness – it acted as something of a vacuum. But if this theatre had not been available, another would have been found through which the deep seated conflict of interest between the major powers would have been acted out. Indeed, Eastern Europe was not the only region to find itself playing battlefield – so too did Africa and Asia. It was only the most unfortunate, in that it was here enacted with particular ferocity.

In fact, the failure of interwar democracy in the region, presumably the development that 'invited' destruction, was not the product of peculiar Eastern forces or any predisposition towards 'authoritarianism'. The failure of democracy was a universal feature of European and United States politics. In Italy it began in the early 1920s with Mussolini's march on Rome – long before any glimmer of 'native authoritarianism' in the East. While less dramatic elsewhere in the West (apart from Germany of course), democracy was universally called into question in the interwar period. What is more, failure in Eastern Europe was largely a response to this political crisis.

It was made clear from their very creation after the First World War that the existence of independent states in Eastern Europe was conditional upon more important developments. From the Treaty of Locarno in 1923 onward, all the countries of the region were considered dispensable. The international priority remained the resolution of the German question: how to fit this new, and as yet excluded, power into a world order that had already divided the spoils. If resolving this issue required that Germany be redirected eastwards to take over her 'natural colonial zone' – Eastern Europe, then so be it, was the dominant sensibility in the West. Particularly for Britain, with its colonies further afield, Eastern Europe remained of marginal importance. It seemed straightforward, therefore, to assume that it would be the most obvious, and least problematic locus of German expansion.

It is not surprising that Eastern Europe was already by the mid-1930s a de facto German colony – before that status was formalised by occupation in the war. Nor is it surprising that politics in Eastern Europe largely revolved around foreign alliances, rather than democratic domestic politics. In particular, those parties that identified with an increasingly authoritarian Germany were clearly those that had a future. 'Democratic', or rather pro-French or pro-British, parties were hardly likely to flourish where the British, and increasingly the French also, made it plain that they were prepared to abandon the region to satiate Germany. The infamous betrayal of Munich was the logical consequence of what had gone before. Domestic politics was seen by all the parties as relatively trivial in the context of passing the region from one set of powers to another.

This is in addition to the economic devastation wrought upon the region by a world recession that was not of their making. The German economy collapsed following the United States stock market crash of 1929. Unsurprisingly, this impacted upon Eastern Europe in an especially dramatic way, given that the region was already designated little more than an outpost of the German economy, and was accordingly fragile and dependent. Again, these were hardly ideal circumstances for the growth of democracy. As Harry Schwartz put it in *Eastern Europe in the Soviet Shadow*, back in the time when the region was formally acknowledged to have been a victim of circumstance, 'It is amazing in retrospect that anyone should have expected democracy to flourish in the region after World War One.' This was not because of collective stupidity, or a 'native authoritarianism', '... much more important were the pressures flowing from military, economic, and political developments elsewhere'.[23]

In reality, the region has never had the capacity to determine its own future, let alone the destiny of Europe as a whole. As a German and Russian academic put it recently, 'It never managed to become a subject rather than an object of world politics ....'[24] Rather, history suggests that it is only when the region has become a focus for great power competition that conflict has ensued. Historically, it has been whenever East and Central European states have been dragooned into the service of a great power, that catastrophe has followed. Indigenous factors in this respect are quite irrelevant; they are only the form, not the substance of the problem. Insofar as we can speak of an indigenous factor, it is that of a power vacuum – a weak and largely powerless area unfortunately positioned adjacent to the most destructive world powers – providing a field of battle for wider quarrels.

Writing the West Out of the Picture

As has been discussed, the most prolific and longstanding premise of a European divide is, and has been, that of the civilised West encountering the barbarous East. Interference in the region has, in various ways, been shaped by this discourse of civilisation versus semi barbarism. But there is an obvious tension, however, between such a discourse and the culpability of the West for wreaking havoc through the region before, during and after the Second World War. The economic and political abandonment of the region to Hitler's Germany in the 1930s, let alone the subsequent carnage, hardly squares with the notion of an especially civilised West. And of course, even if we imagine the outlook of the Allied powers to have been clearly distinguishable from that of their German rivals, we are still left with the fact that Germany is as much a part of the West as any other nation. In this context, any (re)interpretation of the interwar period and especially the war itself, which might cast the great powers in a more flattering light, or one which at least obfuscates Western responsibility, is attractive. It does not require a conspiratorial view of how the past is presented and interpreted, to suggest that its implications for the authority of a society are reflective of that society's concerns. Historical scholarship is always informed by particular norms, values and given priorities.

In this respect there appears to be an attempt, conscious or otherwise, to write the West out of the picture, particularly in relation to the wars fought on East European soil. This tendency is centred most clearly on the redefinition of the experience of the Second World War – which still stands as the greatest challenge to the West's image as 'civilised' in contrast to the East. Particularly for Germany, that experience continues to be a reminder of an embarrassing past which can act as a brake on the future. It remains problematic to match its economic importance with political and indeed military projection, while it remains associated with its wartime experience. Any attempt therefore to shift responsibility for that conflict, or even merely relativise it by establishing that others, like the Serbs, have also carried out their own holocausts, is intuitively welcomed on their part.

The contemporary preoccupation with the shortcomings of 'the East' offers original opportunities to put forward new theories of culpability for acts of the Second World War. During the communist years, the peoples of Eastern Europe remained cast as victims of external forces, and the devastation that had resulted from the West's intervention could only be relativised indirectly through the discourse of the lesser of two evils – communism versus the West. The portrayal of East European victims of Soviet 'totalitarianism' made it difficult, at the same time, to emphasise their alleged responsibility for causing Europe's wars. The West had to make do with the sense that anything we did in the past, is surpassed by what the USSR is doing in the present. This sensibility could never quite eliminate the discomfort with the recent history of the West's wartime activities. But this was hardly a pressing concern while the spectre of communism dominated the political agenda.

The end of Soviet domination presents the need to renegotiate the West's relationship to the Eastern past. It also presents the possibility of sharing out some of the blame for the war. In its most extreme form, playing up the alleged horrors of the Serbs in the Yugoslav conflict – to the extent that they are somehow comparable with those of the Nazis – lessens the singularity of that experience, and therefore the particular obstacle the past represents today. The insistence that Eastern Europe 'made itself', and indeed continues to do so, not only removes responsibility, but provides a means through which the historical legacies of the past can be renegotiated. This is perhaps the real process of so-called 'holocaust denial', or rather what is more accurately described as the 'relativisation of the holocaust'.

Having largely concerned ourselves with the perception and presentation of the East, we now need to hold this against the real impact that the West has had on the East. The region has taken on unique contours and reflexes. While it is irrational to speak of this marginalised region somehow having the capacity to shape the destiny of Europe and the world as a whole, in a sense it is quite unique. The intensity of the West's impact upon the region has distorted these societies in unusual ways.

7

A Colonial Object

Looking for Sponsors

The idea that East Europe is a product of its own past is, then, self-serving for the West. It excuses the devastation wrought by the major powers, by pointing to a native 'East European-ness'. It is, though, possible to identify elements of continuity that have maintained the region as, in some sense, distinct. Crucially, these are not features derived from something innate, but nor can they be dismissed as the creation of prejudicial interpretation in the literature on the subject. The region's continued subordination to the West has given rise to a number of enduring realities. These have changed significantly over time. Nevertheless, at the risk of too general a presentation, highlighting them throws light on the otherwise apparently natural peculiarities of the region. The first feature that needs to be grasped is the virtually colonial character of relations between the two halves of the continent. This is a part of the world where even relations between neighbouring states come a very poor second to the overwhelming significance of relations with the West – where Czech President Havel's first visit in his new role was to Germany, rather than Slovakia – what was until only a few months before, the other half of Czechoslovakia.

The relative weakness of social development from the nineteenth century, itself very much a product of the increasing domination of the leading European powers, meant that marginalised Eastern elites were forced to appeal to the major Western powers to build their nations. In what was to become Romania, for example, there was a long tradition of looking to France to help the local elite consolidate their control. If, in the process, this involved de facto colonial status, then so be it. Thus Prince Cuza, a key architect of Romanian nation building and self-proclaimed 'lieutenant of the Emperor Napoleon', could make the following appeal to his beloved France in 1856:

Romania would be for France a force and a glory. You would have more than a colony, more than a fortress ... France has no need to make a conquest of us: we are open to her, let her come and recognise herself in us ... we have always loved and hoped in her.[1]

Even to this day, Romania makes much of its supposedly special relationship with 'mother' France.

The leaders of the future Czechoslovakia also appealed to the French for support in creating a nation for themselves. Their appeal was not based on becoming a simple colony however. Czech leaders made geo-strategic appeals, touting their potential to assist in the containment of Germany. Thus the Czech leader Kramar, in the late nineteenth century, tried to advertise his potential nation in French newspapers as a barrier to German ambitions. Such appeals proved prophetic. The creation of Czechoslovakia from the ruins of the Austro Hungarian empire after the First World War was indeed the result of great power strategic thinking. The country's role in containing both Bolshevik Russia and a defeated Germany was central to its birth at the Paris Peace Conference. In particular, American misgivings about bestowing independence were largely overcome by the role of the Czech legions in causing problems for the Bolsheviks, as they fought their way back home through Russia towards the end of the war. The Czechs provided clear evidence of their utility, and were rewarded with recognition by Woodrow Wilson in 1919. The roots of Czech 'independence' are still reflected in the Prague landmark which bears his name to this day.

Such appeals were not confined to the Czechs, nor to the period leading up to independence. The Poles, too, made much of their potential to keep the Soviets out of Europe, particularly as they had driven the Red Army back into Russia at the end of the First World War. The formal independence they were granted, partly as a result of such appeals, solved little however, as they were left at the mercy of Germany in the troubled interwar years that were to follow. They had little option but to prostrate themselves. Thus the Polish Minister to Washington, Prince Kazimierz offered United States businessmen an 'opportunity to start some kind of colony for [your] nation', coupled with the traditional offer to act as a barrier to Bolshevism.[2]

A Return of Direct Domination?

Eastern Europe's inferior position, and in particular their proximity to Germany, lent this peculiarly prostrate character to their relations with the West. Nothing was too much to please potential sponsors and allies in the West, even if the interests of the nation were openly subordinated in order to present themselves as an attractive proposition. To some extent, this direct subordination has returned. The observation that the region has now only swapped Soviet for German and a wider Western domination is clearly apposite, even if it overestimates the much weaker impact that the USSR made by comparison (it is because of this weakness that they had to resort to force). Bosnia is of course the most extreme example. The OSCE decided, when the September 1996 elections took place, which parties were eligible and how they organised their campaigns, the priorities of reconstruction in the country are also being determined by Western institutions.

Other virtually neocolonial relationships are less well known. On the assumption that, without American involvement, societies in the Balkans would relapse back into authoritarianism, the United States set about reshaping the countries of the region in their own image with fervent anti-communist zeal. Thomas Carothers, for example, in his interesting survey of American 'democracy assistance' details the process with particular reference to Romania. The United States created an 'independent' media, sponsored anti-government political parties such as the Democratic Convention and much more – at the same time as they were also monitoring the elections to ensure 'fairness' and a 'level playing field'! The extent of this involvement is indicated by one representative from the International Republican Institute – responsible for the training of the opposition. 'We taught them what to say, how to say it, and even what to wear when saying it', he said. After all, 'They were like children. They were at the sixth grade level politically.'[3] (One wonders whether the notion of national sovereignty is taught in the United States curriculum!) The numerous farcical failures of United States interference, where they 'backed the wrong horse', or were themselves taken for a ride, do not, in the context of this sort of arrogance, inspire much sympathy.

The United States laid claim to the Southern Balkans as its own sphere of influence in the East. Its experts have been ensconced at every level of the Albanian administration with ministries having their own United States adviser. The United States military has had a significant presence also – especially with a view to preventing any attempt to absorb the ethnic Albanians of Kosovo into a Greater Albania. So too has Bulgaria been subjected to American tutelage. As in Albania, United States advisers have been everywhere in the Bulgarian administration. The United States embassy in Sofia occupies the same position as the Soviet embassy of old – although now that their advice has apparently led to economic collapse, American interest has noticeably diminished. Overall, however, their influence, especially at the military level, has intensified. Particularly through the elaborate anti-Serb containment policy which has developed in the Clinton years, involvement has increased to the point where American military advisers are questioning it's extent of involvement. Ted Galen Carpenter of the Cato Institute, and Amos Perlmutter, editor of the *Journal of Strategic Studies*, express dismay at '... moving toward making that volatile region a zone of extensive US influence – perhaps ultimately a virtual American protectorate – with the goal of containing Serb power'.[4] Carpenter and Perlmutter, like many others, are alarmed at such extensive United States involvement in a region of little strategic value.

Parallel – and potentially conflictual – spheres of influence exist elsewhere in Eastern Europe. Germany has taken on the Baltics for example: their advisers frame legal systems, train army and police personnel; German financial institutions have developed the banking system; and cultural organisations like the Goethe Institute has expanded. Weaker powers like France meanwhile have made some moves to fill the void in the more marginalised countries like Romania and Slovakia.

On a more general and systematic level, Western institutions are now central to determining policy throughout the region. British academic Bob Deacon, for example, has detailed the extent to which social policy in the CIS and Eastern Europe is now shaped by the EU, the Council of Europe, the OECD and the World Bank. Interestingly, European institutions in particular have been keen to impress the need for 'the social dimension' on Eastern regimes, and not simply allow economic efficiency to determine priorities. The concern, as ever, of Western institutions is of a primitive backlash against democracy (and the West) if the impact of the market is not cushioned. The Commission of the EU explained that, 'Co-operation between the EU and CEE countries on the social dimension of transition is essential to reduce the risk of the population rejecting democracy and the market economy because the social and human costs are too high.'[5] Interference is based upon the unsupported prejudice that the peoples of the region are prone to 'reject democracy'. They therefore need educating in the benefits of European social policy.

Such interference is regarded as benign, and there is certainly little protest from the likes of Albania or Bulgaria who, because of their own marginalisation, have proven glad of any interest – on virtually any terms. The West is on a moral mission to bring economic know-how and prevent them from slaughtering each other. But it is important to recall that even classical nineteenth century imperialism was inseparable from crusading morality. It was bringing education, Christianity and the like to the unfortunates. And no doubt many, such as the missionaries, fervently believed in what we now recognise to have been little more than self-congratulatory propaganda. Simply because Western interference declares that it is there to do good, to catch 'war criminals' or whatever, does not mean that this is indeed beneficial, unladen and assures a beneficial outcome. Just as we can regard the teaching of 'tolerance' as the contemporary equivalent of exporting more traditional Christian values, so the punishment of Serbian miscreants shows the harsh side of the colonial patron – much as punishment was periodically dished out under classical imperialism as a lesson to the potentially 'unruly' natives.

Nor does the moral presentation of the Western presence in the East preclude the more or less open domination of these societies. Some even make this virtually colonial relationship plain, where it was once emphatically dismissed for fear that it would encourage the alignment of these states with the Soviet Union. In this new climate, barely disguised calls for recolonisation are now made routinely – from those of a 'liberal' persuasion perhaps more than from those of a more traditionally conservative outlook. For example, the *Guardian*'s East European correspondent, Julian Borger, called for a 'benign colonial regime' or an 'international protectorate' in order to bring democracy to Bosnia.[6] His colleague on the paper, Martin Woollacott, meanwhile declared that '... an open ended occupation, with no specific time for elections' would have been more desirable.[7] With remarkable lack of embarrassment then, there are again calls for open domination of parts of the region. There is little to inhibit the extension of this demand to other states, given the Western assumptions that cultural deficiencies are profound and prevalent.

The imperative for greater interference is insatiable. Since it is not so much driven by any specific difficulties on the ground, as a wider conviction of superiority, no amount of interference goes far enough for the likes of these commentators. Bosnia Herzegovina is already a de facto international protectorate. This was established by the Dayton Accord. The UN determines the government policy agenda, and has the power of veto over elected representatives. Meanwhile, the IMF has installed a non citizen governor of the Central Bank, and the EBRD has assumed responsibility for privatisation and public utilities. The original civilian and military mandates have been extended for up to two years. Still, the constant refrain is that 'we are not doing enough', or 'standing by as powerless onlookers' – meaning that there remain some developments which are not taking place under the aegis of the 'international community', and are therefore likely to spin out of control. One could be forgiven a powerful sense of deja vu here, particularly for those familiar with the more traditional colonial literature.

The Competition for Favours

This is not to say that nothing has changed. Appeals to act as a barrier to German or Russian expansion, for example, could hardly make any sense in the 1990s. The contemporary vernacular of the marginalised East in its dialogue with the West has been a more general claim to represent civilised Western values. In response to the politicisation of values by the West, each player in the region is forced to pitch their claims for inclusion in the language of 'who is more civilised than whom'. As Slavoj Zizek has pointed out, 'Every participant ... tries to legitimise their place "inside" by presenting themselves as the last bastion of European civilisation ... in the face of Oriental barbarism.'[8] Claims, such as those made by Romanians to represent an island of Latin civilisation in a sea of Slav barbarism, have been made since the region's original peripheralisation in the nineteenth century. But in today's conditions they have taken centre stage – displacing the discourse of 'who is best equipped to help contain Russia and Germany' that prevailed before the war.

The desperation to gain admittance to the West, even on belittling terms, is such that politics is becoming peculiarly degraded. The financial and political programmes of these societies often do not even pay lip service to the interests of the people. The international circus of 'election monitoring' is a case in point. Here the democratic wishes of the electorate come a poor second to international etiquette. Carothers refers to Romanian critics who have pointed out for example, that in the 1992 elections foreign observers were allowed good access to the electoral commission, while Romanian journalists and other representatives were not. Even copies of the electoral law '... were for some time easier to obtain in English than in Romanian, reflecting the government's eagerness to please the foreigners and its indifference to aiding Romanians'.[9]

This was no accidental oversight, but a logical consequence of the degradation of democracy intrinsic to the intense supervision of these elections by the major powers. The logic here, is to bypass any pretence of national representation whatsoever. One of the candidates in the 1995 elections in Latvia for example, was Joachim Siegerist –

a German who spoke no Latvian. On the basis of being the man best equipped to guarantee German interest (wrongly as it happens, because he was then a discredited figure back home) he came second. Elsewhere in the region, returning 'prodigal sons' have also fared well. The Californian Milan Panic for example, was temporarily premier of the reconstituted 'Yugoslavia'.

The more important process of undermining democracy which flows from international interference is the way in which 'democracy' is now legitimised only through foreign institutions. Under these circumstances, the fate of elected governments hangs on the word from Brussels or Washington like the gladiatorial thumbs down from the Roman senator. In a sense now, the opposition, indeed anyone with a grievance throughout the region against elected authority, only has to cry foul play to the major powers to potentially undermine governmental legitimacy. The net effect is for opposition parties to not bother seeking the support of, or justifying themselves to, the people. Friends in high, international places count for far more than the respect of the electorate. This is not to suggest that the West always responds to these external standards by undermining ruling regimes. As we can see from the example of Albania (elaborated in Chapter 10), Western pressure is dependent upon their own geo-political priorities.

'Only the Anti-Democratic Protest?'

Given this subordinate relationship, it is necessary even at the best of times for governments to speak two different languages: a relatively combative one for the domestic audience, at the same time as demonstrating a ritualistic love of all things Western for the 'international community'. Without understanding the split personality that is necessary for any Eastern politician, political discourse would seem strange indeed. Romanian leaders, for example, routinely announce their desire for reconciliation with Hungary regarding the contested region of Transylvania when Western ears are listening. Yet the very same politicians may then speak harshly of 'Hungarian expansionism' for the benefit of their domestic audience. With little authority to be derived from any other sphere, posturing over territory is sometimes the only option. This is particularly because of the need to over-compensate for the embarrassing extent to which, in every other respect, political forces have to organise themselves around an agenda set by Western institutions.

In the face of demands to behave as the West desires, protests of independence are rare, and largely for limited domestic consumption. Complaints are rarely heard about the extraordinary conditions placed upon regimes if they wish to gain admittance to even the more decorative Western institutions like the Council of Europe, for example. Anything less than a compliant response tends to be diagnosed as the work of a demagogue. If a Slovak or Romanian politician expresses disquiet at having national policy determined by the EU or the United States, this only confirms what we knew all along; that they are anti-democratic, and need to be forced to behave properly. This is particularly clear in the case of the disquiet voiced by many in the region at the incredible influence of George Soros. In a sycophantic article for the *Guardian*, for example, Ian Traynor waxed lyrical about the apparently selfless philanthropy of '... eastern Europe's Robin Hood ...'. Traynor paints a fanciful picture of Soros' Open Society projects battling, against the odds, with authoritarian governmental intolerance. Soros, a man whose '... tone was quiet, self-deprecatory, but the determination ... steely', is '... greeted with fear, hatred and ingratitude'.[10] Governmental figures in Slovakia, Hungary, Croatia, Serbia and Belarus are singled out as being particularly 'ungrateful' – they instead indulge in what Traynor sees as anti-Semitic conspiracy theories. Traynor constructs a conspiracy theory of his own, where the impression is created of a poor old Soros under the cosh – which entirely ignores the fact that he wields more influence than many governments in the region.

Traynor attributes no significance to the few reactions against Soros' activities – for example as he mentions, 16 pro-government newspapers in Albania published a blank page last summer to protest at Soros' money going to save a single opposition newspaper. Or the fact that more broadly, as a critic responded in the paper's letters page: 'Millions of his dollars have been used to shore up politically aligned papers and even parties.'[11] More broadly, the massive involvement of Soros in the region – in 1993 his foundations were operating in some 23 countries with a budget of $300 million – is inseparable from the political and commercial leverage created by such power.

Whatever we might think of the individuals concerned, it is remarkable that the complaints of Eastern Europe's elected representatives count for nothing, while the unelected businessman's extraordinary interference in sovereign societies is beyond reproach. As the extension of Soros' power goes under the banner of the 'open society', anyone who expresses even concern can only be for a 'closed society'. Complaining about the colonisation of your society makes you a 'totalitarian'. We are left with only the occasional expression of wry reflection, such as from Ardil Kalenovic, a radio station chief in Bosnia, commenting upon the carve up of his country. 'Only English colonial minds could have drawn a map like this', he laughed. 'The problem is, this is not Africa.'[12]

An End to Great Power Rivalries?

Great power involvement in Eastern Europe has been recast by the end of Soviet domination. The elevation of an 'Eastern-ness' has put Western interference in a 'no lose' situation. When intervention is unsuccessful, or worse, destabilising, the blame is laid squarely with the region's intrinsic Eastern qualities.

The West's ability to intervene with impunity is further assured by the apparent lack of great power conflict over the region. Away from alarmism about 'Balkanisation' infecting Europe as a whole, more sober voices have counselled a degree of optimism with regard to any repeat of old mistakes. In particular, there is now seen to be relative harmony among the great powers – certainly to the extent that there will never again be world conflict over East and Central Europe. The 'moral to be drawn' by Professor Gregory Flynn at Georgetown University, for example, is that 'Eastern and Central Europe are safe for local wars because no one will get involved'.[13] Similarly for another analyst, 'The principal difference between the violent chaos of 1914 and 1991 is that no great power has an alliance with either the Serbs or Croats, so what is happening now will continue to happen only in the Balkans and spread no further.'[14] Notwithstanding the implicit recognition that great power rivalries are indeed the problem, and apparently oblivious to the massive involvement which has escalated the war in the former Yugoslavia, Robert Kaplan here suggests confidence that today's Balkan conflicts can be safely contained.

In fact, only rarely have any of the major powers consciously sought to 'get involved'. The British in particular have always sought to keep out. Benjamin Strong, for example, a Bank of England representative, argued back in 1921: '... people are now learning that the political risks inherent in Central Europe are still so grave as to require insurance before capital can be invested in such enterprises'. Meanwhile the British minister in Belgrade made clear a year later that this was not the sort of place one would naturally seek influence, explaining that '... were it not for the desperate desire of HM government to get British trade going again at almost any price,

I should have strongly deprecated in principle the guarantee by the British government of a loan made to a foreign country like this one'.[15] The region has always been a bad financial risk for all but the most desperate of imperial powers.

More importantly, there is the realisation – sometimes conscious, sometimes not – that involvement is likely to trigger wider conflict. Thus the demise of the Ottoman empire in the late nineteenth century provoked concern not because it was likely to create conflict in itself, but that it might trigger rivalries between the major powers – all with different ideas about how to maintain the status quo. In this spirit, Sir Edward Grey congratulated all the powers in the pages of *The Times* for their restraint in 1913. Grey was impressed that they had not clumsily rushed in, disregarding the sensibilities of their rivals. Instead, common sense had prevailed, as the gentlemen had kept to their agreement not to let any conflicts of interest get out of hand: 'To the "two most interested powers", Austria Hungary and Russia, special credit is due for the moderation and self-restraint which ultimately prevailed in their counsels ....'[16] In more contemporary times, the same can be said of the hard line that the United States, under both Bush and Clinton, took with Serbia over Kosovo. As they feared that Serbian attack on the unruly Albanian Kosovars would potentially lead to wider intra Western conflict, the United States threatened Milošović with direct attack on Christmas Day 1992 (further belying the myth that the United States was soft on the Serbs at this stage). What stimulated such a decisive response was, as David Gompert, a senior policy maker in Bush's administration makes clear, the perception that this conflict '... could consume the entire southern Balkan region in a conflagration that would pit one Nato ally against another'.[17] Even in the early 1990s, the fear that inspires action like no other in the East, is West versus West confrontation being brought to the surface through the vacuum of the East.

Intervention 'to Stop Intervention'

This concern has not prevented such involvement, however. Ironically, so often in the name of limiting involvement (of others), various Western nations have found themselves embroiled in the region, as, for example, with the Balkan wars of the early twentieth century. In general, the great powers have not trusted their rivals to maintain the status quo, and prevent the outbreak of conflict into which they would inevitably be drawn. This was very much the essence of the 'Eastern question'. As one historian explains, 'The reason why there was an "Eastern question" throughout the 19th century was that the great powers could not agree what to do about these problems.'[18] The particular problem was the disintegration of the Ottoman empire. Especially after the agreements which terminated the Crimean War in 1852, the very essence of 'Europe' became the attempt to prevent the regulation of affairs – particularly in the East – according to the interests of a single power.

To some extent the same problem exists today. It was evident in the barely disguised rivalry between United States and Europe over the conflict in Yugoslavia. The driving force is not some abstract desire to have control or influence – after all who wants responsibility for the Balkan states? Rather, there is a lack of trust. This is illustrated by the way in which the United States was drawn into the conflict. As a report in *Newsweek* described, 'The Pentagon is now drawing up scenarios for how American military power can support an international relief operation. Ten days ago the JSC was saying "Hey, no way," said a Bush official. Now they're saying, "If it has to be done, we'd better do it."'[19] It can't be left to the Europeans, they'll inflame the situation, so we'll get involved ourselves (and inflame the situation ourselves), is the logic here. The unseemly scramble among the powers to claim the cause of Sarajevo, and the mantle of most vociferous opponent of the Serbs, has proven irresistible to the major players in the world. While they have agreed on the general problems, they have proven reluctant to allow their rivals to 'do it'.

Because of the concentration of great power energies in the region, otherwise insignificant events get blown out of all proportion – local conflict becomes international war. Back in the nineteenth century, the Habsburg administrator of Bosnia once satirised a report received from one of his Belgrade agents. 'Great excitement among the population. Jovo has been robbed of two more oxen. What will Europe say to this?'[20] Clearly, 'Jovo's oxen' might only lead to 'great excitement' because great power reputations, not just parochial grievances, were potentially at stake.

In a more contemporary Balkan conflict, that in the former Yugoslavia, no one bothers to ask why it is that a local civil war excited such interest, or why conversely, in those countries marginalised from the diplomatic circus like Italy, there was comparatively little concern (despite the country's proximity to Yugoslavia). Wars in Afghanistan, Sri Lanka and elsewhere are more generally neglected. It is only because the region, and in particular the war in the former Yugoslavia, became an arena for wider rivalries that a local civil war became so important – and inflamed. Now, as back in the times of the original Eastern question, the great powers have proven incapable of agreement, and as a consequence, have upped the stakes to gain an edge over competitors. Those in too weak a position to generate prestige from this process, like Italy, have politicised the issue neither internationally nor domestically.

This is not to say that little has changed. Principally, what is new is the unparalleled extent to which interference is seen as a positive necessity: as a moral imperative of a 'reluctant imperialism'. Most remarkable is the extent to which Germany has been left with a free hand to do as it pleases in the region. Such is the confidence in the moral mission of the West, that even Germany – with its highly sensitive history as regards the East – can be left to dominate unimpeded. In this sense, the reassurance that local wars can now be contained has an element of truth. Any German expansion into the region will not necessarily bring it into conflict with rivals. There is no 'German question' in its traditional sense of an excluded great power whose expansion necessarily challenges the established division of influence. The first real act of Germany striking out on its own, the recognition of Croatia, did trigger a competitive response from the United States in the shape of their own sponsoring of Bosnian 'independence'. Nevertheless, in general, it is clear that potential confrontation between the established powers can be managed for the foreseeable future. Germany and the United States have even gone on to form something of a partnership in the management of the former communist bloc.

An Open Field

There remains a residual unease about this open field, however – particularly in Germany itself. 'Why on earth leave Central Europe to the Germans? It's crazy. It repeats old mistakes, They fear it, we fear it, but very often unfortunately, the only country interested in the region is Germany', exclaimed Friedbert Pflugar, a foreign policy analyst and MP in Kohl's CDU.[21] A fear of the largely unspecified consequences of unhindered expansion underpins an anxiety at the core of, at least declared, contemporary German foreign policy. As one analyst put it,

> In other words, if the EU fails to integrate East Europe, Germany will feel forced to go it alone. This irresistibility triggers Germany's

great post-war neurosis. Help us not to be ourselves runs the troubled sub text of German European policy! Tie us to the mast like Ulysses, that we are not tempted to pursue our interests.[22]

In the same spirit, even former German diplomats, as Timothy Garton Ash has pointed out, declare the aim of German foreign policy must be to prevent German hegemony. Kohl appears to see that the EU should play this role of 'saving Germany from itself'.

Understanding that it is this 'reluctant' great power interference that accounts for the tragedy of Central Europe rather than some peculiar culture, we can see that such fears are not without foundation. The German recognition of Croatia ignited the conflict in the former Yugoslavia more than any other single event. Because of the unquestioned support for Western intervention in all parts of the world including Eastern Europe, the most remarkable and dangerous meddling can take place without anyone batting an eyelid. It is well known for example that is was the United States which not only gave the go ahead for, but played a large part in the training of the Croatian army which drove the Krajina Serbs from their homes in 1995. Thus the mass expulsion of between 150 to 200,000 Serbs (described by the *Guardian*'s correspondent as the product of Serbian 'herd instinct') was effectively organised from Washington.[23] As the *Observer* newspaper headlined the story, 'Invisible US Army defeats Serbs'.[24] Complacency is then not justified – despite the end of the traditional German question. Dangers are not now even recognised, let alone prevented from happening. Dangerous alliances have been cemented, and tragedies swept under the carpet when the victims are on the wrong side.

It is not a question of suggesting that there is likely to be a third world war breaking out in Europe, or even that we are likely to see more wars like that in the former Yugoslavia. The remarkable degree of international cooperation between the major powers, at least partly refashioned through the course of the Yugoslav war, means that differences rarely get out of hand. Nevertheless, given the total lack of opposition to the Western reshaping of the East, there is little barrier to even the most naked domination.

At the time of writing, 'the West' is sending 6000 troops into Albania. Three aspects of this intervention demand particular attention. All indicate an arrogance whereby it is not even felt necessary to explain or seriously justify such extraordinary actions. Operation Alba was undertaken with indecent haste. Remarkably, it has not even been made clear how, and by whom, this action was authorised. It was scarcely felt necessary to even go through the motions of grounding the operation in international law – certainly of making that public. Second, the 'multinational' force comprises principally the most self-interested regional parties. There is little pretence that this is essentially an Italian undertaking (on the anniversary of Mussolini's own invasion of the country!). Their principal partners are the Greeks – the other neighbour most concerned with limiting immigration from Albania – together with the other Europeans charged with policing 'Fortress Europe's' Southern 'flank', France and Spain. Unlike other contemporary neocolonial ventures, there is little pretence of this being a multinational force which represents a wider good. Instead, Albania's more powerful neighbours have been allowed a free hand to do as they please in that troubled country – all apparently with the open ended sanction of the 'international community'.

Finally, what is the purpose of Operation Alba? Insofar as any justification has been presented, it is that of safeguarding food supplies. Yet there is no evidence of food shortages in the first place. Far from being the result of detailed investigation into what is needed in Albania, the legitimising of Operation Alba through the 'need' for food supplies appears to have been casually dreamt up as a thinly disguised cover for a self-interested policing operation by the country's historic enemies. Given the lack of even tokenistic scrutiny of Operation Alba, the Italians, Greeks, French and Spanish will be able to do as they please to Albanians already written off as lawless criminals in Western eyes. It is hardly surprising that the French have already made clear they will use maximum force if they deem it necessary. The conflicts and tensions which are likely to arise through the sudden arrival of free food, for example, will undoubtedly be controlled with an iron fist by Albania's self-appointed guardians.

I now turn to the alleged deficiency of Eastern Europe which has most commonly set it apart from the rest of Europe in Western eyes, and thereby demanded 'benign intervention' – the East as a cauldron of ethnic nationalism.

8

The Weakness of Nationalism

The Discrediting of Nationalism in the West

The discussion of 'nationalism' and 'ethnicity' is long and confused. There is much disagreement between for example the radical Eric Hobsbawm and the more conservative approach of British theorist Anthony Smith. Opinions differ widely over whether nationalism is an elite creation, or something more given by basic group solidarity. One area where there is something of a consensus, however, is that it has evolved quite differently in Eastern and Western Europe. Much is made of the historically different relation between state and society in the two halves of Europe. The more fragile basis of the nation in the East is seen to account for nationalism's exaggerated and xenophobic character in comparison to the more balanced and organic nature of the Western variant. Particularly since the Second World War this has been codified into a distinction between a relatively healthy 'patriotism' in the West, and a dangerous 'ethnic nationalism' prevalent in the East. An academic consensus sees the latter as an exclusivist product of the racial conception of the nation, whereas the former is imperfectly derived from the inclusive idea of a nation that comprises citizens whose racial origin is essentially irrelevant.

There are undoubtedly differences between the national development of, for example, Britain and Hungary. And nor are these without consequence in relation to nationalism. The historically powerful development of Britain has assured a more confident and relaxed national identity, whereas in Hungary, particularly with their dismemberment after the First World War, the sense of the nation has necessarily been more fraught and problematic. At the same time of course, there are significant distinctions between the development of the Czech nation and its nationalism for example, and that of Romania or the Ukraine. Equally, there is little common pattern to 'Western nationalism' if we scrutinise the evolution of Finland, Spain or Austria.

121

There is no qualitative distinction which neatly divides East from West. In fact any general formulas regarding nationalism make little sense in themselves. The impulse to argue that such a line can be drawn is only explicable in the context of being able to write off an increasingly discredited nationalism to the East, and in the process salvage authority for the West. To look at this question we need to begin by briefly charting the increasingly negative light in which nationalism has been seen in the West as the century has progressed.

Besides a handful of well known essays, the nation and nationalism was not a subject of widespread discussion before the First World War. The very success of nation building in Italy and Germany, and the continued expansion of more established states like Britain meant that the question of 'what is the nation' was rarely posed. As we know from history, it is only when something becomes problematic that it becomes a focus for debate. From the turn of the century, however, it did become a cause for considerable disquiet. With the democratisation of Western societies, elite fear of the masses intensified: control became less assured than in the past. Fear of socialism gripping the masses was one obvious worry. Less obvious, perhaps, was the extent to which nationalism among the masses appeared increasingly out of control in countries like Britain. While the elite generally held to a utilitarian and pragmatic approach toward national sentiment, the masses appeared to them incapable of exercising such restraint.

Thus one of the pioneers of nationalism studies, Carlton Hayes, spoke in the mid-1920s of the 'laughing gas' of nationalism which had 'possessed the masses'.[1] Such worries were heightened through the experience of popular expressions of nationalism seen in Britain during the Boer War for example. Consternation about the drift towards more military conflicts (particularly when these proved not so easily winnable as in the past) became intertwined with the 'unseemly' expressions of support for such enterprises among some of the working class.

Nationalism took on increasingly negative connotations throughout the century. Any usefulness in maintaining social cohesion appeared more and more peripheral. Particularly with the First World War, nationalism began to appear as the root of all evil – rather than a potentially civilising force – one that could undermine civilisation's very basis. This was something of a misinterpretation we should note, akin to blaming the messenger rather than the message. War, and indeed the expressions of chauvinism that went along with war, are not in themselves the problem. The market system is based upon competitive international rivalry, and in this respect military conflict, as Clausewitz pointed out a long time ago, is only the continuation of politics, and indeed also economics, by other means. But the elite were hardly likely to question the very foundation upon which their domination of society was built, even if they did find it distasteful to 'dirty one's hands' with the rallying of the masses for war. Instead, it was more comfortable to believe that war and nationalism were something of an aberration from the normal course of events. This perspective helped resolve the contradiction between the centrality of family, church and nation with sending the masses off to fight in war, and by so doing disrupting these, the foundations of society as far as the elite were concerned.

If nationalism became discredited through association with the First World War, it was further undermined with the failure to restore international harmony in the interwar years. In addition to its association with the masses and military conflict, economic nationalism became the bugbear of the 1920s and 1930s. The threat of renewed conflict was not dispelled as the international system quickly returned to open competitive rivalries. An important focus for this concern was Eastern Europe. The irrationality of economic division was most graphic in the newly created states of East and Central Europe, where the multinational empires had been replaced by small states which made little economic sense, and could only survive through intense and dangerous competition. The attentions of Carlton Hayes increasingly turned eastwards, for, as he explained, '... perhaps most strikingly, it [nationalism] has invaded non national states, such as the Habsburg, Muscovite, and Ottoman empires, and broken them into fragments'.[2]

By the Second World War, writers found it difficult to retain any enthusiasm for national sentiment, as it had yet again apparently plunged the world into conflict. The measure of this disillusionment is that it became increasingly awkward to maintain the traditional distinction between the positive and negative aspects of nationalism. As the Royal Institute of International Affairs' treatise on the subject noted at the time: 'In particular, the popular distinction between "good" and "bad" nationalism, or between "pacific" and "aggressive" nationalism, should be treated with great caution.'[3] The general solution to this problem (after all, nationalism could hardly be dispensed with altogether given its role in cohering society) was to effect a geographical distinction. The principle of nationalism was saved by arguing that it was primarily when it got into the wrong hands that it ended in calamity. German hands figured prominently in this equation of course – given the Nazi experience – but in the post-war years this gave way to a more general targeting of the East.

Writing off Nationalism to the East

In an important sense, as we shall also suggest later, 'the East' became the inheritor of this (supposedly German) tradition of nationalism-as-xenophobia. Post-war writings on nationalism hammered the point home that nationalism had been distorted in the wrong, Eastern context. It was there after all, that the nation had 'proven' most artificial, as a mere creation of the 1919 peace settlement. Thus the renowned expert on nationalism, and in many ways the originator of the East–West distinction, Hans Kohn, introducing *The Meaning of Nationalism* in 1954, argued that the problem was not so much with the principle, as with who was applying it. He added the flourish that the East was fundamentally opposed to the enlightened modernity of the West.

> In the 19th and 20th century nationalism spread to Central and Eastern Europe, to lands of entirely different traditions and social structure from those in the modern West and frequently hostile to, and contemptuous of, modern Western ways. In these lands nationalism became a trend toward collective self assertion, towards a closed society, in which the individual counted for less than the strengthened authority of the national whole.[4]

Speaking primarily of nationalism's adoption by anti-colonialist movements, he concluded that 'Contemporary nationalism is a destructive force that often contains a high degree of xenophobia ....'[5]

Nationalism could not be entirely repudiated, but it was clearly problematic not to do so given its continued association with Nazism. This dilemma was resolved by insisting on a distinction between East and West, initially within Europe, and later between the West and the whole of the non Western world. While this perception had a real basis in its more artificial and compromised nature in the East, it was a dramatic reformulation of that difference which owed much to the imperative to salvage something of this important Western concept. Louis Snyder, in the same volume, made this plain, declaring that 'Much of the difficulty now encountered in the use of the generic term "nationalism" could be dispelled by qualifying its use according to the Kohn formula of Western nationalism and non Western nationalism.'[6] Others, such as the political theorist John Plamenatz, similarly insisted on the centrality of distinction between a 'nice' Western nationalism, and the 'nasty' Eastern distortion. On the basis of this duality, Snyder was able to go on and conclude his study with a section headed 'Patriotism as an ennobling virtue'.

Discussion about nationalism has remained uncertain – which is hardly surprising given its association with the devastation of the Second World War, and the subsequent barely disguised hatred of post-war anti-colonial movements in the Third World. Nevertheless, the East–West distinction went some way to at least distancing the West from its most negative associations, and allowing its 'patriotism' a degree of authority which it might otherwise not have had. To this day, a Western constitutional, civic, and therefore at least potentially positive, 'patriotism' is counterposed to an altogether more dangerous variety that persists in the East (and the rest of the non Western world). This distinction has now gone so far that the national identity of a Western society such as Britain is now defined partly by its hostility to aggressive nationalism. We have the curious anomaly of an 'anti-nationalist nationalism', whereby national pride is expressed through an acclaimed absence of the extreme chauvinism which supposedly characterises 'foreigners'. Like the man who prides himself on his immense modesty, Western nationalisms are now frequently communicated through a unique ability to rise above the petty hatreds of others.

In the cold light of day, this distinction between a relaxed and harmless Western patriotism and the dangerous Eastern variety does not stand up to scrutiny. The United States reverently worships the Stars and Stripes, and one only has to ask a Mexican whether United States citizenship is open to all. France now miss no opportunity to aggressively defend the most apparently trivial aspect of their culture from foreign infection. 'German-ness' remains closed to all those not 'racially' and, increasingly as we shall later point out, 'culturally' German. As of 1997, even the German born and raised offspring of long established immigrants need to obtain, and regularly renew, residence permits. German citizenship has long been withheld from the 'gastarbeiter' who helped rebuild the country. The criminalisation of immigrants to 'multicultural' Britain has intensified during 1996. These are only a few examples which clearly contradict the flattering depiction of a benign Western patriotism.

The Weakness of Nationalism in the East

Historically it is true that 'the nation' has been more secure in many countries of Western Europe. However, it is patently false to imply, as is generally done, that it is the less dangerous for having been so.

The great calamities of this century have been driven by the national ambitions of the major powers. It is precisely because of their relative power, and the consequent ability to defend themselves from outside influence, that Western powers' conflicts have been played out elsewhere – on the territories of those whose lack of resources to uphold sovereign integrity has left them vulnerable to international pressure. This is not to say that elites in Eastern Europe would not have liked to similarly instil in their own populations such a certain sense of national pride. The problem has always been that these countries lacked the dynamism to really involve the whole of society in their national ambitions.

If anything, 'nationalism' has always been weak as a social force in the East. Its changes in 'form, weight and impact' have generally been the product of wider influences; the impact of the world market and the specific involvement of the dominant powers. The Balkan wars which broke out at the turn of the century, for example, were directly related to the increasing scramble for influence among the great powers, as the disintegration of the Ottoman empire loomed. This was not an explosion of powerful local nationalisms which gripped society as a whole. Although fought through local actors, that is precisely what they were – clients for competing international players. This may not have been how it always appeared, as the major powers often avoided too direct an involvement. But it was they that activated local disputes and conflicts behind the scenes. Speaking of nationalism in interwar Bulgaria, for example, Walter Kolarz in his important *Myths and Realities in Eastern Europe* explained, 'No doubt this ideology did not originate with the powers in question but without their intervention it would have remained a mere chimera instead of becoming one of the watchwords of actual politics.'[7] In other words, it was only with the intervention of external forces that a previously insignificant ideology became animated. Even when local squabbling appeared to take on a life of its own, invariably there were more powerful forces behind the scenes. Indeed, the very expression of national aspiration has to be located within the context of appeals to these wider influences.

International manoeuvring lay behind the otherwise mysterious inability of regimes to establish cooperation or any sort of federation along the lines of the European Union – despite attempts to do so. As one historian, documenting the longstanding failure to establish regional cooperation, pointed out at the end of the war, 'The great powers behind the scenes had been able to mobilise so much local resistance that the failure of all projects of co-operation appeared to be caused by the inability of the Danube nations to agree among themselves.'[8] With rival powers backing particular clients in the region against others, it might appear that it was purely local pig headedness and insularity that prevented more harmonious relations. Invariably, however, there would be one great power backing one local player, and another backing their competitor. While it might make sense for local rivals to overcome their differences, for their backers there was invariably more at stake – with local influence only forming part of a broader strategy of establishing influence.

To some extent the contrived character of Eastern nationalism is now acknowledged. In the now popular emphasis on 'constructed identities', identities are seen to be the product of intellectual and social invention – often by elites for purposes of legitimacy. Even the discussion of East Europe has not remained immune from this contemporary outlook. There is too, a trend towards identifying the crisis of legitimacy among the communist elites as predating the opportunistic emergence of nationalism – therefore providing the trigger for a resurgence of ethnicity. However, the popularity of isolating the artificial character of nationalism is still generally blind to the determining role played by external forces. Such studies generally examine the internal process of identity creation, ignoring its animation by wider influences. There is an emphasis upon the 'symbolic', as if the mere creation of symbols by an elite can account for their apparent cohesive power. What is more, the role of the past often remains assumed as a transcendental force, whether conjured by a devious political elite, or simply 'arising from slumber'.

The centrality of the past is still unexplored in the most contemporary writing. Even those who sense that its importance is overstated, find it difficult to transcend this outlook, because they are bound to the fundamental consensus that 'the East' is shaped by forces of its own making. Even when history and nationalism are downplayed, the problem of 'culture' – in many ways a different way of elevating the same problems – remains popular. While more sensitive analysts now acknowledge that aggressive nationalism is not an innate characteristic of East Europeans, and instead emphasise its created character, there is still little recognition of its fundamental weakness – created or not. Often bewitched by the force of the symbolic, sight is lost of the crucial fact that nationalism as a social force in the East is generally weak, and only responsive to more decisive developments further afield. This is partly why it has often had little but symbols to rely on and, as we can see from the period of Stalinist domination, the desperate search by the elite for even symbolic means of suggesting a common national purpose was generally unsuccessful. Not that this stopped these 'communists' from trying, however.

The Stalinist Encouragement of Nationalism

There is then a longstanding duality established in the understanding of nationalism between different Eastern and Western forms. This has provided the framework for the misrepresentation of contemporary Eastern Europe as a cauldron of ethnic tension. More specifically, this established wisdom about the region is backed up by two factors: first, the proposition that communism suppressed national sentiment, and this led to a 'bottling up' of national feeling; second, that the peoples of the region themselves are gripped by a fierce ethnic, tribal loyalty. I now turn to the first of these ideas, to illustrate how it involves a significant misreading of the communist period.

In one sense it seems commonsensical to suggest that communism – internationalist, and traditionally hostile to a nationalism which it viewed as a tool of the elite – would have suppressed expressions of nationalism under its rule. This is perhaps why we might be prepared to believe there was the systematic denial of nationalism under Stalinism that many claim took place, without even inspecting the facts of the matter. It is unsurprising then that it should burst asunder once the constraint of communist dogma was removed. We might even expect that nationalism would have attained a particular ferocity which was largely absent in the past. Aggravated and bottled up, perhaps we need look no further than this prolonged suppression of nationality to explain conflicts which have 'emerged' with the collapse of Soviet control.

We can indeed find evidence of ill treatment of nationalities under communism, and attempts to deny the legitimacy of particular national aspirations. The emergence of 'great Russian chauvinism' was evident even under Lenin, and reached its apogee in the Second World War as Russia was proclaimed the 'guiding force of the Soviet people'. Allegedly 'traitorous' groups like the Crimean Tartars and Chechens on the other hand, were forcibly relocated. In Eastern Europe too, various expressions of nationality were dealt with harshly, as for example, with the response of the Yugoslav federal authorities to attempts to revive Croatian nationalism in the 1970s. More widely, the Comecon trading bloc which organised economic relations within the region, at least initially involved the subordination of national economic strategies to a cooperative regional division of labour.

More striking, however, are the countless examples which suggest there was little principled opposition to nationalism: that a dogma of 'international brotherhood' was far from being a 'guiding principle'. From the 1930s, internal Soviet passports declared ethnic identity. The whole policy of 'nativisation' pursued by the Soviet authorities encouraged local ethnic elites. Even at the height of his powers, Stalin, far from taking the opportunity to create a unitary state encouraged more languages and more states – as was the case with the Turkmen and Uzbeks. Stalin's policy was one of divide and rule, and the divisive encouragement of yet more ethnic groups and languages if such a course was considered necessary.

There were changes of policy, moves in favour of, and against, 'localism' under subsequent leaders, as the encouragement of local ethnic elites in places like Georgia and Armenia led to fragmentation. But the essentially multiethnic approach continued into the 1970s and 1980s. As Tom Nairn has pointed out, 'It is simply untrue that nationality was "repressed" under Titoism, any more than it was in the old USSR or any other parts of the Communist emporium.' Overall, as he continues, '... a kind of castrated nationalism was, if anything, over-cultivated in a cultural sense', there were always '... the interminable folk dancers' and other desperately summoned symbols of the past.[9]

Attempts to substantiate the notion of the Stalinist denial of nationalism frequently rely upon definitional contestation, rather than a survey of practical policy. Great importance is attributed to the Soviet term 'nationalities' for example. According to some authors the existence of this term meant that most ethnic groups were effectively denied their right of self-determination through their redefinition as 'nationalities'. Even in its own terms, however, this proposition, that the definition of 'nationalities' necessarily indicates a denial of national aspiration, is questionable. More fundamentally, it forgets that the whole essence of Stalinism was as *national* communism with the emphasis far more on the former than the latter.

In the satellite states of Eastern Europe this emphasis upon the national was equally pronounced, as these supposedly 'communist' countries lacked even the limited legitimacy of the Soviet Union – which was at least founded on the authority of a real revolution. As a consequence, they frequently had to fall back on the encouragement and manipulation of national feeling. The cosy relationship established in Poland between the Catholic Church as symbol of the nation, and the authorities, is well known and documented. Poland was, however, something of an exception – not in the sense that it was an isolated example of national communism, but that playing the nationalist card was relatively straightforward. Elsewhere, suitable symbols and institutions were lacking. Quite peculiar paths had to be followed in order to emulate what the Polish elite had achieved by aligning themselves with the Catholic Church and anti-Semitism. In Romania, an independent foreign policy and ruinous autarky were pursued as the symbol of national uniqueness, while in Hungary, traditional territorial grievances stemming from the settlement after the First World War were played up in the name of Hungarian communism. No matter how absurd, each regime had its own brand of nationalism – even if some were more viable than others.

This is not to say that Stalinism was any more principled in its encouragement of a nationalist substitute than it was in pursuing 'international working-class solidarity'. Stalin, the native of Georgia, yet figurehead of Great Russian patriotism, was no 'multiculturalist' – despite his encouragement of various nationalities. His was an essentially pragmatic approach dictated by the fundamental lack of viability of the society which emerged out of the Russian revolution. The Stalinist social system was never sufficiently dynamic to systematically transform the Soviet republics and satellites in its own image. It was a question of managing the chaos given by the crisis and stagnation which characterised the system from the mid-1920s onwards. In this context, there was a frequent reliance upon divide and rule – setting one group against another as was particularly evident in the 'Asian' republics of the USSR. Elsewhere, the strategy was to buttress a profound lack of social dynamism and cohesion with appeals to nationalism.

Where the symbols of the nation, sometimes even the nation itself, did not exist the authorities had to manufacture these themselves in the hope of securing a wider stability. An important contemporary example are the Muslims of the former Yugoslavia. As a stratum, they were '... historically associated with class and religion rather than nationhood' as Misha Glenny has explained.[10] The idea of a Muslim 'nation' was only introduced by the constitution of 1963, and their elevation to nationhood enshrined in the famous constitution of 1974 (leading to the peculiarity that in Yugoslavia Muslims were a nationality rather than a religion). These were means of attempting to preserve the ethnic tranquillity of Bosnia and Herzegovina, specifically to prevent a contest for their loyalty between Serb and Croat.

Ultimately this was a dangerous course to pursue. National communism was a contradiction in terms, not least in the fact that

Stalinism's claim to embody national particularism was always likely
to be challenged by those who could lay claim to national traditions
more directly. In the case of Yugoslavia, of course, the overall policy
of conceding ground and recognition to numerous nationalities
paved the way for later dissolution. This did not prevent systematic
attempts to pursue this course, however, particularly as the Stalinist
bureaucracies invariably managed their survival on a very short term
basis, with little consideration to the longer term implications of
encouraging potentially disintegrative forces.

Insofar as we can speak of general tendencies then, nationalism
was not suppressed in any meaningful sense. As we have suggested,
it was often nurtured to shore up regimes which had little else
available around which to cohere society. But nor is this to suggest
that communist Europe and the USSR were a seething mass of
nationalism waiting to explode as a result of these policies. The
Stalinist encouragement of nationalism was most important with
regard to the cohering of regional and national elites. For the rest of
society, profoundly estranged as they were, such manoeuvres were
often recognised as transparent attempts to garner support and were
treated accordingly. The access to resources which helped secure the
support and creation of new elites was not available for society as a
whole. It is quite clear in retrospect that the manipulation of
nationalism was in no way sufficient to properly legitimise these
regimes which could offer little but a peculiar mix of laughable
Stalinist ideology and the 'interminable folk dancers' endured by
Tom Nairn.

In the post-communist period, it is hardly surprising that the
surge of 'nationalism' which gripped the Western imagination was
primarily among politicians and officials. The process was essentially
one of former Stalinist apparatchiks formalising an ethnic identity
in an attempt to relocate themselves in the new political environment.
Their Stalinist trappings were rapidly abandoned, and the nationalist
card played to the full, in the hope of out-manoeuvring opponents.
The former Chechen leader Dudayev, for example, was actually a
former Soviet air force commander who saw a brighter future for
himself as leader of a nation, rather than staying on in the crumbling
Russian military. There are countless other examples of such
opportunism. In the process of reforming themselves in the 1980s,
the Hungarian communists even had the audacity to indentify
themselves with the 1956 revolution (through praise for the reformist
leader Imre Nagy, for example) which their predecessors had so
bloodily suppressed with considerable Russian assistance.

It is equally striking how short lived the efficacy of this strategy proved, however. There was indeed an initial wave of support for politicians who proclaimed the national interest above all others. This was largely based upon the hope that the loosening of old arrangements with the former Soviet bloc, and within the various federations, might secure more resources and perhaps even privileged relations with the West. Going it alone suggested the possibility of keeping funds otherwise to be diverted to federal authorities, even worse to subsidise Russia in some way. In this respect it would be more accurate to describe a wave of anti-centralism, than nationalism per se. But even anti-centralist nationalism has proven to have had a short shelf life – the popularity of some form of reunion with Russia in the former Soviet republic of Belarus being the most extreme example. In general, hopes for better economic prospects being secured simply by severing ties with the federal authorities or/and the USSR proved illusory. It is largely only where a national strategy has been rewarded with better relations with the West that it has retained purchase among the population. Elsewhere, more straight-forward promises are now more popular with the voters. Parties promising financial subsidies or favours from Germany, not heroic national destiny became typical after an initial wave of anti-centralist nationalism.

This should come as no surprise. Precisely because of the weakness of loyalties to relatively fragile nations, allegiances have always proven shallow and subject to change. Now, even more so than in the past, pragmatism rules among the peoples of Eastern Europe – even to the extent of some places accepting with resignation the renewed domination of their former Stalinist rulers in new democratic garb.

Shifting Allegiances

Turning to the resonance of nationalism and ethnic loyalties among the people more widely, we have to ask where is, even was, all the 'ethno-nationalism' that so excited Western observers? It is surprising how rarely it is acknowledged that the fears of post-communist ethnic turmoil – of a Bosnia writ large – have proven to be largely groundless. Francis Fukuyama is one exception, perhaps because of his determination to challenge pessimism in the name of his (relatively) optimistic 'end of history'. 'If we look carefully,' he points out, 'what is striking is not the strength of intolerant nationalism but its weakness .... There have been any number of conflicts that have so far failed to materialise in the former Soviet bloc.'[11] Thomas Simons Jr goes a step further, arguing as I have done above, that even those movements deemed 'nationalist', might more accurately be understood simply as expressions of the collapse of old arrangements, rather than an upsurge of strident ethnicity. 'But given its history, what is equally striking to me is how little nationalism has conquered area wide ... even in the former Soviet Union, it is worth pointing out, much of the surge has been anti-centralist rather than classically nationalist', he says.[12] We face a curious dichotomy then between the relative weakness of nationalism in the region, alongside the perception that nationalist forces are, historically, a dominant feature of Eastern Europe.

In fact, ethnic loyalties have often proven negotiable in this part of the world – partly because they are so frequently hard to determine. Hence in the 1991 Yugoslav census almost half a million people were nationally 'undecided'. This indeterminacy is illustrated by the mystery of the Rusyns, or Ruthenians as they are sometimes known. Frustrating those who wish to announce the existence of another ethnic group (the Canadian academic Paul Magosci has embarked upon a one man crusade to have them recognised – to the point of codifying a language), this group of Slavic people have changed their identity on a number of occasions.[13] With regard to those in present day Slovakia, ... sometimes they have been Ukrainian; sometimes Slovak; sometimes Ruthenian or Russian. As one expert notes of the nominally Slovak Ruthenes: 'When we compare the rubric "nationality" in census [sic] from different dates, we find an incredible fluctuation: inhabitants of the same village are mentioned once as Rusyns, ten years later as Slovaks, a further ten years later as Russians, later still as Ukrainians, then again as Slovaks.'[14] Insofar as their designation has been of any concern, it is evident that these changes are the product of wider developments. For example, the renunciation of Ukrainian identity was very much linked to the anti-Ukrainian feeling in post-war Czechoslovakia as a result of Ukrainian support for Nazis. 'The ethnonym "Ukrainian" was often identified here with the name "banderovec", just as "German" was with "Nazi"', as one Slovak expert explained.[15]

Even in contested areas, loyalties have proven flexible. After the Second World War, the Hungarian Prime Minister recalled asking a Czech politician how many Poles there were in the disputed Teschen border region. His answer was less than certain; '... perhaps 40,000, perhaps 100,000 ... the peoples of certain villages are changing their nationality every week according to their economic interests and sometimes the economic interests of the mayor of the village'.[16] With little to choose between the advantages of accepting one nationality over another, identities have often been difficult to determine. Some villagers on the Czech/Slovak border were still undecided over which to choose following the split of the two countries in 1993. Weighing it all up comes down to a close run cost–benefit analysis of one country's European status, social provision, economic prospects and preferences in matters of culture. 'Nationalism' is very much negotiable, and unlikely to be a cause in the abstract for which one might lay down one's life.

A Bark Louder Than the Bite

This is not to say that people do not express national allegiances. Many do so, and in the most extravagant terms, listing their hated neighbouring nationalities in descending order. But it is precisely because of the fragility of nationality – that it is so difficult to state clearly, and with conviction, what one's nation represents and has achieved over and above others – that one can resort only to colourful denunciations of obviously more or less identical neighbours. Thus in Romania for example, many will routinely denounce Hungarians, gypsies, Jews etc. This does not necessarily attest to the power of nationalism however. Romania is a country which appears to have little future – even the peoples of neighbouring Moldavia have preferred 'independence' and close relations with Russia to unification with the country to which they were historically attached. The same Romanians who might indulge in these denunciations, might well exchange their identity for another if it meant a better lifestyle. One is reminded of the old saying; those who talk about it most, do it the least. An analogy can be made between this Eastern type of nationalism and football crowd ribaldry: it can be frightening, especially to the middle class, but is ultimately inconsequential and long forgotten at work the next day.

It is precisely because these nations have proven so weak, that there is often much to say on the subject, especially among the intelligentsia. As one observer noted about Poland in the late 1950s, '... more books and articles have been written on questions of nationalism in Polish than in any other language'. Why? As the author goes on to explain, 'By contrast, in England ... nationalism so pervaded the mind that it ceased to be problematic.'[17] Nationalism saturates the very fabric of Britain, France, the United States and other major powers to the point where it is not recognised as such. This is not a sign of its weakness, however, but of its dormant strength.

Meanwhile, even in the most powerful state of the East, Russia, soldiers are so indifferent to such calls that they suffered complete moral collapse during the war in Chechnya. If we measure nationalism not by the intensity of its rhetoric, but the real capacity to mobilise and cohere, it is Western not Eastern nationalism that is the more powerful.

And in the ultra pragmatic 1990s, these national identities are as flexible as ever. Particularly for those nationalities seen to have little to offer economically, such as in Belarus or the Ukraine, identity can prove remarkably flexible – even tradable. 'Independence' is of little interest in itself to the majority of people in these societies. If better prospects involve closer ties with Russia, or even a rejuvenated USSR, it is a price easily worth paying for many in these former Soviet republics. An interesting feature in virtually all the countries of the former communist bloc is that historical animosities toward the Germans as a result of two world wars have largely been put to one side. 'History' and 'tribal nationalism' do not seem to count for much here. Far from this real grievance from the past determining the outlook of the present, the influence of contemporary factors has decisively reshaped old loyalties and animosities as they are swept aside by the allure of German wealth. Indeed, there is something of a scramble to prove German ancestry in order to secure passage to the West as it (just about) remains constitutionally binding for the German state to accept 'ethnic Germans' from the East. As ever, economics has the last word in identity formation – as Karl Deutsch once put it, nationalism is 'an implied claim to privilege'. Without any privilege, nationalism does not add up to a great deal. On the other hand, once it becomes officially sanctioned by the predominant power in the region as was the case with the German backing of Croatia, nationalism can become all.

Explosive External Interference – The Yugoslav War

It is only under the most extreme and extraordinary circumstances, where conflict has spiralled out of control as a result of wider politicisation and internationalisation, that we see identities become fixed and potentially explosive. In understanding why one potential 'ethnic' confrontation escalates into war and another is settled relatively easily, it is crucial to unravel the interplay of domestic with more decisive international influence. Wars, even ostensibly 'civil wars' in the non Western world such as that in Angola, need to be understood in a wider context. And in stark contrast to the contemporary understanding of the Yugoslav war, it was acknowledged that this war was indeed driven by external, in this case South African, interference, rather than being explicable as simply another 'ethnic feud'. Otherwise, in attempting to grasp why, for example, the breakups of the Czechoslovak and Yugoslav federations took such a different course, it can only be concluded that the 'culture', nay the 'blood' of one is predisposed to violence, where the other is inherently peaceable. A tautological 'explanation' is the result. Ignoring the impact of wider forces, we must conclude that the dissolution of Czechoslovakia was peaceful because the Czechs and Slovaks are congenitally peaceful, and by contrast that the South Slavs, in particular the Serbs, are simply given to violence against others. Even disregarding the fatuous nature of such reasoning, how this accounts for the historically widespread recognition by the South Slavs of the need for cooperation embodied by the Yugoslav federation is left a mystery. If it is merely 'in the blood', why did Slovenes, Croats, Serbs and the rest peacefully coexist for so long? The now popular assertion that this was a largely forced union does not account for the very high rates of intermarriage between different 'nationalities' (certainly higher than those between 'Ossies' and 'Wessies' in present day Berlin) which were a consistent feature of the former Yugoslavia, and partly explains the difficulty so many people had in determining their ethnic identity.

The decisive impact of international pressures in the Yugoslav war is acknowledged in the dominant consensus that Western inaction emboldened the Serbs to act with impunity. Had the 'international community' in its American or European forms been more decisive, and made it clear they would not tolerate Serbian aggression, tragedy could have been averted according to this version of events. As an argument this proposition makes no sense. It rests upon the curious idea that greater violence leads to peace – that had the Nato bombing campaign of the Serbs happened earlier than August/September 1995, or had the arming of the Croats and Muslims also been carried out sooner, again, a more peaceful outcome would have been the result. Further, it assumes, a priori, that Serbian action was driven by nothing else but mindless expansionism (why did they not then go to war with Slovenia if this was the case?).

While the argument does not stand up to scrutiny, it is significant that the centrality of Western reaction is sensed – the problem is that the real course of events is stood on its head. The pro Slovene and Croat signals sent out even before the outbreak of war by European powers decisively shaped the course of events that then followed.

As Gompert explains, '"Unofficial" Austrian and German encouragement spoke louder than American caution to Slovene nationalists, who hoped to see their Alpine nation soon tucked safely into a close economic and political relationship with Germany, en route to membership in the European Community (EC).'[18] The course of secession was set, and the war that followed was as much a propaganda war to legitimise Slovene, and later Croatian and Bosnian independence. This was a case of too much, rather than too little intervention, even if that interference took the form of a diplomatic and propaganda, rather than a military, offensive – in support of the breakaway republics on Austria and Germany's part.

This is not to argue that local factors were unimportant. In the Yugoslav context it was crucial that the consolidation of nationally charged independent states immediately threatened conflict, given the delicate ethnic balance of the constituent states. Perhaps most decisively, an assertive independent Croatia immediately threatened the substantial Serb minority in the Krajina region. Bosnian 'independence' and the calling of a referendum in a territory so potentially ethnically divided, was not only pointless and contrary to the constitution of that state, but would again, necessarily lead to confrontation. Hardly surprising then, that Bosnian President Alia Izetbegovic requested that recognition of Croatia and Slovenia be withheld for fear of the impact on his own republic. In this context it was the international weight thrown behind the two projects that rendered compromise impossible and war inevitable. Suddenly it became in the interests of both the Croats and Bosnian Muslims to escalate and politicise events, and refuse dialogue. Once it had been made plain that international recognition was possible if they could successfully portray the Serbs as aggressors, keeping the violence going, even to the point of inviting and provoking Serbian destruction, became a strategic goal of Croatia and later, the Bosnian Muslims.

Without the international encouragement of Croatian and Bosnian Muslim nationalism, deals could have been struck at any number of points. The tragic escalation of these two situations which followed, and which largely accounts for the scale of the war, need not have been. The very intractability of these thorny problems dictated that compromise was virtually given, if local actors were left to their own devices. Instead, tensions were inflamed by the international stamp of approval for these nationalisms, and the most extreme forces on every side – Serb, Croat, and Bosnian Muslim – were given free rein. In the case of the Serbs, their vilification only confirmed and strengthened the influence of the most alarmist Serbian nationalists.

As the American commander Charles Boyd has put it, 'Demonization has unleashed demons.'[19] Particularly once it became clear to Serbs that anything they did would be distorted – that they would only ever be the aggressor in the eyes of the world – the initiative fell to those who argued for a war against a world which had turned against them.

The first war – that between Serbs and Croats which began in earnest in August 1991 – was particularly important as it set the pattern for the future. Initially Croatia was in no position, especially because of military weakness, to provoke confrontation, and therefore pursued a less provocative strategy than the unilateral secession and seizing of boundaries undertaken by Slovenia. Croatia did not want at this stage to preclude even the maintenance of some form of relationship with Serbia. What was decisive in determining Croatia's course was international, particularly German, reaction. Croatia tested the water by concentrating efforts on the propaganda war. The Croatian leadership dramatised, and to an extent even provoked, the attacks on the cities of Vukovar and Dubrovnik by the Yugoslav army. The international, particularly German, response was to accept that these confrontations, and increasingly that the overall situation, was simply one of Serbian aggression and Croatian victimhood. This emboldened the Croats to go further. Through Vukovar and Dubrovnik, the Croats confirmed for themselves that propaganda and presentation to the 'international community' were their key resources. Such a concerted propaganda offensive came relatively naturally to the Croats as it does to many other elites in Eastern Europe because, as I shall indicate later, exclusion from the West has created a discourse of 'who is less civilised and Eastern than whom'. Denigrating neighbours is an almost instinctive elite reflex in a region where the fortunes of individual countries are seen to depend upon leapfrogging over competitors for limited Western attentions.

Especially once officially sanctioned with German recognition of independence, 'Croatian-ness' was blessed and politicised. Being Croatian took on unheard of significance. Croatia became a cause worth killing for, especially as it was virtually guaranteed that your actions would not be subject to scrutiny. Given the moralisation of the war as one between Serbian evil and their victims, even the most extreme acts could be portrayed as understandable reactions to aggression – that is if they were publicised at all. As a consequence, possibilities opened up of which even the extreme nationalist leader Franco Tudjiman might otherwise not have dreamt. This international backing reached its apogee in the later invasion of the Krajina.

Once events spiral out of control through such charged politicisation it is possible for ethnic identity to become decisive. It was thus that the cosmopolitan Yugoslavs, traditionally indifferent to individual particularisms, fell victim to the cementing of loyalties. With sorrow and regret, a Serb by birth, married to a Muslim, explained his own predicament well. 'We feel neither Muslim nor Serb, yet these nationalities are imposed upon us.' A friend added that, 'The more this war goes on, the more nationalistic I become. My husband was killed by a Muslim sniper and my son was maltreated in a Croatian camp. How can I embrace our enemy? ... Separation is the only option.'[20] Of course, for those in the former Yugoslavia who, mistakenly or otherwise, felt that they did not have to fight to retain their land or livelihood, escape to the cities, or abroad proved the preferred option. Ethnic hatred is no more in their blood than in people in any other part of the world. Nationalists are not born, they are created.

The process of Yugoslav disintegration illustrates acutely a wider trend where it is the major powers whose influence is more decisive than that of local actors. This is not to argue that it is only their involvement that can, and has, inflamed conflicts in the region. Russia too, through its interference in Georgia for example, has created military conflict out of local tension by backing one side against another. Nevertheless, the Russians generally lack the status and resources to make as decisive and dramatic an impact as the big league of international players. Their limited influence was dramatically illustrated by their role in the Yugoslav war, where they were rarely even seriously consulted by the West. Russian weakness means that interference is crude and barely disguised. By contrast, Western players are able to operate more discreetly – particularly as they are backed up by the weight and 'pulling power' of the world market. Even without direct interference, the impact of the West is very important and often decisive. It was the opportunity to 'join the West' by ditching 'Eastern' Slovakia that led the Czech leadership to force the disagreements with their federal partners to the point of an open split. Czechoslovakia's end thus had far more to do with Czech attempts to 'rejoin Europe' than with Slovak nationalism.

The virulent ethnic nationalism said to characterise the East is a myth. Insofar as it has been created, most dramatically today in the former Yugoslavia, it is the product of a process of externally driven politicisation. Its apparent autonomy is explained by the characteristic refusal of the great powers animating conflict to formally acknowledge their role. The alliance between the Croats and Germans, for example, was never officially ratified – especially due to the sensitivity of

German involvement in the region (given Croatia's wartime past as a Nazi puppet state). Nor was the client relationship established between the Bosnian Muslims and the United States. They were to all appearances acting entirely independently. The war could thus be presented as either 'Serbian expansionism' (why would they seek to 'expand'?) or simply an obscure historical feud between Serb and Croat. Confronting what are in effect the consequences of their own interference, the West can then throw their hands up in exasperation at the pettiness of these neighbours who insist upon settling their 'blood feuds'. That these 'blood feuds' would have been largely inconsequential without the meddling of the self-ordained 'international community' is rarely recognised. 'Criticism' of the Western role only succeeds in turning reality on its head – invariably charging that the West has 'not done enough' when in fact it has done far too much. Such is the confusion that even those on the receiving end of this supposed 'too little, too late' interference, in this case the Serbs, have been left only with elaborate conspiracy theories about Nazi/Vatican plots to colonise the Balkans, as a means of making sense of their experience.

The myth of a uniquely destructive Eastern nationalism thus endures. Indeed this perception has led to a tendency for the West to not only deny responsibility, but to react to the destructive consequences of their involvement by denying that the West has anything to do with the East. On a wider level, perhaps the most important feature of East–West relations which requires elaboration is the impulse for the West to disassociate itself from an East that is all too clearly an expression of its own contradictions. The East, this 'especially clear case of the modern world', or 'heart of darkness' as it has also been known, has acted as something of an embarrassment to the West – particularly as so much Western driven devastation has repeatedly wreaked havoc. The response has been to deny any relationship between West and East – not only between the nationalisms of the two halves of Europe, but their whole character.

'An Especially Clear Case of the Modern World'

The 'Mirror' of the East

The enduring weakness of affiliations and arrangements discussed in previous sections, compounded by economic fragility, has meant that developments in the East did not proceed so smoothly as in the West. Power relations are more naked, and the elite has not managed to successfully present its own interests as the interests of all. In the West, the same basic relations within society are more mediated and disguised. Greater social integration was made possible by economic dynamism. Hegemony, as Gramsci described, is exercised indirectly. In this context, the East has presented an embarrassing distortion, or perhaps more accurately, given an ugly reality to Western principles and mores. In a number of different ways, Russia and Eastern Europe have demonstrated most starkly the contradictions of modernity. There, the destructive consequences of the world market, and the competitive rivalries which followed have been laid bare. Society itself in the East has been stunted and distorted to a greater degree than in the West. These societies have then acted as an ugly mirror image of the West. The naked capitalism of contemporary Russia where wealth is concentrated in only a few hands, for example, creates considerable discomfort in the West – especially now that the West is quite hostile to unregulated capitalism. A general response has been to deny that the West was anything to do with the East – let alone its creation – in an attempt to remove this unflattering self-image. In the case of the Russian financial oligarchy, the Western response is now to insist that this is not 'proper' capitalism. This impulse has been a feature of East–West relations since the nineteenth century. Only in the Cold War could it convincingly be argued that 'the East' really was 'nothing to do with us' without this insistence.

Throughout that century, as powers in the West like Britain led the way in the transformation of society, the relative lack of change in the empires of the East was striking. Particularly for those concerned with progress and reform, the apparent stagnation in Central and Eastern Europe was something of a disappointment. Even where there were attempts to reproduce developments from the West, particularly in the area of political change, its weakness was striking. Karl Marx, for example, was continually frustrated by the weakness of the feeble capitalist class, particularly with their role in the revolutionary events of 1830 and 1848. Not only were they incapable of mounting a serious challenge to the old empires, but they actively assisted in the crushing of movements for change.

'Liberals' and reformers in the East seemed so far removed from their Western equivalents, that they were perhaps a different animal altogether. 'No radical in England can inveigh more violently against tax than do the liberals of Hungary', wrote the Englishman Paget of his observations on the Hungarian Diet of 1835. 'But they mix up their invective so strongly with the privileges of nobility, that it would be difficult to recognise anything like the same principle in their opposition to it.'[1] Of course, liberalism in England was hardly implacable in its opposition to privilege. Indeed, shorn of its pretensions, liberalism in Hungary stood as a painful reminder for Paget of the compromise at the heart of the liberal project, so much so that Paget refused to recognise it as the same animal; instead seeing it as quite distinct. In so doing, he reassures himself that the project is an essentially healthy one – in the proper hands.

Western liberals were not alone in identifying in the East the most crude and monstrous manifestations of discomforting features that could be associated with their own societies. The old European elites, preoccupied with the way their world was being destroyed by emerging and dynamic nationalisms in the nineteenth century, experienced this most sharply in relation to the East. The famous Austrian Grillparzer, for example, described the descent of civilisation as one from 'nationality to bestiality'. The force of nineteenth century nationalism appeared to many to bear testimony to this image of destruction most pointedly in Central and Eastern Europe. There, the old empires, particularly the grand old Habsburg monarchy which epitomised traditional order and culture, were disintegrating. From Grillparzer's point of view this was the result of the nationalisms embodied by Eastern Europe, rather than the more general process of decay that was really responsible.

In the twentieth century the region was even more pointedly the domain in which the decline of Europe was experienced. For the novelist Robert Musil, the old Austria was 'an especially clear case of the modern world'.[2] He might instead have said contemporary malaise, as it was to the dilemmas and contradictions of modern capitalism that he was referring, and which he saw so starkly in the empires of 'the East'. The very foundations of European dominance and superiority were found wanting most graphically in the East. Ivan Berend suggests that 'Central and Eastern Europe's feeling of being pushed to the periphery prepared the ground for the revolt against liberalism, free market economics, parliamentary democracy and rationalism in the Western world ... obvious during the 30 years from 1880s to World War One.'[3] While it is an overstatement to talk of a 'revolt' rather than simply graphic failure, we can agree that it was here that these fundamentals were found most wanting. The general response, however, was not to acknowledge the fundamental flaws at the heart of the liberal project. Rather than question the viability of these ideas themselves – an exercise which would have put to question the structures of moral superiority in Europe and much more – it proved more comforting to locate the problem within peoples. They were incapable of applying essentially sound ideas and principles. Rationalising, or rather naturalising, the problem in this way rendered the ideas of parliamentary democracy, liberalism, free market economics and rationalism salvageable, even if it then seemed that they could only be correctly applied by those in the West, which represented a considerable limiting of earlier claims to embody universal principles.

The Blow to Self-Confidence

The inability to carry over West European dynamism into the East, then, had already set in motion a process of disassociation of the West from the East by the late nineteenth century. But until the First World War, the West retained in itself a qualified confidence about the future. Given the depth of pessimism in the late twentieth century, it is now difficult to recall the optimism that still reigned in pre-war Europe. It certainly now requires something of a leap of the imagination to capture the consequences this optimism had for the sense of Europe and its boundaries. Quoting an eloquent contemporary European of the time, Stefan Zweig, is perhaps most useful in this regard.

In Vienna we shouted with joy when Bleriot flew over the Channel as if he had been our hero; because of our pride in the successive triumphs of our technics, our science, a European community spirit, a European national consciousness was coming into being. How useless, we said to ourselves, are frontiers when any plane can fly over them with ease, how provincial and artificial are customs duties, guards and border patrols, how incongruous in the spirit of these times which seeks unity and brotherhood! This soaring of our feelings was no less wonderful than that of the planes, and I pity those who were not young during those last years of confidence in Europe.[4]

The onset of war dealt a significant blow to Western self-confidence. This had a particular impact on the view of the non Western world, as Rodinson explains: 'In the field of Oriental studies, as in other fields, the First World War shattered the self confident belief of European civilisation in the continuity and limitlessness of its own progress, and in so doing shook European ethnocentrism.'[5] The response to this weakness was withdrawal; as we have suggested elsewhere, a battening down of the hatches. But in some ways, this only added to the West's sense of vulnerability. In its weakened state, the East now appeared distinctly threatening to 'the West'. Not only was it increasingly unrecognisable, but as is the wont of created demons, it even began to even take on threatening dimensions.

For Hans Kohn, in his famous *History of Nationalism in the East*, the First World War ushered in a new era of struggle between East and West. The East had awoken – evidenced by the much discussed triumph of Japan over Russia. Significantly, in Kohn's illustrations, he shows a world now divided into separate cultural areas – principally the Anglo Saxon pitted against the rest. A new spirit of nationalism was seen to be sweeping the Asian and North African worlds, where they saw themselves capable of running their own affairs without the white man. Although the West European hold on the colonies was still secure, the sense of domestic decay lent this experience frightening dimensions. 'What we see from a distance, in the Orient, is the destruction of Europe', noted a French intellectual in 1924.[6]

While 'the East' described is the 'the Orient', this concern with rising danger also had an impact upon the sense of the East within Europe – a nether world between Ottoman and Western orbits. As a result, a fortress mentality evolved, defined today by Brzezinski as the 'weak ramparts of the permissive West'.[7] In this context, all that lay outside this new defensive barrier became increasingly separate.

This tendency, through which a distinct division of Europe was becoming eminently more acceptable, was only consolidated in the period following the Second World War, however. The aftermath of this war was burdened with the awkwardness of the catastrophe that great power conflict had brought to the East. It was through the intensity of this experience that Eastern Europe was truly written off as something unrecognisable and, by direct implication of course, having no relationship to the West. This important moment therefore deserves special attention.

Post-War Despair

Introspection was already very much the order of the day in the troubled climate of the 1930s. Historians indulged in wide ranging historical generalisations and overtly partisan conclusions in a way that would in the past have been considered a betrayal of scholarship. The response to the difficult interwar years was to draw upon history as a resource for the present – to bolster a troubled 'West'. The Italian Benedetto Croce's 1934 history of Europe as the unfolding of liberty is one such example. Intrinsic to this approach was an emphasis on unique cultural inheritances. The relationship between a sense of crisis and the turn to history and culture is illustrated by the case of France. Commentators noted in the late 1930s that 'A few years ago an anniversary of 1789 would have been just another anniversary. Today we hail it as a portentous event.' What stimulated this discovery? As the same author tells us, the '... feeling that something essential to our civilisation is dying. With that feeling has come the realisation that this civilisation is immeasurably precious to us.'[8] This discovery of a rich heritage of a 'Western tradition' was especially marked after the Second World War. Then, in looking for where 'we had gone so wrong', the answer was found in a mythical departure from our spiritual roots in the traditions of Greece and Rome.

The immediate post-war period, in many ways the culmination of the terrible interwar years, was Europe's darkest hour. Despite victory in the war, the mood, even among the non German Western elites, was decidedly bleak. Pessimistic forebodings about the future were the standard fare in the books and journals of the mid to late 1940s. The sense of decline stimulated by the First World War was now more pervasive and mainstream. Many writers expressed a pessimism about the future even more closed than 30 years earlier. The 'decline of the West' anticipated after 1919 was not now postponed to the future as it had been in the writings of Oswald Spengler, but was apparently staring us in the face. 'The West' appeared to be not merely in steady, though inexorable decline, but already exhausted. This was particularly acute from a German perspective. The sociologist Alfred Weber proclaimed the first 'end of history' in 1947: the '... end of history as moulded by the West'.[9]

If the reaction to the First World War was one of shock, reaction to the Second was one of virtual despair for the Western world. Despite victory in the war for the non German West, the titles of the books and articles of the war and immediate post-war years spoke of 'crisis' and wondered what was to become of our 'civilisation'. The historian Geoffrey Barraclough asked himself a question that was not far from the minds of much Western opinion. 'May it not be that, in a couple of centuries', he wondered, that 'the war of 1939–45 will appear not as the last in a long succession of successful struggles to prevent European hegemony, but rather as the decisive conflict in which Europe, committing suicide, surrendered mastery to the coloured peoples?'[10]

This despair cannot be written off as the product of strictly economic factors. Particularly with American Marshall Aid, there was no reason to believe that the devastation of war could not be overcome relatively quickly. Alan Milward, in his authoritative examination of the period for example, has shown that the apocalyptic protestations about the dire condition of Western civilisation were not based on any absolute deterioration in real European conditions.[11] Recovery was evident by 1947. The problem was ideological – particularly with regard to reconstruction. 'Our principal weakness is not economic or military, but ideological ... of ideas', wrote one commentator anticipating 'The Ideological Combat' of the Cold War, that would be necessary to redress the problem.[12] The immediate issue to be faced was that the West was associated with fascism, collaboration, economic slump and elitism. In the longer term, the task was one of evolving a new, non racial self-identity for Western society.

Many writers sensed that it was not the real threat of the USSR that led to widespread alarmism developing so rapidly, but the ideological insecurity of the West. It was perhaps the fact that the USSR was not tainted with regard to these ideas, and stood as a principled opponent of fascism and elitism (no matter how false this was in reality), that it presented itself as a threat – simply by its very existence. Similarly, during this period, the Soviet Union was perceived as an economic success. Few bothered to inspect the real economic chaos of the interwar Soviet Union. It was surely only the aggravated sense of economic decline in the West that led so many to convince themselves that things were better in Russia. The British historian of 'civilisations' Arnold Toynbee was particularly sensitive to these weaknesses (and the fact that a new Western identity would have to be developed in response). For him, '... the fact that our adversary threatens us by showing up our defects ... is proof that the challenge he presents to us comes ultimately not from him, but from ourselves'.[13]

This challenge was, above all, the widespread discrediting of the racial and elitist world view which had dominated the Anglo-American outlook since the nineteenth century, and which now stood irrevocably compromised by the Nazi genocide.[14] As Janos notes, the First World War had been problematic enough. Then the 'remarkable' domination of the East, legitimised by a powerful sense of moral superiority, was thrown into disarray: 'When this war came in 1914–18, it destroyed half of a continent and with it the Spencerian myth. It also tarnished the global image of the Occident.'[15] The Second World War was if anything even more of a blow to Western self-esteem and the Spencerian world view of racial superiority. Exactly how the West was to extricate itself from any responsibility for the ultimate implementation of their own ideas of eugenics and racial superiority was unclear. What is more, what was to replace the old elitist ideology? The response was, as we have already indicated in relation to the writing off of nationalism to the East, to at least establish geographical distance from now compromising ideas.

'Totalitarianism' in the East

A great deal of intellectual energy went into trying to prove that fascism was a uniquely German aberration that bore not the slightest resemblance to, or relationship with, the rest of the West. Many of the books written about fascism in the late 1940s and 1950s were, consciously or otherwise, written with this in mind. Increasingly, the idea of 'totalitarianism' emerged from these studies. The unmistakable message was of fascism being the blood brother of communism were in fact the real blood brothers, rather than the social Darwinist and imperialist outlook shared by Nazi Germany with the rest of the West.[16] In this intellectual scramble to rescue an aggravated form of the Western reputation, Eastern Europe stood as an uncomfortable reminder of the past that the West was attempting to discard. Elite domination in the East had coarsely aped Western elitism, and the region was a tragic reminder of Western destructiveness. Now as never before, Eastern Europe epitomised all these embarrassments of the interwar, and in fact, the wartime period itself.

The impulse to set the region apart intensified in the immediate post-war years – particularly in relation to the most sensitive issue of all – collaboration. A writer for *Foreign Affairs*, for example, writing in late 1946, considered that 'It would be an exaggeration to say that these social groups collaborated with the Nazis en bloc – as a class. It is for instance, obviously untrue of either Holland or Belgium. But the generalisation comes nearer the truth in Eastern Europe ....'[17] Of course, the European elites had collaborated with the Nazis everywhere, and this stood as a severe problem in re-establishing authority. It remains a highly sensitive issue to this day in countries like France, and it was understandable that there were attempts to show that collaboration had been much worse elsewhere – namely in Eastern Europe. The proposition that collaboration was really a problem particular to the East, was a compelling one in the immediate post-war years.

If collaboration, and indeed the wider affinity with racial intolerance, was particular to the East, then it would be no surprise to find that these values had outlasted even the Nazi regime. Such a formulation was advanced, and eventually systematised into the division between the nationalisms of East and West that has already been mentioned. A key work was Walter Kolarz's 1946 volume, *Myths and Realities in Eastern Europe*, a book expressly concerned with warning the West of the continued presence of 'totalitarian' ideas and dangers on their doorstep. 'It was but logical to believe', explained Kolarz, 'that the bestialities of Nazism and fascism – the final culmination of aggressive nationalism – would have compromised chauvinism and racial megalomania all over the world ... Unfortunately, this expectation has turned out to be wrong.'[18] These values lived on in Eastern Europe according to Kolarz.

In fact, 'Eastern' Europe and its peoples came to be seen as 'nothing to do with us' – even if they had foolishly convinced themselves otherwise. *The Economist* decided in 1947 that 'Their enthusiasm for Western values is recent, and has less to do with Shakespeare and Leonardo than with the atom bomb.' Invoking a West defined by its classical 'traditions' rather than an intensifying militarism, provided a measure of exclusion for Easterners who '... make up in passionate hatred what they lack in understanding. All who stand in their way are "Jewish scum" and "Moscow agents." Whether they be communist or neo fascist, the demagogue and the police though are confident that the future belongs to them.'[19] So different were they in the eyes of *The Economist*, that '... for Balkan citizens, personal contacts with Westerners are deadlier than the plague'.[20] This was because they had become 'totalitarians'. In the remarkably (and somewhat cumbersomely) titled 'Hungary's and Romania's Nazis in Red – Hitler's Graduates Staff Stalin's New Order', Bela Fabian in *Commentary* explained that, 'East may be East, and West, West; and perhaps the twain never shall meet. But in such countries as Hungary and

Romania, left is not left; nor is right, right. The twain – being totalitarian twins – have met, mingled, and merged into a regime of uniform terror.'[21]

Evidently it was Western commentators who were convincing themselves of something, namely that they were a race apart from the peoples in the Western created democracies of the East. This was not the product of some abstract dislike. To the critical eye it is clearly the onerous problems of association with the Nazi experience that loomed large in the thinking of the time. Thus Frederick Hertz, for example, pondering *Nationality in History and Politics* in 1944 regretted that 'It is probably the most widespread view of the causes of Nazism that Hitler merely was the tool of the capitalists who financed him for their purposes.'[22] This association between fascism and capitalism had to be addressed if Western authority was to be restored. As the historian Gaddis Smith puts it, the West at this time was driven by the 'ghost of Hitler' more than hatred of the USSR.[23] Exorcising this ghost required a 'fall guy'. The 'tiresome, squabbling' peoples of the East were to play this role, whether they liked it or not.

The important component of this presentation was the corollary that these compromising values no longer existed in the West. In other words, associations with the racism of Western empires were obfuscated in the relocation of 'totalitarianism' to the East. Meanwhile, the West became synonymous with democratic pluralism. Having raised the spectre of 'totalitarianism', the West could then 'revive the cult of liberty, equality, law, justice and honour' as one observer had already anticipated as necessary back in 1939.[24] Or as another, explaining the necessity for 'ideological combat', put it, 'The Soviet Union is challenging the US to renew and develop for our time the magnificent inheritance of Western individualism ... the faith and morals of Christianity, the rationalism of the Renaissance and the Enlightenment, the English gift for compromise, the liberty of the democratic revolutions ....'[25] This new Western ideology was only made possible by the presentation of the East as the antithesis of supposedly historic Western values. It was rendered necessary by the embarrassment of the war, and possible, by the existence of the USSR as a counterpoint to newly created values.

Abandoning Eastern Europe

It was in the context of this developing Western sensibility that the region was more or less abandoned to its fate – as a defensive barrier for a Soviet Union keen to avoid a third German invasion. Notwithstanding anti-Soviet rhetoric, there was no real effort made to integrate the region. The slightest excuse, such as timid questioning by East European leaders of the terms of Marshall Aid, was used to deny funds, and thereby leave them to the Soviet orbit. The West had more pressing matters – its own reconstitution. Joyce and Gabriel Kolko document this process excellently in *The Limits of Power*. They describe, for example, how the Americans – who had assumed responsibility for the reconstruction of 'the West' – saw the need to draw definite lines. American Secretary of State Byrnes was clear about his priorities. 'In a word, we must help our friends in every way and refrain from assisting those who either from helplessness or for other reasons are opposing the principles for which we stand.'[26] More accurately, Byrnes should have said 'principles for which we would like to stand, and perhaps may be able to stand, if we can distance ourselves from fascism'.

Clearly, Eastern Europe embodied a past that the United States was were keen to forget. Energies were therefore concentrated on the more pressing problems of France and Italy. Aid to the region was largely terminated as early as 1946. If the Soviets wanted to try their luck with this troublesome part of Europe, they were to find little resistance from the West – at least initially. This is not to suggest a conscious conspiracy to hand over the region to the USSR, even if Churchill's agreements would suggest otherwise. The region embodied a past which had to be buried if the West was to undergo revival. The American political class in particular instinctively grasped this imperative. At the very least, little attention was paid to unfolding developments in the region in 1946 and 1947. Much to the fury and despair of what was left of the old elites in Eastern Europe, they were sacrificed for the cause of Western revival.

Having made it clear that the West would do little to integrate the region back into their orbit, and that they were largely indifferent to the fate of the region, developments in Central and East Europe did not take place under Western control. Particularly under these circumstances, it proved impossible to revive the old interwar order. Much of the old capitalist class had been wiped out, and those that remained stood isolated and fatally compromised by collaboration, and the general experience of interwar collapse. There was a general desire for change. In some cases this meant considerable support for Stalinist parties – as in Czechoslovakia. We should note, however, that virtually nowhere did this mean automatic hostility to the West. Stalin himself did not envisage exclusive control, particularly of a troublesome neighbour like Poland – a country where he famously described attempting to introduce communism as comparable to trying to saddle a cow. The Soviet Union we should recall, had completely thrown in its lot with the West through its wartime alliance. There was every indication that Stalin was obsessively interested in maintaining this arrangement. Allowing the British to wipe out the significant Greek communist movement, for example, was considered a small price to pay for the continued recognition of Stalin's Russia as the equal of Britain and the United States.

The blind eye was not sustained for long however. When the West did turn its gaze once more to what was going on in Eastern Europe in the later 1940s – now with domestic anti-communism gathering momentum – Stalin's Russia appeared strong and purposeful, where the West had been ineffective. Already highly sensitised to the way in which the USSR 'showed up our faults', and engaged in the militant anti-communism announced by Churchill's 'iron curtain' speech, the West viewed events in the region in an entirely different, alarmist light. Where they had previously proven indifferent (and still were in any meaningful sense – there was still no support available for the Eastern elites), now there was widespread fear at the slightest indication of encroaching Soviet power.

The key event was the reaction to the coup in Prague. 'Coup', let alone 'revolution', is a somewhat important and exaggerated title for what was a rather more unexciting turn of events. The Czechoslovakian 'coup' was the resignation of most of the old bourgeois section of the government. They hoped to draw attention to their isolation, by walking out en masse, thereby embarrassing the pro Russian faction, and most importantly, gaining attention in the West. They succeeded in little but confirming their own irrelevance however. But if the West was not forthcoming with practical support, they certainly began to raise the propaganda alarm, as this event was rapidly presented as step one of a quest for communist domination of Europe. Alarmist talk of Soviet takeover was not justified by events however. No wonder *The Economist* pondered: 'What has happened to make the feeling suddenly become much worse?' when they considered the reaction to events in Prague.[27] Western politicians had proven largely disinterested in the prior course of developments. This was precisely why the Czech old guard felt they had to do something drastic to gain attention.

The talk of Soviet takeover was more a reflection of preoccupations nearer to home. Far from radical observers like Sir Robert Lockhart realised that events such as the coup in Prague were not the product of any Soviet conspiracy. Rather, the defensive mind-set of the West was interpreting the slightest change as a challenge to their fragile ideological position. More obviously, it provided the first real fuel and vocabulary for the developing anti-communist consensus that was to become central to the ideology of the new West. The 'salami tactics' slogan used to describe the allegedly devious plot to erode democracy in Hungary, for example, was later to become the 'domino theory' in the anti-communist lexicon.

Communism as 'Organic' to Eastern Europe

While such events were used, and to some extent experienced, as a challenge, there was little suggestion that serious efforts be undertaken to restore Western influence in the region. Rhetoric about Soviet world takeover aside, there was an accepted inevitability to this strange land – home to, and originator of, extreme nationalism and intolerance – becoming part of an Asiatic East. According to the new Western consensus it was no accident of history that Eastern Europe had become more a part of the East than the West. As Elizabeth Wiskeman, in her renowned *Europe of the Dictators* put it, 'World opinion is not unwilling for communist Russia to try its hand at developing Eastern Europe.'[28] More critically, reflecting his own roots in the region, Hubert Ripka saw in 1961 that 'The conversion to communism of the countries of East Central Europe has to some extent been considered by some Western experts as a sort of natural stage in their development.'[29]

In this light we can also understand the way in which during the Cold War – despite the occasional 'Captive Nations Week' and the like – the West regarded Eastern Europe as a real part of the 'Eastern bloc'. Rhetoric, as in Eisenhower's 1952 election campaign, may have hinted at 'rollback' and the liberation of Eastern Europe, but the true Eastern policy of the United States was revealed in an embarrassing leak from the State Department in the 1970s, in the rarely discussed 'Sonnenfeldt Doctrine'. Paul Latawski, in his recent book on the problem of nationalism, is one of the few to draw attention to this interesting episode. 'At a meeting in London of American ambassadors to Europe', he explains, 'Helmut Sonnenfeldt, a counsellor at the State Department, suggested to his colleagues that the aim of American policy ought to be to transform the "inorganic, unnatural relationship" between the Soviet and Eastern Europe to one that was "organic" for the sake of peace and stability.'[30]

There was predictable outrage at these candid remarks. Complaints were longstanding, particularly from expatriate East Europeans, that the region was being ignored. In 1957, George Kennan, attacked a Western policy '... which left no room, even in concept, for the East European peoples, which would have no place for them even should they be able to liberate themselves ...'.[31] Few were even going through the motions of declaring support for our supposed kindred spirits in the East. Some, like Senator Fullbright, were even for closing down Radio Free Europe. It was in this context that Joseph Rothschild's book on Eastern Europe as a region of diversity had such a positive reception in the academic community.[32] It did not treat the region as a uniform, and therefore presumably Stalinised, bloc. Perhaps more calculatedly, old Cold War warriors like Kennan felt it important to make a show of interest in their fate – certainly not spell out the fact that Eastern Europe had long been written off.

Noticeably however, no one felt able or willing to question the central issues revealed in the Sonnenfeldt Doctrine, and disquiet was essentially concerned with the possibility that that candid approach should not be made public. After all, the cause of Eastern Europe remained a significant part of anti-communist propaganda. The core understanding that this was a natural sphere of Soviet influence did not preclude some rhetorical support for Eastern Europe, nor indeed, occasionally more practical measures in order to put pressure on Moscow. As Latawski further notes,

> The silent partnership with the Soviet Union ... did not stop the Western camp from occasionally using it as a means to cause Soviet discomfort. Cynical support for Nicolae Ceaucescu's 'national communism' in Romania and the encouragement of Solidarity in Poland were examples of the West's willingness to play the nationalism card if it made life more difficult for the 'evil empire'.[33]

To openly state in this context that the East was actually regarded as an 'organic' part of the Soviet orbit would hardly have made this task any easier.

Contemporary commentators are now less circumspect about writing off the East. Apart from anything else, it no longer involves an apparent concession to the great enemy – leaving half of Europe to the 'evil empire'. Today, at the end of the twentieth century, with the loss of the Soviet threat, it is perhaps not surprising to find the old conviction about unassailable 'Eastern-ness' becoming explicit. This is particularly so in light of the current need to explain away the West's failure to transform the region after the collapse of communism. Justifying the failure of transformation, the *Sunday Telegraph* speaks for more than eccentric conservatism when it tells us that for these peoples, '... relishing authoritarianism and dictatorship ... huge majorities believe capitalism is a zero sum game'.[34] Writing off the East in response to Western failure, and in the process casting East Europeans as uniquely non disposed to 'our' ways, has a considerable historical pedigree. Having been submerged beneath the 'captive nation' rhetoric of the Cold War, it has now come back into full view. So too have expressions of confidence in the benign character of Western influence.

10

Contemporary Eastern Europe and New Interference

Pragmatism Rules

The lurid portrayals of Russia and Eastern Europe as still in the grip of demonic forces from the past, or even paralysed by a fear of the future, are quite at odds with reality. If politics and society in the post-Cold War West is now largely bereft of competing ideologies – even the basic division between left and right – Eastern Europe, as ever, expresses these trends in an 'especially clear' way. Even the avowedly anti-political forces of the first wave of opposition as embodied by the likes of Vaclav Havel were, ironically, found to be too ideological themselves in their moral and outright anti-ideological approach. They were replaced, in the main, by technocratic management teams. Even those parties retaining 'socialist' or 'social democratic' titles appealed to these same 'who can run the show best' sensibilities, indicating that political labels, as much as in the West, now mean little. Farther East, in Russia meanwhile, there are no parties as such, apart from the so-called 'communists' (the party of the marginalised regions and sectors, and the old), but groups of individuals who more or less directly represent different sections of the elite. This has not unduly upset the electorate. Besides attracting Western interest and recognition, people in the East have proven interested in little beyond the most immediate concerns, never mind ferocious nationalisms, or undying commitments to Marx and Lenin – despite the electoral success of former apparatchiks in countries like Hungary and Poland in the mid-1990s. There is little at stake but personal survival, even at the governmental level.

The much-vaunted 'return of communism' does not indicate the persistence of old ideological passions, but its opposite. As one astute Hungarian observer explains: 'The ex-communist Socialists won because they successfully presented themselves as the least ideological on the market.' He goes on to ridicule the 'Animal Farm' prejudices of Western observers, and the idea that election results bear any

155

relation to their grim forebodings – even the more rational explanation that nostalgia solely accounts for the popularity of the new 'socialist' parties. 'Most striking of all for the Animal Farm prejudices', he explains, 'is the poor showing of populist, authoritarian, anti-semitic, xenophobic, anti-liberal, neo-Communist, and all other varieties of extremism. All these should have been winning cards if the disillusionment or nostalgia theories were to hold.' He concludes with a rhetorical question: 'Isn't this exactly what you would have expected in Central Europe, "The Place Where Wars, Fascism, Communism, Began": an election that wipes extremism out of politics?'[1] What is more, as ever when commentators seize on a new development and declare it to be the shape of things to come, they are inevitably overtaken by events. The 'return of communism' now looks rather less impressive in the light of victory for more traditionally right wing forces in both Romania and Bulgaria in late 1996 for example.

Survival is the name of the game in Russia and Eastern Europe – making ends meet is the general preoccupation. Everything is tempered by these realities. The declared hostility to German influence expressed by many Czechs for example – as I have indicated, a much discussed 'problem' in the region – counts for nothing. Economic realities render such feelings inconsequential. Even Vaclav Havel, a man who has spent so much time moralising about the 'mind-set' of his countrymen, retains a clear sense of proportion in this respect. As he put it, 'I meet people who frighten those around them with talk of the German threat but at the same time hang out signs saying "Zimmer Frei" in their windows and collect rent in DM even from their Czech tenants.'[2]

Only for the minority who managed to cream off old state assets is there perhaps even time for anything but the hard work of getting by. A Polish journalist described the typical entrepreneur in terms which ring true more generally:

The average candidate for a Polish capitalist stands ankle deep in mud, freezes in chilly weather and takes a pee in a staircase nearby. He buys during the night and sells during the day. He has a folding table, a camp bed, a suitcase, then a tent, then a wooden hut. Then maybe a small shop or wholesale operation based in his aunt's apartment. He started trading because others did the same, because the time was right, or simply because he had to survive. If possible he still draws unemployment benefit. Only one in ten, or even one in a hundred, will ever move up the social ladder, open a shop or set up a company.[3]

Even Russia is now littered with thousands of street traders selling imported goods on the streets, much as Poland was in the early 1990s. Life here is dominated by the day to day, even minute to minute, rather than grand visions of the future, and historical enmity. This is not the stuff of more Yugoslavias. Contrary to the suspicions of many commentators, there is evidently no reason why such a second rate capitalism should lead to large scale conflict. In the absence of any sense of alternative possibilities – certainly vehicles through which this might be expressed – the frustrations of personal survival acquire no shape or focus. Particularly because the socialist alternative has apparently been tried and rejected, there is no immediate prospect of anything but the continuation of efforts to 'strike it lucky'.

Insofar as this new capitalism in the East has not met expectations, it is not due to a cultural inability of Easterners to adapt to the ways of the market. It is certainly not because of an ideological opposition. What is often forgotten is that so many East Europeans had been surviving through entrepreneurial ingenuity throughout the years of Stalinism. This was a culture organised around privatised trade and barter, as it was one of holding down two jobs – in addition to tending the home grown vegetables. Wheeling and dealing was a way of life that did not have to be learnt overnight in 1989. There was, and to some extent still is, continued opposition to the withdrawal of state subsidies from certain industries, and a desire for continued social provision in traditional areas. Those who stand to suffer directly from the changes are understandably opposed to cuts, and have often (as in Russia and the Czech Republic for example) been successful at arranging for continued covert government support. But this does not indicate 'cultural' opposition to the market, any more than similar developments in the West. Demands for state protection are a feature of politics in the EU, as is the widespread government help often secretly afforded industry throughout Europe. In the Western setting however, they are unlikely to be held up as evidence of a deep seated hostility to the free market, as is often the case for commentators noting protectionism and state subsidy in the East.

Western investors have an open field. There are no rivals standing in the way of German expansion into the region, nor are there any real obstacles in the region itself. The workforce is well trained and educated, and has proven willing to accept all the sacrifices demanded of it. Limits then are only those of the West itself or, as one observer put it in relation to prospects for the former GDR, 'How far East will Europe extend: as far as German taxpayers want, and that will not be very far.'[4] Any barriers to capitalist development are not essentially internal. Insofar as reticence has developed about the market system, it is in response to disappointing results – too little market, rather than too much. Had it delivered anything like what East Europeans were led to expect, there would have been no greater enthusiasts for the hidden hand of market forces than in Eastern Europe. Even without spectacular success, the enthusiasm that does exist is in marked contrast to the lack of unqualified support in the West for a free market associated with the 'excesses' and 'short termism' of the 1980s. The (nominally) 'socialist' parties fully embrace capitalism – to the point of arguing that it is they who can make it operate most efficiently.

Even without significant Western investment, economic prospects are by no means disastrous. Estimates from PlanEcon, a Washington based consultancy, have assessed 1995 as the second year of widespread economic growth, and anticipate even better results for 1996. The OECD's forecasts for 1996 are similarly positive, anticipating growth rates of between 2.5 per cent and 5 per cent for most of the countries of the region. Reports from the European Bank for Reconstruction and Development and the Economist Intelligence Unit – both also authoritative monitors of economic trends – are equally positive. Such forecasts are partly related to the previous collapse of output. Percentage growth figures are percentages of a smaller economy, and are thus not as impressive as they might appear on paper. Nevertheless, we are not witnessing descent into general economic oblivion. Neither do growth rates follow the pattern one might expect according to prejudice, that the further East one ventures, the lower the figures. Romania and Slovakia for example, are doing relatively well. Economic developments are quite unremarkable, like so much else in the region.

Balkan Exceptionalism? – Albanian Collapse

At the same time, the picture is not even. Significant protests have developed in Serbia, and without the cohering impact of war, Milošović's days look numbered. The economic picture in Bulgaria was disastrous in 1996/7, and anti-government protests, with international pressure, have forced the government into conceding fresh elections. Most seriously of all in the most recent period, Albania has collapsed. From having been held up as a showcase reformer by the IMF between 1992 and 1995, and the United States' favourite Balkan country under the rule of President Sali Berisha, Albania disintegrated in early 1997.

Warnings of wider conflagration throughout the Balkans have been issued, especially by Greece and Italy – the two neighbours most concerned with the potential for large scale immigration from Albania. All in all, the apparent explosion of the country seems to have again confirmed the existence of dangerous forces concentrated in the Balkans, and reminded us of the consequences of complacently assuming that the region might escape its unstable history.

Intellectually, there has been a predictable re-emergence of more focused culturalist 'explanations' in the West, about the congenital backwardness and instability of 'the Balkans' and its peoples. Ottoman and communist legacies, anti-democratic traditions and other indigenous factors have been raised. Jacques Rupnik, now director of research at the Centre for International Research in Paris for example, claims that, 'We're seeing another example of a new Balkan democracy threatening to collapse because it lacks the political foundations and understanding to assimilate quickly Western-style politics and a market economy.'[5] Rupnik suggests that the overreaction to the collapse of the pyramid schemes is founded upon attitudes shaped by communism, whereby the population expect everything to be done for them. As a result they now blame the government for the collapse of the 'get-rich-quick' pyramid credit schemes which precipitated the crisis.

Superficially, there is much to confirm the dramatic prognosis of an 'explosion' in Albania. Since the collapse of the pyramid credit schemes, events escalated to the point where central authority collapsed. Virtual anarchy has followed, with much of the population seizing weapons from the numerous arms dumps left scattered throughout the country by the paranoid Stalinist regime of Enver Hoxha. 'The rebels', as they have been dubbed, are demanding nothing less than the resignation of the President, and threatening to back up their demands with force. There are also potential 'ethnic' and political ingredients which have been highlighted by some observers. Many in the rebellious south are of Greek origin, while the North is more loyal to Berisha. In the context of gun law and the continued refusal of the President to resign, Western nationals were dramatically airlifted from the country by Italian, American and German troops in scenes reminiscent of the fall of Saigon.

On the other hand, there was evidence to suggest that the situation was not as explosive as might have appeared to be the case – particularly before unrest spread from the South to the country as a whole. Certainly this was no ethnic conflict. For all the potential danger posed by the amount of arms now in circulation, casualties in this 'war against the sky' were largely a consequence of stray bullets. By all accounts there was a strangely conciliatory mood in the rebellious South. The resignation of the President, and an enquiry into the operation of the pyramid schemes, was evidently sufficient to defuse the situation, and there has been no wider attempt to challenge the social or territorial character of society at this stage. A curious mismatch is evident between the modest ambitions of opposition to Berisha, and the social collapse which has been the result. This begs the question as to why the failure of a financial scheme should have such dramatic results.

To an extent, the population's anger is simply because almost everyone, especially in the South, had invested their savings in the pyramid schemes. But that this reaction should lead to the collapse of the country indicates the very narrow foundations upon which it was built. Contemporary Albania has little to endow it with any sense of purpose or identity. In the absence of any clearer ideology or purpose, the ruling Democratic Party made much of 'get-rich-quick' schemes: 'everyone wins with the DP' was the electoral message. An illusory 'popular capitalism' became the be all and end all of what democratic Albania was all about. Otherwise, it was a country identified only with the fact that most people want to leave, maybe to join those already scraping a living abroad – in Greece, or further afield. The collapse that followed the end of this dream is more accurately described as an implosion, not an explosion. The country was not so much torn asunder by dynamic forces, ethnic or otherwise, as it simply collapsed.

In understanding this collapse, the cultural explanations put forward by the likes of Rupnik make little sense. Regarding 'overreaction' to the collapse of the pyramid schemes, the idea that Albanians, long accustomed to the security of communism, cannot comprehend that they are now responsible for their own decisions – and their consequences – is ridiculous. Life under the rule of Enver Hoxha was no bed of roses. Perhaps more than in most parts of the communist bloc, survival demanded personal initiative and yes, comprehending that one attempts to gain, financially or otherwise, from any transaction. As for alleged Albanian stupidity in staking their savings on decidedly suspect financial operations, they did not so much make a bad choice, as take the only opportunity available. Albanians did not choose investment in pyramid schemes over shares in Microsoft. Had they made such an unwise decision, there might be some basis for concluding that the intricacies of the market are beyond them.

Blaming the government for wider social problems, an alleged peculiarity singled out by Rupnik among others, is hardly specific to Albania or the former communist bloc. In the West this reflex is, if anything, more developed. The government in Britain is held responsible for 'not doing enough' to check the meat that is consumed, and that schoolchildren's homework is done, to cite only a couple of examples. An almost universal response in the West to the most insignificant or isolated problem is to demand greater government regulation for even the most intimate aspects of life. By comparison, Albanians attacking a government for not checking the activities of financial operations in which they were directly involved, is hardly exceptional. Even the strange sight of men, women and children looting arms, and then firing wildly into the air is not inexplicable under the circumstances. With the collapse of authority, grabbing food, and then the weapons which offer both protection and a potential object of barter, is hardly surprising given that it was only arms that were readily available (gold bullion would no doubt have been preferable). Shooting into the sky is for the benefit of excitable Western journalists; for the criminal gangs which have emerged in some towns to establish their authority; and as a show of strength to the hated secret police. Overall, none of the allegedly peculiar 'cultural' traits highlighted in the Western presentation of Albanian collapse are particular to, or explain the actions of, Albanian people themselves.

International factors are, as ever in this part of the world, crucial. In the most immediate sense, they account for Berisha's stubborn refusal to back down and resign. The virulently anti-communist, former communist Berisha was firmly backed by the West, to the point where he refused to recognise that his time was up, and that his former sponsors had now abandoned him. But there is a wider picture here. Albania, together with the other Southern Balkan states, was treated differentially by the West in comparison to the rest of the region from the very beginning. It was deemed to be incapable of absorption into Europe, certainly the EU, from the word go. This exclusion was ratified in late 1995 when Carl Bildt, EU special envoy to Yugoslavia, called for a common set of 'Balkan agreements' for those not covered by 'Europe agreements'. As a result, Albania has been so desperate to join any international body, and thereby become fully recognised in the world, that they applied to attend the 1997 Francophone summit. Despite never having been a French colony, they were left only with the French equivalent of the British Commonwealth as a means of escaping an isolation no longer self-imposed as it had been under the former communist regime.

With no place to turn, the Albanian, like the Bulgarian elite, has lacked any sense of purpose, even orientation or coherence. Excluded from Europe, the country has figured only as a piece in a Balkan security jigsaw created by the destruction of Yugoslavia. The country's stability, or at least containment, was seen to limit the potential for conflict in Macedonia and Kosovo. Berisha was supported on the basis that he would not politicise the situation of Albanians in Kosovo and Macedonia. The United States took the lead in this process, but given the security priorities, this was essentially military involvement, rather than an intervention involving significant trade or investment. United States involvement cooled somewhat under Clinton, however, and Germany became an increasingly important supporter, particularly as a bulwark against Serbia. Advisers from the Konrad Adanauer Institute helped in Berisha's re-election; economic influence has increased; and army officers were reportedly trained in Germany. This involvement has clearly affected policy toward the country. The Germans (along with the other most interested European party, Italy) pressurised the OSCE not to invalidate the May 1996 elections. It is also not surprising that German criticism of Berisha's hardline response to protest has been muted, and they have sought to ensure that European pressure was not seriously brought to bear.

Albania's implosion proves very little about the region in itself. As Martin Woollacott put it in the *Guardian*: 'Albania is not so much a failed state as a state which has never had a chance to succeed.'[6] The poorest European state has remained in pretty much the same condition since the collapse of communism – not spectacular or dangerous, but simply sad. It has been integrated into international relations only insofar as cynical realpolitik has demanded. With no internal dynamic, the country will for the time being lack any organising principle or mechanism, other than limited force. Areas of the South are likely become more a part of Greece than Albania, while towns like Vlore will possibly consolidate relations with Italy.

Eight years on from '1989 and all that', a fragmented Balkan state whose peoples are prevented from escape by hostile neighbours is a fitting epitaph to the very divisive approach taken to the whole former Eastern bloc by a self-absorbed Western Europe. The predictable response, led by Italy, has been to criminalise the Albanians. The Italians declared a state of emergency because an alleged 10,000 impoverished Albanians arrived by sea. A prominent Italian MP said that refugees should be thrown into the sea – something which already happened to the 80 or more Albanians who drowned after their boat was sunk by an Italian corvette. While the MP's remarks provoked some condemnation, support for the plight of Albanians was almost entirely absent, largely on the assumption that they can only be criminals. The Italians, at the time of writing, are set to send troops, ostensibly to 'protect aid delivery'. Having invaded the country in both world wars, they are venturing uninvited once again into the country – motivated, according to them, by humanitarian considerations.

New Divisions

Whatever seems to happen within the region, instead of finding themselves increasingly an integral part of Europe, the countries of the former Eastern bloc have, to one extent or another, been determinedly confined to the margins. Two of the most renowned commentators on the region have noted the process of exclusion that has gone on since being 'welcomed back' at the end of the 1980s. Part of Misha Glenny's conclusion to *The Rebirth of History* is that 'The West deals with each country according to a flexible, sliding scale of merit, which is guaranteed to provoke existing regional tension.'[7] Mihaly Vajda saw, even before the wall came down, that 'Quite a few people and nations having failed to establish a "democratic" political system in their countries, find themselves – willy nilly – excluded from Europe. Barbed wire divides Europe from "not yet Europe" or "not any more Europe".'[8] An economic report back in 1992 noted that, while 'Some are being helped and welcomed by Western institutions, ... others are finding themselves the target of a multinational form of "differentiation".'[9]

The most important feature of East–West relations is that the region remains excluded from Europe proper. Chancellor Kohl's assurance that, 'There must be no borders which perpetuate the prosperity divide', now sounds distinctly hollow.[10] So does his declaration that the final overcoming of the division of the continent between East and West is one of the two objectives in clearing a path to the 'Europe of the future'. Even more cynical is the self-congratulatory idea that, 'The "pull" of the EC is instilling discipline and hope', which was suggested by one United States academic, and widely shared by the consensus of policy makers and scholars.[11] Apart from anything else, East Europeans are often not allowed to even visit the West of which they are now said to be a part.

Restricting freedom of movement is a central concern in the new Europe of the 1990s. It overshadows much of the diplomatic activity that goes on – especially between the new democracies of Central and Eastern Europe, and the states of the EU. The pattern that has emerged is one of increasing exclusion for those from furthest East, with the more favoured states – Poland, Hungary and the Czech

Republic – being drawn into exclusionary arrangements in return for diplomatic favour. One expert on the contours of the new 'Fortress Europe' describes their role as one where they '... act as a de facto buffer zone between Western and Eastern Europe in respect of sanitising the West from the "threat from the East" in terms of refugees and asylum seekers'. The result: '... greater inner Europe is "protected" by an exclusionary buffer zone on its periphery with outer Europe'.[12]

In this arrangement, the states of 'Central Europe' have taken on a policing role for this 'greater inner Europe'. Thus the Poles and Czechs have agreed to take back 'illegal immigrants' expelled from their Western neighbours. They, in turn, have agreements with those to the East such as Bulgaria, to allow the repatriation of their citizens from the Central European countries through which they travelled to get to Germany or some other Western destination. If a Bulgarian is expelled from Germany to Poland, they are then swiftly deported further East. Increasingly, the Czechs and Poles in particular have taken it upon themselves to prevent Easterners even getting as far as Germany by sealing borders and keeping them stuck 'in the middle' – in Slovakia for example. This process of exclusion does not only take place directly, but is systematically woven into the very fabric of the new pattern of relations established between the two halves of Europe.

In many ways, the most ideological and potentially damaging aspects of political culture revolve around establishing 'civil society' and proving who is most advanced in this regard. Although referred to in the opening chapters, this trend demands greater attention. The Czechs, for example, make much of their greater affinity with the West and of course, by implication, that their neighbours are more backward and belong confined to the East. Virtually every other state reproduces this discourse in one way or another. But the overblown preoccupations among the elites in Eastern Europe with putting down their neighbours are not signs of impending conflict, only a disguised appeal for resources. Christopher Lord from the Charles University demystifies much of the talk of the search for a democratic 'Central Europe'.

> Democratically, of course! Oh yes. Again, the inner meaning of this term is simply: 'Can we have some more dollars please?' And the appeal of 'Central Europe'? 'If they want their goodies from Washington', it is obligatory to establish a safe distance from 'the East'. 'And the idea that you can escape the horrible "Eastern Europe" label just by announcing that you were never part of it

in the first place has an undeniably attractive simplicity...' The trick of this 'impressive sounding region', is maintain 'a vague and ill defined picture' so that you might be included.[13]

Insofar as we can identify potentially divisive ideological posturing, it is in the widespread talk of who is more Western, and therefore less Eastern, than whom.[14] It is quite clear, however, that this is really about a barely disguised appeal for special treatment by the West – 'look, we are more Western, so we deserve to be first in line for any money that is available'. It is manifestly not a mysterious product of an Eastern obsession with history and culture. It is the consequence of exclusion by the West. Because it has been made clear that not all the countries of the area will be admitted to Western institutions, or even gain access to investment, a competitive struggle has inevitably ensued where all parties are forced to advance their claims for inclusion in the language of 'who is more Western than whom?' The Czechs express this necessarily competitive process very clearly. 'We refuse to make some sort of gentleman's agreement that we will all go together into the European Union', said Miroslav Somol, the Czech deputy minister of trade and industry for example. This was justified as a question of cultural superiority. 'We think there are many differences between the countries, economically and philosophically' continued the official.[15] Before we begin condemning Czechs, Hungarians and Poles for such silliness, however, we should remember that had this exclusion not taken place, there would have been no divisive ideological talk of competing historical claims for inclusion in the West clouding the atmosphere of regional politics.

Lord illustrates this important feature of East–West relations with his discussion of Nato membership – an otherwise apparently irrational preoccupation for nations against whom the Western defence institution was designed. It is only because 'West European enthusiasm for subsidising the modernisation of potential competitors from the former East bloc is virtually nil', he explains, that Nato membership has taken on symbolic significance as the only point of entry to the West. Thus the fractious competition, particularly between Russia and her former satellites, is not the result of collective stupidity, but the product of exclusion. There would be little interest in joining Nato, and the damaging quarrels, particularly between East European states and Russia, would not have happened had they been allowed to join the West proper. It is only because of being denied access to the key institutions of the West, particularly the European Union itself, that such a premium has been placed on membership of even a largely symbolic body like Nato. Gaining acceptance to any important Western institution, even a military one, is seen to be of moment because it suggests a way out of isolation; a definite head start in getting to the front of the queue for membership of the EU. Disputes over Nato are thus not really about 'squabbling little nations' fighting over access to a redundant military alliance, or insofar as they are, it is the inevitable consequence of policies of exclusion made in the West.

The New East–West Discourse

It is not only the discussion of Nato membership that has been the hidden agenda for East Europeans of at least establishing a foot in the door – virtually all points of contact between East and West have this undercurrent. This is why Eastern 'partners' are prepared to put up with the dehumanising assumptions which invariably accompany westernisation. The United States has been busy drafting constitutions throughout the region for example. Indeed, as one professor from the Virginia School of Law put it, it is the '... most active period for American revisers in this century. It's a new cottage industry.' Are we to believe that the Hungarians, the particular subject of revision discussed by this author, are incapable of writing a constitution? The nation that has produced more Nobel prize winners per head of population than any other, cannot translate the United States constitution into Hungarian? In fact, as Robert Bigler continued, this particular exercise was about something quite different. As he politely puts it, '... public relations were also involved, and they hoped that by hiring American experts they bolstered their image and increased their chances for winning foreign aid'.[16]

As is so often the case, highly educated East Europeans are forced to act like children in order to gain a competitive advantage over their rivals in the queue for limited Western favours. The same can be said for many aspects of the establishment of 'civil society', a term which has become little more than a catch all euphemism for shaping the East in the image of the West. The new language of East–West relations revolves around the aping of Western concerns. For those enterprising enough to try and advance their careers through Western NGOs, this is especially important. Fine explains that 'By now ... almost everyone in ECE knows that projects structured around the needs of the Roma, or containing elaborate plans for reeducation containing the catchwords "civil society" or "rights" or "democracy" will receive funding.'[17] The likes of Fine may complain about such naked opportunism, but it is the inevitable consequence of contemporary relations between East and West.

While a handful of resourceful East Europeans may gain lucrative employment from this process, the majority do not. Indeed, the patronising assumptions of this new discourse (and practice) reinforce further their status as first class idiots in need of 'education'. Many of the initiatives of westernisation are quite absurd if we realise that the peoples of the region are much like ourselves. As part of its sinisterly named Marshall Plan of the Mind for example (a Foreign Office funded organisation driven only by 'old fashioned philanthropy' according to their publicity), the BBC, with funding from the European Union, has developed a version of its famous radio show 'The Archers' especially for Romanians. This saga of rural life is to teach ignorant Romanians the mechanics of the market economy. As one account explained, 'Set in a Bucharest apartment block the saga will also include storylines on shop keeping and importing from overseas.'[18] Similar soap operas are intended to help bring about agricultural reform in the Ukraine. Without the help of the BBC they seemingly cannot grasp the benefits of selling goods for more than they paid. Why do people go along with this nonsense? From the BBC's point of view it is because they must be convinced of their inherent superiority. For Romanians, Ukrainians and others, because any contact with the West is preferable to isolation – it appears to be at least an opening which might lead to better things. Any interest is better than none – even if it does involve the self-humiliation of going along with the idea that you do not comprehend the basics of human existence.

The BBC's gift to Romania is by no means exceptional in its absurdity. Besides imparting such economic 'know-how', another particular focus for Western projects is teaching 'tolerance'. The Project on Ethnic Relations, for example, has held police training seminars (as does the British 'know-how' fund), where American police management specialists 'present tolerance and training seminars' to the country's police and justice officials. The concept of American police officers, notorious for their virtual war with young blacks, lecturing anybody about 'tolerance' is strange indeed. Always however, we should remember that there is a disguised dynamic at play in these otherwise farcical interchanges.

The ostensible purpose of this process of jumping through hoops to prove that one is civilised, or at least aspires to be so, is to make the East more like the West. But this has proved to be an illusion. Why else, after some six years of this 'democratisation' is Europe now more firmly divided than it was back in the 1980s? As countries in the East are forced to make fools of themselves, aping Western concerns and accepting the most humiliating demands, their preparedness to do so only confirms the prejudice that they inhabit a different moral universe to our own.

In a self-fulfilling prophecy, we see that they really were not like us in the first place. As an illustration, take the association agreements drawn up by the EC for the Czech and Slovak republics which included special 'human rights' obligations. Refusal to sign would mark out either country as distinctly uncivilised. But on the other hand, the agreements rightly '... sent some Czech delegates reeling at the implications and worried about what the world would think' according to the *Prague Post*. Their fears were proved justified as EC Commissioner Leon Brittan made their status apparent in an intended reassurance. He explained that the EC's policy was to include the clause in every agreement '... signed with third world countries'.[19] This was particularly galling for the Czechs who had done little to prevent their split with Slovakia, precisely because going it alone and ditching the supposedly more 'Eastern' Slovaks suggested greater opportunities for becoming Western in the eyes of the EU. Instead they found themselves explicitly labelled as a 'Third World' country – a fate which awaits all who accept that they are in need of supervision over the treatment of their citizens. On the other hand it is interesting to note that the Czechs have in other respects been quite successful at promoting themselves as distinct, precisely because the combative Klaus has shown himself very sensitive to the ramifications of such measures. He has often refused to accept differential treatment – to the point of stating that they do not need aid or investment, and have completed 'transition'.

Westernisation Through 'Civil Society'

I have already indicated in a previous chapter what we might term a return of a neocolonial relationship between East and West. The governments of countries like Bulgaria and Albania have been virtually run from Washington, and United States military involvement has been extensive throughout the Southern Balkans, for example. This type of involvement is distinctly out of fashion however. Straightforward democracy promotion in the Balkans and elsewhere was in many respects a last gasp of the Cold War. Even its promoters, like USAID, no longer believe in its efficacy. On the ground, the limitations of the 'drop in and host a seminar on the wonders of America' approach has led to a reorientation toward a more sustained penetration of society. Rather than creating democracy from the top by training the old elite, encouraging 'civil society' through a 'bottom up' decentralisation of power is the order of the day. The approach pioneered by George Soros' institutions, where initiatives are staffed by local recruits and there is generally a much more organic relationship to society, is now in favour. At the same time as the type of approach is changing, there is more emphasis on issues such as minority rights, which are seen as helping effect a more long term change of political culture in these societies.

It would be wrong to draw too dramatic a distinction between old and new forms of interference. American intervention has blended traditional anti-communist democracy building through government bodies, with the work of the 'advocacy', political lobbying NGOs which are such a feature of United States politics. A key instrument of United States involvement in the region, the National Endowment for Democracy, now focuses on disbursing funds to NGOs to build 'civil society'. Everyone from the World Bank to the IMF is now keen on imposing 'civil society' rather than traditional austerity packages, or at least combining the two.

However we understand it, whether it is old institutions modernising their agendas or new ones coming to the fore, it is clear that Western involvement in the East is changing. The cutting edge is through far more contemporary concerns: 'retraining' of the workforce; the 'counselling' of despair and 'trauma'; support for women, children and minorities. These are generally regarded as being above criticism because a focus on the disadvantaged is not so obviously partisan as other forms of establishing domination. This type of interference was first vividly brought to my attention by my old Romanian language teacher, fuming at the translation work she was undertaking to top up her wages. It consisted of texts teaching Romanian mothers how to bring up children. As she rightly pointed out, 'they' have been bringing up children for a very long time without the aid of British advice. The implications are far more dehumanising than those of political and military domination, painting as they do a portrait of the East as now incapable of even rearing its own children.

There is now a multitude of NGOs operating in the region. According to some recent figures, the Czech Republic has some two thousand, Hungary has one thousand registered, and Poland a massive twenty thousand (other estimates are much higher). A sense of the focus of these organisations that are busy building the new 'civil society' can be gleaned from looking at the list of projects organised by the British Charities Aid Foundation and funded largely by the Foreign Office. They include: paying for members of 'Childline' to get telephone counselling for children set up in the Ukraine; workshops on incontinence in Romania; an Association for the 'Child's Right to Play' established in Russia and Romania; developing 'advocacy skills' for the disabled, establishing alcoholics' groups in Moscow; and support groups for widows. There is the Estonian Family Therapy Union; groups taking photos of disabled people to promote positive images; environmental education centres; workshops for health professionals on 'breaking bad news'; and paying for visits of East Europeans to Edinburgh's multiethnic play schemes.

Considerable claims are being made for the potential of this reorientation. Typically, a recent book by the United States Brookings Institution concluded with a resounding call for greater support for Western NGO involvement in the region. 'NGOs operating close to problems at grassroots level', claim the editors, 'can play a key role in helping to resolve low level conflict before it becomes violent and intractable.' Already, they are '... beginning to help, barnacle like, to educate and build the skills for civil societies that can manage conflict through their own institutions'.[20] In the same volume, Fine tells us that 'In environments fraught with conflicts, there are certain functions that some kinds of local nongovernmental organisations seem best fit to undertake.' They '... can open windows to dialogue ... bear public witness to grievances, ... educate local populations and the next generation about everyone's human and civil rights, and teach some skill sets: how to spot signs of trouble when "hate comes to town"'.[21] Ewa Lés, in her useful examination of the voluntary sector in East Central Europe, makes even greater claims. 'Having been a guardian of a democratic and peaceful transformation', she says, 'the voluntary sector is now a significant source of tradition and force for change in most countries of the region.'[22] The voluntary sector manages to be both a 'force for change' and, more mysteriously given its recent origins, a 'significant source of tradition'.

For all the superficially positive rhetoric involved in the trend toward greater 'grassroots' NGO involvement rather than traditional democracy promotion, this shift is based upon a much greater pessimism, both with regard to the prospects for democracy, and to the peoples of the region. Lés justifies the need for NGOs with the claim that the region is universally '... a politically – still fragile environment, where the number of countries breaking up almost equals those which remain intact, where the democratic systemic transformations are endangered in some countries, where economic crises are a daily occurrence and fundamental changes of societal value systems are underway ...'.[23] Keitha Sapsin Fine's argument for greater NGO interference goes further. It is predicated upon a pessimistic contempt which is extreme even by the standards of typical Western prejudice. These '... people in the so called new democracies have remarkably few legal, political, and civic skills; they hold deep seated prejudices and an enormous reservoir of anxiety about the future. They have as yet little willingness to reconceptualise their prejudices or anxieties in language familiar to westerners.'[24] They have 'internalised' violence en masse according to Fine, and governments whip up ethnic hatreds as a matter of course. Her reading of events is completely fanciful, as she casually throws in incredible assertions – that the region is 'overpopulated' and there is a 'holocaust' in the former Yugoslavia for example.

It is no surprise that such an aggravated sense of 'problem peoples' is evident among those at the centre of 'civil society' promotion. What underlies the shift toward grassroots re-education is a far more patronising and anti-human attitude than even was evident in more traditional democracy promotion. In a sense, this can be thought of as a shift from a more brash and confident United States democratisation, to the more fraught and anxious European effort to only limit the atavistic impulses of the masses through building 'civil society'. Carothers indicates this difference when he points out that Romanians dislike the arrogance of Europeans even more than that of their Atlantic cousins. Whereas Americans operate on the assumption that Romania is a generally disadvantaged country, '... a deprived child to be helped along ... the Western European attitude is much more focused, historical contempt for the Balkans and all things "Eastern" in Europe'.[25]

It should also come as no surprise in this light, that any criticism of NGO activities from the very people these projects are supposed to be helping, can be dismissed. David Samuels of Princeton, for example, describes how the director of a Bosnian radio station explained to United States delegates at an NGO gathering that he did not wish to be invited to any more conferences, as they were of little practical help. 'We feel very stupid, and you are only making our tragedy longer', he complained. The response was telling. 'He is a common East European type, very depressed, very angry', replied one American donor later.[26]

In its own terms, this drive toward grassroots involvement is very much open to question. On what basis can they assume the propensity for conflict that underlies this perspective? Where is the proof? Striking too is the contradiction between greater and greater 'barnacle like' interference, and the strengthening of 'their own institutions'. 'Barnacle like' interference leads to the strengthening of the grip of Western institutions, not those of the people themselves. That is best done of course by leaving people to their own democratic devices.

There is much to be debated about this array of 'politically correct' concerns about counselling, 'advocacy' and 'child protection' – in themselves – let alone their export to the East. Many people consider it 'empowering'. But who asked for it? Who benefits from it? What relation does it bear to the real problems in these societies? Carothers mentions a telling story of a Romanian woman who goes to see an NGO director about problems with her water supply and a neighbourhood quarrel only to be told that it is outside the organisation's brief as it does not concern 'human rights'. David Samuels describes the absurdity of 'conflict resolution' techniques, and the bafflement and irritation of East Europeans being lectured about them. Quoting from 'Towards Sustainable Peace in the Balkans', a pamphlet produced by the Balkans Peace Project NGO, he explains that,

> Foremost among these is 'sculpting', 'a tool used both in psychodrama and family therapy' in which the 'protagonists' form 'living sculptures' from fellow members of the group. 'The use of family or group members as the "clay"' the project instructs, 'allows these individuals to explore for themsel[ves] the physical and psychological feelings generated by their position in the sculpture.' One participant in the workshop stated his suspicion of such psychological techniques for resolving conflict, saying, 'Imagine that this was 1939 and Hitler had just invaded Poland and a group of psychologists were trying to do conflict resolution between Germans and Poles ....' [27]

Other examples are even more perverse. The Unicef drive to force Serbia to respect children's rights not only ignores the fact that this is a society traditionally obsessed with caring for children, but that it was the UN imposed sanctions which were making children's lives more difficult – not irresponsible Serbian parents.

Protecting Minorities?

A much discussed and widely supported example of contemporary Western involvement is the drive to intervene on behalf of national minorities and those designated as ethnic groups 'at risk'. This may well sound laudable in the abstract, but on dispassionate reflection, it raises as many questions as it answers. What is a minority? What about the majority, and its will? Why are they considered to be in danger? By what authority do Western institutions have the right to interfere? Certainly, as I have indicated elsewhere, the history of Western support for minorities in the East is not a proud or productive one. The most authoritative work on the previous, interwar experience with interference to protect minorities in the region concluded that it was '... not very heartening ...' and that '... experience surely justifies the thought that any interference in the affairs of another is provocative of irritation and good feeling, and should not be undertaken without good reason'.[28] It was no accident that the whole idea of international minority rights protection was entirely discredited after the Second World War. More often than not, apparently selfless support for minorities on the part of Western powers has proved to be a cover for ruthless realpolitik.[29] Even if such involvement were driven only by altruism, however, the consequences are invariably divisive.

Selective support for favoured minorities has established relations of patronage for some, while excluding others. The various projects for the Roma are a case in point. The ill treatment of gypsies, or Roma as they are now known, has invited the attentions of Western institutions and benefactors such as Soros. This has been on a limited basis, and one insensitive to the tensions and anxieties created among those left out. Take the case of the Soros financed Roma-only vocational school in Budapest. As *Newsweek* pointed out with regard to the head of the project, 'Yet the most vocal critics of the school are Roma leaders, who accuse Varga of practising segregation.'[30] The handfuls of Roma children taken on – presumably a future elite of the Roma community – are set apart for exclusive privilege denied the majority.

Another exclusively Roma school in southern Hungary is the Gandhi Foundation. This points to one of the most pernicious aspects of the singling out of the Roma as an 'ethnic' group – the creation of a mythical past. There is no clear evidence that the Roma are ethnically, as opposed to socially, distinct – certainly no one is able to convincingly indicate their origins. Yet along with patronage appear to have come attempts to authenticate their legitimate status as an ethnic group. Thus the vague notion that they somehow originated in India is now being promoted – hence the 'Ghandi' school. There has been legitimate and longstanding complaint of a damaging tendency in Eastern Europe to make up mythical pasts which lead to antagonisms with neighbours, slighted by the latest revision of history. In this case, it would appear to be the process of Western involvement that is stimulating such fanciful, and ultimately damaging, interpretations of history. It is but one illustration of how even the most apparently well intentioned involvement by the West – in this case, support for a marginalised social group – can create problems as bad as those that they purport to address.

We should add here that the focus on minorities is also very much an instrument of international realpolitik; it is not only divisive internally, but also in the region as a whole. Demanding cultural privileges for minorities has become an important stick with which to beat regimes. Despite the fact that the Hungarian minority in Slovakia, for example, are not oppressed or denied equal rights, their treatment has been politicised and become an important source of discord between Hungary and Slovakia, and a means of suggesting a lack of democracy for Western powers. Still in February of 1997 the Hungarians were demanding international action – now over the absence of bilingual school reports in Slovakia. Cultural privileges are here equated with equal rights, and Slovakia is condemned for an anti-democratic attitude. No doubt other externally defined cultural minorities will also demand resources, knowing that this is an ideal means of pressurising the government, and appealing to the new consensus that the minority, rather than majority, is all.

Creating a New Elite

This new interference is divisive. It should also be acknowledged that this is a process of westernisation every bit as systematic as the Sovietisation that preceded it. It is interesting in this respect, that a key impulse which led to the United States project of 'exporting democracy' from the early 1980s was the desire to create a Western version of the Soviet programme which brought people from the 'non aligned' world to Moscow. David Samuels describes how, 'The West, Reagan believed, should have a system of its own, one that would teach the young people of the world to be good democrats.'[31] The export of democracy, now 'civil society', was then launched, according to Samuels, with Reagan's 1982 address to the British Parliament. It could be said that sponsoring the establishment of innocuous institutions like the scouts or guides in the region (as is happening) is nothing to be worried about, and in a sense maybe it isn't. Yet the establishment of the Young Pioneers, the Soviet scouts, was understood to be part of the consolidation of Soviet influence. Should we not then regard the export of old imperial institutions such as the scouts, along with their very particular morality, in the same light?

Perhaps a more accurate comparison would be with the missionaries who invariably accompanied the civilising mission of nineteenth century imperialism and who also, 'barnacle like', opened up the pores for settler societies to influence. It would otherwise seem difficult to understand why the normally self-interested British Foreign Office is prepared to pay for teaching East Europeans telephone counselling, incontinence training and 'how to break bad news'. This is not to suggest that this is a wholly cynical exercise, as indeed spreading the gospel of Christianity at an earlier stage was itself heartfelt – if also conveniently complementing more practical aims. Nevertheless, it should at the very least be understood to be as integral a part of westernisation as the spread of McDonald's, or indeed the rather comical presence of American evangelicals, and Salvation Army soldiers 'spreading the word' to 'fallen' Eastern souls.

Institutional interference in Russia and Eastern Europe has given a new lease of life to numerous bodies and individuals in the West. Consultancy firms have prospered through the EU's PHARE and TACIS schemes. United States politicians continue to enjoy luxurious stays in the region through the National Endowment. Opportunities for travel, and boosting authority, through election monitoring with the OSCE have provided academics demoralised by the state of education back home, with some welcome relief. More significant, however, are the consequences of establishing these points of contact for the societies of the East themselves. The upshot of the new pattern of East–West relations is the separation out from society of a new elite steeped in the most contemporary Western concerns and habits. This was a core objective of 'philanthropic' Western influence from the beginning. Kevin Quigley, programme director for the Pew Charitable Trusts for example, notes that 'investing in individuals' (principally through fellowships) has been a guiding principle of Western trusts and foundations. As Quigley describes, the sponsorship of these 'multipliers' as they are called in the business, is however, only a 'means to an end' toward the creation of 'future leaders'.[32] Given the relative simplicity of such a task in the context of such unequal relations of power, it is not surprising that the sponsoring of individuals has been very successful. In Carothers' sober assessment of involvement, it is the 'transformations of talented but inexperienced persons into significant sociopolitical actors' that he singles out as the best achievement.[33]

The process of westernisation creams off the most able and ambitious in the target societies. Particularly in the weaker countries of the region, those with experience and connections are head hunted by Western firms, and otherwise gravitate towards the opportunities offered by links with foreign NGOs. It is thus not surprising to find that the offices of such organisations are often more lavishly equipped than governmental buildings. There is a corresponding drift of personnel toward the former. One can already envisage a situation in a country like Slovakia where the state loses all but the most conservative to these Western firms and charities. As a result, there is greater dependence on the West as the state lacks even the qualified staff, let alone the confidence, to deal with the West on anything like an even footing.

Meanwhile, a new elite is being created – trained by Western grants, charities and corporations. With no ties or loyalty to the people whom they are supposed to ultimately represent, they have free rein to develop the loathing of the Eastern masses so characteristic of their sponsors. Carothers indicates this process well, explaining that,

> The experience of Romanian civil advocacy organisations has had the somewhat paradoxical effect of, on the one hand, empowering their own sense of self and their place in society – while, on the other hand, creating a sense of discouragement among many of these people as to what it will take to change, both more broadly and more deeply, the stunted civic consciousness of most Romanians.[34]

The mentality that goes along with career advancement through Western NGOs is one of frustration at the countrymen they have left behind. 'Why can't they be as "empowered" as me', they sigh, forgetting that their new outlook is very much the product of largess denied the population at large. In this sense their 'empowerment' establishes their distance from, not 'sense of place' in, society. Not only are they under no pressure to win respect from the citizenry whose concerns they now allegedly represent, but they find only disappointment, even embarrassment, in the 'stunted civic consciousness' of the majority of East Europeans.

Building 'Civil Society' – A No Lose Strategy

In their more candid moments, those involved in the Western transformation of the East show little real enthusiasm for the project.

They even indicate some of its destructive dimensions. Carothers notes the creation of a siege mentality among those (the majority) excluded from Western contact, and the creation of dependency among those who do benefit. Fine documents at some length what is, even from her point of view, the often ridiculous charade of interference, to the point of suggesting that,

> Overall, good agencies receive little local support, and foreign support can be contradictory, naive and bumbling. With the best of intentions – and sometimes the worst – legions of foreign consultants and advisers have unintentionally rebuilt walls between East and West, their insistence on certain 'western' procedures, styles and programs engendering more resistance and negativity than constructive change.[35]

Among those on the ground, Carothers notes how when pushed to demonstrate the positive effects of their work, those involved in United States democracy promotion acknowledge it to be a difficult question, '... but then add with a shrug, "at least we're not doing any harm".'[36]

This should come as no surprise. Advocates of interference to build 'civil society' can point to little, even of the most limited and immediate character, which conclusively demonstrates the benefits of this westernisation. More than this, as we have argued, the whole perspective is based on a disdain for the very people they are said to be helping. They do not really believe these people can become as enlightened as themselves, so it is no wonder they expect so little – for all the talk of 'empowerment'. In this respect, the whole exercise is extraordinarily cynical. They do not even believe, as did the missionaries of the nineteenth century, that the 'natives' might one day 'become like us'. Instead, they are simply going through the motions.

But for all the criticism, or rather self-consciousness, they are in a no lose situation, and this is the beauty of the 'civil society' formula from a Western point of view. Any lack of results can always be blamed on East Europeans themselves – or, as they now say, their 'culture'. Fine's portrayal of valiant NGO workers battling against the odds of native backwardness is thus not only a piece of self-flattery, but an abdication of any responsibility for change. 'Human rights and special interest groups do their best in fragile self absorbed environments to raise concerns, develop awareness, protect the interest of foreigners ... but they must, for many reasons, work within the constraints of local laws, little changed from previous regimes.'[37]

Of course there is no question that these activists are on as much of a career trip as any of the locals who also manage to jump aboard the gravy train! More than this, their selflessness is absolved of any need to deliver results – in advance – by reminding us that they have to deal with the 'constraints' of 'self absorbed' East European peoples who are essentially immune to the process of change.

The new Eastern Europe is then an unspectacular world, but one that is in the process of being divided and transformed from below. I now move to the conclusion: to outline in the broadest terms how the creation of a moral division between East and West has become a resource to a flagging West.

11

A Problem With the East, or With the West?

Reposing the Issues

Pondering 'The End of the West', *The Economist* noted that,

> 'The East', as a geopolitical concept is obsolete, it was a synonym
> for the Soviet empire. Where does that leave 'the West', which
> defined itself largely by contrast with 'the East'? Maybe ... bound
> together by a sense of external threat – fear of chaos or Islamic
> extremism, say, from 'the South' rather than the 'East?'[1]

The end of the old divisions has created untold problems for the
West. This is particularly evident for those institutions most closely
bound up with the Cold War, like Nato. August Pradetto, Professor
of International Relations at the University of the Bundeswehr in
Hamburg explains, with reference to the German problem in
particular, that, 'The Bundeswehr shared its legitimacy problems
with the entire Alliance. With the disintegration of the Warsaw pact
and the Soviet Union, Nato's enemy, which for forty years had been
the reason for its existence, was lost.'[2]

It is by no means clear what purpose Nato now serves. The same
can be said for innumerable other Western institutions accepted as
virtually God given, but evidently dependent upon the unique
configuration of politics established after the Second World War. The
two most powerful and durable conservative parties for example, the
American Republicans and British Tories, have now unravelled into
internally warring factions. While not exclusively attributable to
the end of the Cold War, their demise is nevertheless the product of
the end of a political cycle which was ultimately held together by
that ideological confrontation.

Without the counterpoint of 'totalitarianism', self-definition as
'democratic' becomes problematic. This is not simply a problem for
specific political parties, but the whole political landscape. Even the

very notions of 'left' and 'right' now mean little. As a result, particularly in Britain and the United States, a new terrain is, somewhat painfully, taking shape around a highly technocratic, yet also highly moralised 'centre ground'. Elsewhere, the end of the Cold War framework remains at an earlier stage of negotiation. Italy, without the (curious) shape imposed by Catholic versus Marxist, PCI versus Christian Democrat, has descended into uncertainty, instability and, with the rise of the Lombardy League, fragmentation. Of greatest significance, particularly for this discussion, is what is Germany today? This is a question only posed in the 1990s – most obviously because it was not until September 1990 that Germany once again became a sovereign state. With the signing of the 'treaty on the final settlement with respect to Germany', the rights and responsibilities of the Four Powers over Berlin and Germany as a whole were finally ended. Is the newly independent Germany now a country of social consensus permanently humbled by its destructive past? Is it simply a power like any other, or one with special 'responsibilities' to unify the continent and ensure harmony in Europe's Eastern backyard? Even if it is simply to be a legitimate, 'normal' member of the 'international community', the newly reunified state requires some foundation. Especially in the context of problems in the present – the breaking down of social consensus and stalling of the 'economic miracle' – answers are sought in the past. But in looking to some historical continuity as a foundation for contemporary Germany, what tradition is to be drawn upon, even, what symbols?

New Responses – The Left and the Serbs

New responses to the end of the traditional political terrain are evident in every quarter. One of the most dramatic has been among the left. The loss of a cause or purpose has been experienced particularly painfully by radicals who necessarily require a focus in order to sustain some sort of pressure on the status quo. Deprived of the traditional staples of left-wing politics, the search for an alternative became increasingly pronounced in the late 1980s and early 1990s. The left embraced new causes such as environmentalism, which were traditionally associated with a more conservative orientation. It is in this context that sense can be made of the readiness of the left to embrace the anti-Serbian 'cause' with less restraint and qualification than even the rest of society. This is an extreme and important example of the awkward realignments stimulated by the ending of old certainties.

More surprising even than the way in which journalists took sides in the Yugoslav civil war, is that the left, a group in the past so critical of weak non Western states being singled out for criticism, threw their weight determinedly against the Serbs. The radical British MP Ken Livingstone, for example, called for the bombing of the Serbs, in the traditional mouthpiece of British jingoism, the *Sun*. Livingstone not only demanded Western military action against an isolated non Western regime, but found himself aligned with the bete noire of the British left, Margaret Thatcher, who also called for punitive measures against the Serbs. There are countless other examples of the left taking the lead in the moral crusade against the Serbs. And Thatcher's interest pointed to another curiosity in the political alignments stimulated by the war in the former Yugoslavia. For Thatcher more than most, support for the anti-Serbian cause flowed from her embracing of Croatia. As is well known, the last independent Croatia was a Nazi puppet state. Its present day leader Franco Tudjiman, is also a revisionist historian who has sought to deny that wartime Croatia carried out the large scale massacres of Serbs and others, which the majority of scholars agree took place. Croatia today is founded upon a triumphalist nationalism which has long since driven the country's native Serb population abroad.

Indifference to this record, in the light of wider priorities, is perhaps understandable for a politician of the right like Thatcher. They are traditionally less sensitive to such questions. It is far more peculiar that the left, for whom associations with fascism and the repression of minorities shapes alignments and priorities, swept these uncomfortable truths under the carpet. No less inexplicable in its own terms, is that the left was prepared to believe clearly selective information issued by sources which would otherwise be regarded with suspicion. Had aerial CIA photographs of alleged mass graves implicated anyone but the Serbs for example (as were made available at the time of the Croatian invasion of Serbian Krajina), it would be fair to assume that the left would have counselled caution, instead of seizing upon this latest 'evidence' to further indict the 'savagery' of the Serbs.

There is something of a history of taking sides in the Balkans. Rebecca West, in her famous *Black Lamb and Grey Falcon*, described in the early 1940s, how 'English persons, therefore, of humanitarian and reformist disposition constantly went out to the Balkan Peninsula to see who was in fact ill-treating whom ...'. As they were '... unable to accept the horrid hypothesis that everybody was ill-treating everybody else, all came back with a pet Balkan people established in their hearts as suffering and innocent, eternally the massacree and never the massacrer.'[3] But the gusto with which contemporary radicals have taken up the cause of the Bosnian Muslims suggests there to be more at stake than merely the sort of naivete indicated by Rebecca West. Not only did their stance involve the wilful sweeping aside of highly embarrassing alliances, but was evidently more concerned with being anti-Serb, than pro-Muslim or Croat.

The anti-Serbian 'cause' became an attempt to revive the fortunes of the left. With the disintegration of most other movements, even inspirations for change, attacking 'Serbian fascism' acted as a substitute. In the France of the early 1990s, for example, the mark of the radical was an aggressive attitude towards the Serbs, and embracing of the Bosnian Muslims. And despite the absence of anything remotely resembling fascism in Serbia, it is not accidental that this emotive term was so widely used. For many, it was their modern day rerun of Spain in the 1930s. The left-wing film director Ken Loach, for example, indicated that he saw his film *Land and Freedom* about British workers who volunteered to fight Franco, as being relevant to today because of the struggle of Bosnia against the Serbs. For others too, the passion with which the anti-Serbian crusade has been taken up suggests it was understood to be a cause from which only the most apathetic and self-serving could remain immune.

To an extent such a perspective is understandable, particularly if it is regarded as a pro-Muslim, rather than anti-Serb orientation. Muslims in Europe are otherwise denounced as dangerous fanatics, and embracing their cause in the East can seem progressive – especially in France. But it requires considerable self-delusion to see that it is the Muslims rather than the Serbs who have experienced the brunt of Western venom and firepower. It is clear from the actions of the great powers that historical, and indeed wider, affinities and dislikes count for little. Despite any strategic preference in the past for Serbia by the likes of Britain, or more general hostilities towards Muslims in the present, the overwhelming Western consensus was that, on this occasion at least, the Muslims were to be supported. Curiously, in the process, supporting Bosnian Muslims increasingly defined only by their religious allegiance became, at the same time, support for 'multiculturalism'. — LIKE IN SREBRENICA .

The most elaborate conspiracy theories are required to argue that the West has been pro-Serb. The EC took sides against the Serbs with the first large scale actions of the war, the destruction of Vukovar and the bombardment of Dubrovnik by the Yugoslav army (JNA). Punitive measures and an insistence to stop fighting were demanded only of Serbia and the JNA. Croatia was also fighting hard – largely in order to sway international opinion in their favour, and both Croatia and Slovenia had already unilaterally changed international borders. Far from being criticised, however, their provocative actions were accepted as a fait accompli. Later in the war the West went much further, with extensive bombing raids against the Serbs. The United States military trained and extensively equipped both Muslim and Croat – to the point where even European observers complained of the military imbalance against the Serbs which was created. As the deputy commander in chief of the United States European Command in the region between 1992 and 1995 has put it, 'The linchpin of the US approach has been the uninformed notion that this is a war of good versus evil, of aggressor against aggrieved .... Ethnic cleansing evokes condemnation only when it is committed by Serbs, not against them.'[4]

Confronting the Western Past

The ending of old certainties has stimulated novel responses, often leading to political alliances which are quite curious by the standards of traditional post-war politics. But it is of course by no means certain that these will be effective in reviving the fortunes of institutions left exposed in the new environment of the 1990s. It might be relatively easy for the left to so casually disregard its principles and embrace former enemies – they are now under little pressure to account for their actions, or find serious solutions. Matters are not so straightforward for more central institutions – and states – however. Attempts to find a symbol for the new Germany have tended only to bring out the divisions which were contained by the post-war 'economic miracle' and anti-communism. It was proposed in Berlin, for example, that Marlene Dietrich would be an appropriate symbol of a German tradition which transcends the divisions of the past. After all she was a true international figure – as much a Hollywood, as a German, star. But proposals to name even a road after Dietrich have come up against significant local opposition. For the Berlin 'man on the street', Dietrich was a woman who abandoned the country for the comforts of international stardom. Would not the 'unknown woman' who stayed behind and brought up four children through the horrors of Allied bombardment and post-war humiliation be more worthy of honouring?, asks public opinion. In the face of such feelings, suitable candidates for naming after Dietrich have been watered down to the point where a minor rail station forecourt is now being suggested!

As the example of Marlene Dietrich indicates, however, the general Western, and specifically German, problem of identity is not simply one of a vacuum left by the end of anti-communism in its various forms. The reason why the past is so difficult a resource upon which to draw, is that so much of it has been rendered illegitimate and embarrassing. There are far more skeletons in the Western historical cupboard than there are suitable vehicles for cementing national loyalties. It is not just radical critics who question a 'Britishness' bound up with a history of colonial domination, an 'American-ness' inseparable from the racial exclusion and enslavement of a large proportion of the population, or indeed a 'German-ness' which cannot avoid confronting its terrible wartime past. Because the identity of the West for the last 40 years has been organised around 'democracy', even the most conservative are highly sensitive to a far from democratic past which avoided scrutiny so long as 'totalitarianism' stood firm. Without the shadow of communism, the past now has to be confronted. Most importantly for this discussion, Germany cannot now avoid the Nazi experience.

At the time of writing, the most sensitive issue in Germany is the row over the touring photographic exhibition on the wartime activities of the Wehrmacht. The pictures portray the Wehrmacht's role in concentration camps in Eastern Europe, and paint a picture of casual barbarity traditionally associated with the specialised extermination units of the German war against the East. According to post-war consensus, this was 'the decent army', not to be confused with the 'evil' Gestapo and SS. A similar distinction to that drawn elsewhere between German and Western militarism, or Eastern 'totalitarianism' and Western democracy, was made. German authority was partially salvaged by maintaining a moral distinction between the innocent, if imperfect, regular forces of the German state, and the Nazi zealots of the SS and Gestapo, who were presented as something of an aberration.

Apart from calling into question this distinction, and thereby a component of Germany's post-war picture of itself, the photographs of the Serbian victims of German wartime expansion are additionally discomforting. Given the centrality of Serbian demonisation to the contemporary rehabilitation of Germany's armed forces and their right to operate abroad, reminders of Germany's past role in killing Serbs are hardly welcome to the country's leaders. In response to the exhibition, particularly when it was shown in conservative Munich, a demonstration was organised, partly by Kohl's sister party, the CSU. Kohl has refused to condemn the calls for the banning of the exhibition, or the demonstration itself. This controversy, and Kohl's awkward silence on the issue, illustrates in microcosm the problems of identity and legitimacy posed for Germany in the absence of the Cold War.

Divisive Solutions

Current attempts to focus society's attentions on prosecuting former members of the Stasi, and others associated with the GDR, are in this respect an attempt to sustain that old post-war 'German-ness' defined by anti-communism. The problem is that it is now a highly artificial endeavour, particularly as the other ingredient of post-war identity, economic success, is also now no longer assumed. Stripped of this broader framework of a post-war economic miracle and the 'totalitarian menace' on the doorstep, playing the old anti-communist card can only serve to further alienate 'Ossies', already resentful at the persistence of inequality between the two halves of 'united' Germany. There was no love lost, in a different context, between 'Ossies' and the border guards and secret policemen who kept them under control. But some ordinary people in former East Germany feel that the latter's prosecution by Bonn is, to an extent, now also putting them on trial. They are perhaps right in sensing that the German authorities are attempting to relocate the problems of the new Germany on to the shoulders of the old GDR and its peoples.

Beyond Germany, there are wider attempts to recreate old battles. The otherwise peculiar objective of expanding Nato to the East only makes sense in the context of attempting old solutions to the new problems of purpose posed by the Cold War's end. Pradetto, having noted the problems for Germany and the West after the Cold War, explains that 'For Nato, too, enlargement towards the East would be a task which promised to remove at least in part the legitimation deficiency which it has suffered from in recent years.'[5] It is no accident that it was Germany, the country most sensitive to the unravelling of the Cold War, which first pushed for the promotion of Nato enlargement – as a means of prolonging its life. This approach is also limited in what it can achieve. Particularly once the diplomatic show is over, and largely feigned Russian opposition can no longer be sustained – it will be less easy to disguise the fact that this essentially artificial attempt at the revival of outmoded institutions is not a long term solution. Nobody is likely to draw attention for some time to the fact that the Nato emperor has no clothes. The international consensus that the United States and its institutions should continue to organise world affairs, means criticism is virtually non-existent. Nevertheless, institutions such as Nato can hardly act as the organising principle that they once did.

Such partial solutions as reviving Nato, in themselves, avoid rather than confront the problem of the past. They do, however, point toward the fact that it is at the wider international level that renegotiating the problems thrown up by the end of the Cold War can be better managed. The continuation of international cooperation (embodied at the practical level by the anti-Serbian consensus) has opened up possibilities which do not exist at the more immediate domestic level. Even expanding Nato offers more returns than prosecuting former members of the Stasi. No wonder that the West has turned to the international arena to renegotiate some of the dilemmas posed by the 'new world disorder'.

Rehabilitating the German Past

It might appear that moralising over the East is an unsurprising, inevitable, and perhaps an eternal feature of international relations generally. Every power obviously prefers to be cast in the best possible light, and the attempt to do so is a constant feature of self-presentation by virtually every society. The extent to which this is considered essential, and the extent to which it is viable to convincingly strike such a posture, varies considerably with time and place however. During the Cold War, it was simply not possible for the West to stand morally supreme over the non Western world. It remained severely compromised by the experience of racism, both in the colonies and the Holocaust at the heart of 'civilised' Europe. The West was highly defensive in its relations with the 'non aligned' world throughout the Cold War years. Nor was it necessary to have recourse to international authority in quite the same way as today. The post-war boom and the peculiarities of the Cold War created an, admittedly uneasy, compromise where foreign affairs could be left to set piece confrontations between the United States and the USSR.

In appreciating the specific impulse behind the moralisation of international politics through the East, it emerges that it is now both necessary and possible to morally rehabilitate the Western past. Elevating the problem of Eastern backwardness has allowed the rehabilitation of Germany's role in the region. This is a sensitive issue, and it would be absurd to suggest, as British chauvinists are still inclined to do, that Germany is an eternal danger which will always remain on a predetermined course for domination. Nevertheless, it is certainly the case that the German elite would like to eliminate the historical embarrassment that keeps it an 'economic giant and a political dwarf', as it is often expressed. It is in this context that, particularly under Foreign Minister Klaus Kinkel, an explicit policy of 'normalisation' has taken place; in other words, establishing Germany's right to exert its influence in a manner befitting a great power – particularly the 'right' to deploy troops abroad.

Certainly, Germany's newly assertive posture in the East cannot be regarded as simply one of principle. As Garton Ash points out with regard to the defining act of the reassertion of their foreign policy – the recognition of Croatia – it coincided with heavy pressure being put on Bulgaria to prevent, or at least postpone, their recognition of Macedonia. 'Could it, just possibly, be a deal: Germany would not (yet) support the recognition of Macedonia if Greece did not oppose the recognition of Slovenia and Croatia? Oh, brave new world!'[6] So much for 'principle'! The same can be said for Germany's discouragement of independence for the Baltic states, an approach which again stood in stark contrast to support for Slovenian and Croatian secession from the Yugoslav federation.

While Germany took the lead in re-establishing authority through the East, it is not the case that the other powers were any more principled in their approach. The European powers accepted German insistence on the recognition of Croatia in December 1991, only five weeks after the community declared that independence could only be envisaged in the context of an overall settlement. It was passed through on the nod after a tokenistic, and allegedly now 'lost', letter from Croatian President Tudjiman that he would respect the Serb minority in an independent Croatia. Despite the entirely accurate presentiment of the violence that would follow the endorsement of Croatian nationalism, and to the fury of then chief EC negotiator Lord Carrington among others, the other powers went along with Germany, most immediately because of wheeling and dealing over European integration. With the Maastricht summit looming, the other Europeans seemed reluctant to antagonise Germany over its new found cause of Croatian nationalism. More broadly, there developed the recognition of a collective interest in the West standing over a culturally backward East. This demanded a comprehensive condemnation of the Serbs by virtually every major power, not as support for any European national project – the Croats are hardly admired – but as an attempt to cohere a crusade against 'evil'.

More recent German foreign policy initiatives are also driven by a wider agenda. The 'reconciliation' of Germany and the Czech Republic over the retaliatory expulsion of Sudeten Germans after the war should also be understood in the context of the renegotiation of the past. In January of 1997 an accord was signed, where Chancellor Kohl expressed 'sorrow' at the Nazi occupation, and Vaclav Klaus for the Czechs 'regretted' the post-war removal of Germans through the Benes Decrees. In a sense of course, this event has nothing to do with history per se. The German leadership effectively bribed the Czechs with promises to support their membership of the EU if they allowed the establishment of equivalence between the two experiences. Anger at the injustice of establishing this historical parallel was largely dissipated among Czechs for whom it was widely perceived as a price worth paying to get first in the queue for membership of the Union. It was left to a handful of Czech nationalists to protest. Nor was the significance essentially historical for Germany, as *The Times* editorial sensed. 'Yet the accord', they explained, 'does, at last, allow Germany to restore its political and cultural influence to an area where over the centuries it has played a generally determining role.'[7]

But *The Times* and most other commentators have been blind to the remarkable significance of what has happened, and the fact that the normalisation of contemporary German foreign policy does have to take place through a rewriting of the past. This is not the mere settling of an historical argument, but a triumph for Germany which lifts a burden from their shoulders. Germany has cleared the path to 'restoring its political and cultural influence' by pursuing a strategy of moral rehabilitation of its own past through relativising that experience. Significantly, the issue was pursued as one of 'moral restitution' by the German elite. Thus in the talks of January 1996, German foreign minister Klaus Kinkel called on Prague to distance itself 'morally' from the Benes decrees. Demanding the full restitution of property rights, argued for by Sudeten German groups, was not of interest in itself.

This is a project of establishing moral equivalence. Czechs and Germans have become equal partners in crime, equally guilty and responsible. The German dismemberment of Czechoslovakia (with the full cooperation of the other powers) is now just one unfortunate incident, no better or worse than post-war population displacement. More broadly, it establishes equivalence between the historical domination of the East, and the East's own rare and feeble attempts to 'get its own back'. It becomes only a vicious circle, where retribution invites aggression and all sense of proportion is lost. It is not a question of living in the past, still less being anti-German, to insist that equating these two acts, and more broadly the whole wartime experience, is quite grotesque. In codifying the equivalence of aggressor and victim, Germany has in a sense done a service for the West as a whole. As we have explained, it was the whole of the West which was severely compromised by the Nazi experience, and the obfuscation of historical responsibility is of benefit to all the major powers in its obscuring of unequal power relations in the present.

This is not a settling of antiquated historical disputes, but the creation of new ones. Now, the expulsion of Sudeten Germans is indirectly comparable with the Holocaust. There is effectively now another 'holocaust', another experience of so-called 'ethnic cleansing' to be agonised over and debated. And continue it will. Only days after this 'historic reconciliation', it became clear that even the question of property restitution was very much open. The Czech opposition leader and parliamentary speaker Milos Zeman travelled to Germany to try and convince German politicians that a preamble was needed to the agreement that closed the property question, but German parliamentarians ignored his proposal. Having signed the deal believing it to foreclose the possibility of property claims from the Sudeten Germans, the Czechs found that allowing equivalence to be recognised has only led to even greater German drive to maintain a focus on 'Czech crimes'. Property restitution may even become of potential interest to a German elite who have developed a taste for maintaining moral pressure on the East. This is leaving aside the question whether the Germans will fulfil their promise to deliver early EU membership. It would appear that they are in no position to promise any such thing.

The elevation of Eastern backwardness, or simply the establishment of equivalence between the acts of East and West, has allowed Germany to relativise its own past, and in the process do what it has not been able to do for the last 40 years or so. 'Its Balkan success has helped to lift a postwar taboo', as *Newsweek* sub headlined its story on how Germany has managed to 'ease the burden of history'.[8] Indeed, in late 1996 (there had already been more discreet military involvement in the region, and an unsuccessful deployment in Somalia), having successfully overturned the constitutional ban on overseas deployment, the government authorised the stationing of 3000 soldiers in Bosnia. Despite the fact that their Croatian allies embarrassed the Bundeswehr with Nazi salutes, German troops are once again established in the Eastern Europe that they, along with their great power opponents, devastated in the Second World War. The upshot is that whatever benefits we might consider that the new domination of the region by Germany has brought, we should recognise the fact that, as a recent British magazine article put it, 'Thanks to Central Europe, Germany is, in other words, no longer a political dwarf.'[9]

Taking the Moral High Ground

In the absence of more effective, or simply more traditional, domestic solutions to the problems of the post-Cold War period, the West has instinctively gravitated towards taking the moral high ground over 'the East', as a resource for Western society and its leaders. This was particularly evident through the course of the Yugoslav war. Tory leader John Major in 1993, for example, under severe political pressure two days after the attack from former Chancellor Lamont, saved the day at the Welsh Conservative conference by dwelling on the exploits of British forces in the Yugoslav war. The opportunities provided by the moralisation of the war relaunched careers, as with the former British politician David Owen who became central to the 'peace process'. He acquired a gravitas through lecturing Slavs which he sorely lacked back home. More recently, it has played a central role in restoring the fortunes of United States President Clinton. The Dayton 'Peace' was a triumph for United States power over Europe. As such it wrong footed his domestic rivals, and established a hitherto elusive popularity among United States voters.

Given the easy returns possible in this arena, it is hardly surprising that the initial conflict over the approach to be taken towards the disintegration of Yugoslavia was eclipsed by a shared appreciation of the benefits of moralising the conflict. Unlike so many times in the past, competing major powers did not take different sides in the conflict, but established a consensus between themselves that moral authority was paramount, and that therefore a common barbaric enemy was required. Competition was not entirely subsumed, as each attempted to outdo the other in striving for the highest moral ground of all – by being most vociferous in denunciation of Serbs, and embracing of Muslims. Nevertheless, by historical standards, rivalries between the major players were remarkably restrained. Indeed, the moral consensus which developed through Yugoslavia went a long way toward maintaining international cooperation – specifically that Germany and the other powers would continue to allow the United States to remain guarantor of world affairs. It also helps explain why there has been virtually no challenge to the extraordinary presentation of the Yugoslav war. Historically, even accurate information about non Western affairs has only come to light in the context of rivalries between the major powers. Where one power has sought to supplant or limit the influence of another, they have allowed the circulation of information which contradicted the necessarily flattering portrayal of involvement developed by their rivals. Such a competitive dynamic was effectively ended with United States acceptance of Germany's aggressive stance over Croatia, and subsequently the complex truths about the war have been universally suppressed.

With such a pay-off for the United States, it is perhaps unsurprising that Clinton has begun his second term with an even clearer declaration of the centrality of foreign policy for his administration. Madeline Albright has declared that while foreign policy might form only 1 per cent of the federal budget, it nevertheless accounts for 50 per cent of the history and legacy of our times. For a relatively small price, largely paid by those on the receiving end, a sense of purpose is restored. Assessing United States democracy assistance, Carothers opens with what is in many ways the most important point. 'In America, it's hard to go wrong selling democracy abroad, even to the cost conscious Congress and a domestically oriented public ... .Propounding the virtues of democracy makes us feel good and it's relatively cheap besides.'[10] In itself, the West may lack self-belief to the extent that Ken Jowitt recently regretted that, 'As long as the West is ill at ease with itself and operates within institutions that are subject to substantial domestic challenge, it is highly doubtful that we can successfully export an idealised version of what we once were.'[11] But it is precisely because the West is 'ill at ease with itself' that taking the moral high ground is so important. While 'successful export' may occur as an unintended outcome, this is not the essence of the matter. Rather, it is in the process of 'going through the motions' of civilising, that it at least deflects attention, and even allows Western institutions, principles and individuals some much needed flattery. If there are still peoples in the world in need of Western ways, surely these ways cannot be so bad after all?

The consequence of this moral posturing and rewriting of the past is the establishment of a divided Europe. The process of 'consolidating' democracy, building 'civil society' or any other of the now countless terms, is presented as a useful goal setting exercise for Eastern Europe. But it is more accurately described as a process of moving the goal posts. Where democracy was good enough, now only 'civil society' will do for the stern judges of Western standards. Ultimately, nothing will satisfy, for, after all, these societies will never be as good as our own as far as those already convinced of their own superiority are concerned. This is reflected in the now tautological formulations of the academic 'democratisation' industry where, to quote one recent contribution, 'Only democracies can become consolidated democracies.'[12] Only the West can be as good as the West runs the wisdom here. In the heartland of the democratisation thinkers, Bill Clinton's new 'mandate' rests on a minority of citizens – 44.6 million of America's 250 million citizens voted for him. In practice, United States politics, even more than Britain's, looks far from 'consolidated'. It is now an almost exclusively middle-class pastime.

The pretensions that surround the goal of establishing 'civil society' in Eastern Europe need to be stripped away, and it made plain that they are ultimately only a vehicle for condemnation. In its original usage, civil or political society was a means of contrasting the development of state and society to the uncivilised condition of humanity in its natural state or under the rule of despotism. As Kumar put it, 'Civil society in this conception expresses the growth of civilisation to the point where society is "civilised".'[13] In this sense we have returned to its original meaning as a contrast between the civilised and uncivilised, only now it has a fixed geographical expression in the contrast between East and West. The well known American columnist William Pfaff expresses this sense of superiority with admirable clarity:

> The unstated barrier to the unification of Eastern Europe with Western Europe is moral and intellectual. The crucial distinction today is between those Europeans who believe in ethnic politics, ethnic exclusion and an intolerant nationalism, and those who understand that the members of a common European civilisation owe themselves and each other a commitment to national reconciliation ... . This is an essential distinction. If the East European and Balkan nations wish to be members of 'Europe', they must understand that the challenge is to reconcile their nations ... . If they are not prepared to change in this respect, they automatically exclude themselves from a changed Europe ... the Eastern countries have to understand that the indispensable reform is one of political morality and national assumption.[14]

In Pfaff's scenario all has neatly been resolved in favour of the West. They are not excluded by trade and other economic barriers, but by themselves – by their own deplorable 'political morality and national assumption'. Not only is the West written out of the picture and responsibility shifted entirely on to Eastern shoulders, but the West stands as the judge of Eastern moral progress. Given these revived moral certainties in the superiority of the West, it is perhaps not surprising that Pfaff has called elsewhere for a 'new colonialism' regarding the 'Third World' proper. 'Europe must go back into Africa', he insists.[15]

We have a return to the Western moral superiority of old. As the historian Pocock puts it, '... in late 1991 it seems apparent that "Europe" – both with and without North America whose addition turns it from "Europe" into "Western civilisation" – is once again an empire in the sense of a civilised and stabilised zone which must decide whether to extend or refuse its political power over violent and unstable cultures along its borders but not yet within the system ...'.[16] Despite its significant internal troubles, in relation to the world at large the West now stands unopposed. It has free licence to interfere when and where it likes and, precisely because it is so unquestioned, present such meddling as a moral imperative; bringing civilised values to the 'intolerant'.

The New Moral Division – The War Crimes Tribunal

In the sharpest practical terms this moral division is embodied by the War Crimes Tribunal set up by the UN in The Hague. The Tribunal is the first collective 'war crimes' trial since Nuremburg and Tokyo after the Second World War, and has a budget of $30 million for the first four years of its work. Its brief is to prosecute those, principally Serbs (of the tribunal's 74 suspects the vast majority are Serbs – the trial of the first Bosnian Muslims to be charged began in March 1997 with the prosecutor insisting that, unlike with the Serbs, the trial should focus only on the alleged crimes of the four defendants, not overall ethnic responsibility for the war), deemed 'war criminals'. While the trial has its precedent in the post-war prosecution of the Japanese and Germans, its remit is even wider. For the first time, rape can now constitute a 'war crime', for example. Prosecution witnesses can retain anonymity on the basis of an alleged threat to their family, not only themselves. This innovation runs contrary to international human rights, as the defence is effectively denied the opportunity to properly investigate witnesses. The dangers of such extensive witness protection have already been illustrated. The chief prosecution witness in the trial of Dusan Tadic was only exposed as a liar by the defence after they decided to break the court's restrictions, and interview the witness's family members.

Who is defined as a 'war criminal' evidently depends upon who is making the judgment. The imitative showcase trials run by the Bosnian Muslims are based on similarly dubious evidence – Sretko Damjanovic for example, a Bosnian Serb was convicted in 1993 of war crimes, despite the fact that two of the men he allegedly murdered are apparently alive and well. Most importantly, the very creation of a War Crimes Tribunal is based upon an a priori judgement that 'war crimes' were committed, and it is only a question of finding the right culprits. At the time of writing, the first trial – that of Tadic – has ended. He was found guilty on 11 of the 31 counts he faced. Significantly in the first judgement, he was cleared of the murder and torture charges which justified his prosecution as a 'war criminal' in the first place, and was effectively only found guilty of beating and persecuting civilians while serving as a police reservist. Regardless, the cafe proprietor Tadic now stands in a hall of infamy with the likes of Rudolf Hess. Tadic is now an international 'war criminal'. The Tribunal spokesman has gone even further and declared the verdict to be a condemnation of Serbian policy in Bosnia. Under other circumstances, such a procedure would be condemned as a kangaroo court – only no kangaroo court in history has managed to condemn a whole people on the basis of relatively minor crimes judged to have been committed by one man.

The attractiveness to the West of the Tribunal has little to do with the needs of, or justice for, the peoples of the former Yugoslavia. It is simply illogical to suppose that these trials will lead to reconciliation – as is claimed by its supporters. If anything, only further bitterness can be created, as the reconstruction of the former Yugoslavia proceeds according to the extent that the Serbs comply with demands to deliver their 'war criminals' to the Tribunal, and in the process concede their fundamental criminality. In fact, the trial serves little practical purpose other than to create 'war criminals' – no matter how insignificant the individuals concerned. It is this construction of 'evil' which is so appealing to Western sensibilities, codifying as it does the authority of Western institutions which stand in judgment. As a typically glowing account of the tribunal's work recently put it, 'Punishing war criminals has a strong moral and political appeal.'[17] Justice has little to do with it.

It is by no means clear why this conflict (along with that in Rwanda) as compared to countless others in the post-war years should be singled out as demanding the international recognition of war crimes. The scale, intensity and savagery of wars in Vietnam and Iraq to name only two, are hardly less deserving of such scrutiny. The double standard at play is illustrated by the involvement of Judge Richard Goldstone of the South African constitutional court as Chief Prosecutor. Back in South Africa, the constitutional court is central to the Truth Commission concerned with looking into the war against the black population waged by the apartheid regime. There, however, an entirely different principle is in operation. 'Forgive and forget' is the modus operandi of the Truth Commission. Those who confess to the murders they carried out for the apartheid regime are subject to immunity from prosecution, and potential amnesty. A very different 'principle' operates with the War Crimes Tribunal however, where confession does not secure immunity, it only saves the tribunal a lot of work.

Western praise for the spirit of reconciliation evident in the South African Truth Commission is fulsome indeed. The West is clearly attracted by the idea of drawing a line under the embarrassing experience of white domination through apartheid. Codifying the supposed savagery of those in the East, and by implication the moral superiority of the West, is an equally attractive proposition. No wonder the Germans – who are particularly sensitive to both these imperatives – have now set up their own war crimes trials. It is no longer they that are in the dock, as after the Second World War, but 'Eastern savagery'. Most remarkable of all are the calls in late March 1997 by EU Commissioner Hans van der Broek to establish a permanent international criminal court. Clearly, his call is not based on foreknowledge of 'international crimes' to be committed in the future. The desire to fully institutionalise the notion of (non Western) 'war crimes' is driven by the impulse to continue indefinitely the reversal of moral fortunes represented by the current tribunals. Van der Broek's call will most probably be implemented. Meanwhile, any prosection of criminal elements which scavenged upon the Yugoslav civil war – be they Serb, Croat or Muslim – should remain a matter for the peoples of those societies themselves.

Culturally Dividing Europe

Putting non Western cultures on trial in order to salvage authority for a disorientated West, highlights perhaps the most central theme of this book. The consequence of elevating the cultural backwardness of 'others' means that 'culture' plays a similar role to that of 'race' in the past. Indeed, the emphasis upon, and invention of, 'cultural' differences divides humanity more effectively today than the language of biology or traditional racism.

Few people recognise the prejudice on display against people from Eastern Europe because it is not expressed in what is traditionally recognised as the language of racism. Virtually no one openly states that they consider Slavs to be biologically inferior. This is hardly surprising, as the whole of this vocabulary is discredited. But it would be extremely naive to imagine that these sentiments have entirely disappeared. Social inequality, and indeed the inequality between different parts of the world, still needs to be accounted for. What is more, it needs to be accounted for by those who regard this society as the best on offer in such a way that the structures of society and the international division of labour are not held responsible.

In other words, inequality still needs to be naturalised: presented as an unfortunate consequence of the limitations of those who find themselves excluded from opportunity. This need not be in an overtly racial form. For example, the continued inequality of blacks in the United States is no longer explained as the result of their natural inferiority. Instead it is attributed to their culture: the supposedly unique weakness of the family and irresponsibility of black fathers; their rejection of entrepreneurial values, etc. A similar effect is achieved, however, not least in the fact that the structural problems of American society are conveniently ignored. But this is not done through a focus on race, so much as culture: they are a morally feeble 'underclass'.

The contemporary problem of German identity is now understood to be one of blending the differing cultural traditions of East and West. There is indeed a powerful sense of difference between 'Ossies' and 'Wessies' in Berlin. Even those Germans most intent on forgetting the past are struck by the apparent gulf between those in East and West. For many this is not merely 'interesting' but a problem, and one that might even go some way to explaining the difficulties of reunification. But it is necessary to take a step back from such reactions and remember that the way things are experienced is not always the same as the way they really are. As with immigration, where 'too many foreigners' rather than the lack of economic opportunities for 'foreigner' and 'native' alike might appear to be the problem, so we must repose the question of the apparent cultural gulf between 'Ossies' and 'Wessies'. The substantive difficulty is the profound uncertainty about what it means to be German in the 1990s, especially when economic progress, which might otherwise render the issue of identity less important, can no longer be assumed. This is a country where even honouring a long departed film star only brings out new divisions – importantly not between East and West, but the past and present.

These are issues which are difficult to confront directly, and so all that is left, on a day to day level, is the consequence that those from East and West still seem miles apart. But we should understand that were it not for economic slowdown and the re-presentation of Germany's thorny problem of identity, the sense of geographical division would hardly be of concern, or only of interest in the same way that divisions between 'liberal' North and 'conservative' South also figure in the German make up.

Certainly in the abstract, 'Ossies' have no pre-given determination to hold on to their 'culture' or identity. They overwhelmingly voted for Kohl's conservative CDU immediately after reunification, and it was made plain at the ballot box that they wanted to ditch the past and share in (West) German success. The problem has been that the end of the old divisions has created a vacuum around what it means to be German. Implicitly, and sometimes explicitly, targeting the alleged cultural deficiencies of 'Ossies' has acted as a short term substitute for not knowing, certainly with regard to 'explaining' the continued difficulties of reunification. There is here something of a self-fulfilling prophecy, as some of the same 'Ossies' who voted for unity now respond to Western politicians' elevation of their supposedly unique cultural problems by retreating into the past themselves. Maybe the old GDR wasn't so bad after all, is an increasingly common sentiment even among the younger generation of 'Ossies', sick of criticism about their failure to adapt to a supposedly new Germany.

The language of cultural difference not only provides a substitute for a discredited vocabulary of race however. Ironically, it can extend the boundaries of division further than was possible with the old racial approach. Through the Cold War, Germany held up the possibility of all Germans joining the 'free world', and as a consequence there was a somewhat anomalous retention of a racial definition of nationality little different from the Nazis. Citizenship was theoretically open to all ethnic Germans in Eastern Europe according to this Cold War advertisement, even if they had lost many of the ways of their 'motherland' along the way. This is now changing, as Germany no longer needs to define itself against the restriction of movement embodied by the old GDR. The Social Democrats in particular have argued that these people are not 'real Germans' on the basis '... that they did not speak the German language, that they had different ways of living, did not fit into the market economy, believed in traditional values etc.'. In the process, as a recent article on the subject argues, '... those traits were transformed into quasi natural categories. They became static features which one could either possess or not.' The author concludes perceptively that 'In other words, what could be observed was a struggle between an old genetic racism and a new so-called cultural racism, and the latter was more exclusionary than the first.'[18]

It is the 'liberal' notion which identifies a lack of democratic values that is being used to legitimise the failure of Germany to effect real unification between Eastern and Western halves. Peter O'Brien of Trinity University rightly notes that hyped-up discussion of the return of traditional racism is not the real problem in Germany. Rather, it is the notion of '... the alleged illiberalism of East Germans and foreigners which distinguishes them from West Germans ...'. It is this which '... ideologically motivates and rationalises inequality between the groups'.[19] Why is this so? Both are of course 'racially' German. So how can continued inequality be rationalised without questioning more fundamentally the character of contemporary German society? 'Culture' here provides the answer, through fixing a dichotomy between the liberalism of Westerners and the mythical illiberalism of those in the East (similar of course to the idea of patriotism versus intolerant nationalism mentioned earlier). Ironically, as O'Brien notes, these '... rationalisations of postponed equality for East Germans sound unmistakably similar to those resident aliens have heard for years'.[20] One could forgive 'Ossies' a certain nostalgia for the racism of old, as the new intolerance of liberalism is both more hypocritical, and exclusionary!

Towards the end of his life in 1985, the eminent historian of Eastern Europe Hugh Seton Watson rethought his view of the division of Europe. 'I used to think one could divide Europe into West and East ... but as I have thought and learned more, I have become rather skeptical ... there is nothing specifically "Eastern" about either ....'[21]

These moral divisions are no more real than my undoubted favourite drawing of lines. A journalist in Prague suggested one based upon alcohol.[22] There would be a vodka zone (Russia and Poland), a fiery and passionate zone where everyone likes a strong man rather than parliament. Then, a wine zone of instability (Romania and Yugoslavia), followed by a beer zone – dependable Czechs. The West would presumably here be strictly teetotal – pure as the driven snow, or at least compared to the gigantic drinking house of Eastern Europe.

Notes

Introduction

1. Ken Jowitt, *New World Disorder: The Leninist Extinction* (Berkeley, CA: University of California Press, 1992) p.299.
2. Gale Stokes, 'East European History After 1989', in John R. Lampe and Paula Bailey Smith (eds) *East European Studies in the United States: Making its Own Transition After 1989* (Washington: East European Studies, The Woodrow Wilson International Center for Scholars, 1993) p.35.
3. Michael Henry Hein, 'Humanities and East-Central Europe: The State of the Field', in Lampe and Smith, *East European Studies*, p.41.
4. Richard H. Ullman (ed.), *The World and Yugoslavia's Wars* (New York: Council on Foreign Relations Press, 1996).
5. Tad Szulc, 'Unpleasant Truths about Eastern Europe', *Foreign Policy*, No.102 (Spring 1996) p.61.
6. Jowitt, *Disorder*, p.305.
7. *The Economist*, 13 March 1993.

Chapter 1

1. *Financial Times*, 29 April 1993.
2. Quoted in *New York Post*, 3 March 1992.
3. *The Times*, 28 October 1996.
4. *Evening Standard*, 26 March 1996.
5. Quoted in *Daily Telegraph*, 17 March 1997.
6. *London Review of Books*, 25 January 1996.
7. Riccardo Faini and Richard Portes (eds), *European Trade with Eastern Europe* (London: Centre for Economic Policy Research, 1995) p.16.
8. Helmut Leipold, 'The Eastward Enlargement of the European Union: Opportunities and Obstacles', *Aussenpolitik*, No.11 (1995) p.130.
9. Timothy Garton Ash, *In Europe's Name* (London: Vintage, 1994) p.391.
10. Quoted in Charles Gati, *Eastern Europe and the World* (New York: Cliff's Notes, 1978) p.56.
11. R.V. Banks, *The Dynamics of Communism in Eastern Europe* (Princeton, NJ: Princeton University Press, 1961) p.198.
12. Harry Schwartz, *Eastern Europe in the Soviet Shadow* (New York: Abelard-Schuman, 1973) p.7.
13. Schwartz, *Shadow*, pp.97–8.

14. *The Community and its Eastern Neighbours*, (Luxembourg: EC, 1991) p.3.
15. Ronald H. Linden, 'The New International Political Economy of Eastern Europe', *Studies in Comparative Communism*, Vol.XXV, No.1 (March 1992) p.7.
16. *Guardian*, 3 January 1992.
17. *The Economist*, 15 March 1993.
18. Quoted in J. Jedlicki, 'The Unbearable Burden of History', *Problems of Communism*, Vol.XXXIX (July/August 1990) p.43.
19. Slavoj Zizek, 'Eastern Europe's Republic of Gilead', *New Left Review*, No.183 (September/October 1990) p.50.
20. Misha Glenny, *The Rebirth of History* (Harmondsworth: Penguin, 1990) p.197.
21. Quoted in Glenny, *Rebirth*, p.198.
22. Paul G. Lewis, 'Democracy and Its Future in Eastern Europe', in David Held (ed.) *Prospects for Democracy* (Oxford: Polity, 1993) p.291.
23. *Guardian*, 1 April 1996.
24. *Sunday Telegraph*, 22 September 1991.
25. *The Times Atlas of European History* (London: Times Books, 1994) p.188.
26. *The Economist*, 1 February 1992.
27. *The Economist*, 12 August 1989.
28. John R. Lampe, 'East European Studies in the United States: What is to be Done?', in Lampe and Smith, *East European Studies*, p.11.
29. Vladimir Tismaneanu, *Reinventing Politics* (New York: Free Press, 1993) p.243.
30. Zbigniew Brzezinski, 'The Great Transformation', *The National Interest*, No.33 (Fall 1993) p.3.
31. *Sunday Times*, 29 September 1996.
32. Daniel Nelson, 'Europe's Unstable East', *Foreign Policy*, No.82 (Spring 1991) p.146.
33. Philip Longworth, *The Making of Eastern Europe* (London: Macmillan, 1992) p.7.
34. Tad Szulc, 'Unpleasant Truths about Eastern Europe', *Foreign Policy*, No. 102 (Spring 1996) p.54.
35. Michael Walzer, 'The New Tribalism', *Dissent*, (Spring 1992) p.164.
36. Piotr Sztompka, 'Looking Back: The Year 1989 as a Cultural and Civilizational Break', *Communist and Post-Communist Studies*, Vol.29, No.2 (1996) p.116.
37. Sztompka, 'Looking Back', p.119.
38. Krishan Kumar, 'Civil Society: An Inquiry into the Usefulness of an Historical Term', *British Journal of Sociology*, Vol.44, No.3 (September 1993) p.388.
39. Vaclav Havel, Vaclav Klaus and Piotr Pithart, 'Debate on Civil Society', *Journal of Democracy*, Vol.7, No.1 (January 1996) p.18.
40. Keitha Sapsin Fine, 'Fragile Stability and Change: Understanding Conflict during the Transitions in East Central Europe', in Abram and Antonia Handler Chayes (eds) *Preventing Conflict in the Post-Communist World* (Washington: Brookings Institution, 1996) p.563.

41. *Guardian*, 3 November 1994.
42. Paul Hockenos, *Free to Hate* (London: Routledge, 1994).
43. *The Economist*, 13 March 1993.

Chapter 2

1. John Lukacs, 'The Other Europe at Century's End', *The Wilson Quarterly*, (Autumn 1991) p.118.
2. K. Jowitt, *New World Disorder: The Leninist Extinction* (Berkeley, CA: University of California Press, 1992) p.304.
3. P. Longworth, *The Making of Eastern Europe* (London: Macmillan, 1992), p.5 and p.292.
4. *Guardian*, 10 May 1991.
5. *Guardian*, 12 July 1991.
6. *Sunday Telegraph*, 22 September 1991.
7. Charles Gati, 'East Central Europe', *Foreign Affairs*, Vol.69, No.5 (Winter 1990/91) p.136.
8. Jowitt, *Leninist Extinction*, p.291.
9. Radmilla Nakavada, 'The Mystery of Nationalism: The Paramount Case of Yugoslavia', *Millennium*, Vol.20, No.3 (Winter 1991) p.380.
10. Keitha Sapsin Fine, 'Fragile Stability and Change: Understanding Conflict during the Transitions in East Central Europe', in Abram and Antonia Handler Chayes (eds) *Preventing Conflict in the Post-Communist World* (Washington: Brookings Institution, 1996) p.543.
11. *US News and World Report*, 4 January 1993.
12. Quoted in Patrick Glynn, 'The Age of Balkanization', *Commentary*, Vol.1, No.1 (July 1993) p.24.
13. *Independent*, 29 May 1992.
14. *International Herald Tribune*, 11 December 1996.
15. Philip J. Cohen, *Serbia's Secret War: Propaganda and the Deceit of History* (Texas: A. and M. Press, 1996).
16. Michael A. Sells, *The Bridge Betrayed: Religion and Genocide in Bosnia* (Berkeley, CA: University of California Press, 1997).
17. *Guardian*, 23 November 1996.
18. *Guardian*, 8 March 1997.
19. *The Times*, 7 February 1997.
20. *Guardian*, 28 August 1992.
21. Quoted in *Guardian*, 30 December 1995.
22. Quoted in *The Times*, 7 January 1995.
23. Quoted in *Guardian*, 2 April 1996.
24. *Guardian*, 30 December 1995.
25. Vladimir Tismaneanu, *Reinventing Politics* (New York: Free Press, 1993) p.290.
26. Tismaneanu, *Reinventing*, p.244.
27. Quoted in Stephen Borsody, *The New Central Europe* (New York: Columbia University Press, 1993) p.282.
28. Bram Stoker, *Dracula* (Hertfordshire: Wordsworth, 1993) p.5.
29. Stoker, *Dracula*, p.6.

30. From Anatol Lieven, *The Baltic Revolution*, quoted in review, *Guardian*, 8 June 1995.
31. Quoted in Gordon East, 'The Concept and Status of the Shatter Zone', in Norman J.G. Pounds (ed.) *Geographical Essays on Eastern Europe* (Bloomington: Indiana University Press, 1961) p.16.
32. Comte de Gobineau, *The Inequality of Races* (Los Angeles: Noontide Press, 1966) p.83.
33. Quoted in W. Fest, *Peace or Partition: The Habsburg Monarchy and British Policy 1914–1918* (London: George Prior Publishers, 1978) p.98.
34. Quoted in Daniel Patrick Moynihan, *Pandaemonium: Ethnicity in International Politics* (Oxford: Oxford University Press, 1993) p.83.
35. N. Pease, *Poland, The US and the Stabilisation of Europe* (Oxford: Oxford University Press, 1986) p.12.
36. F. Gregory Campbell, *Confrontation in Central Europe: Weimar Germany and Czechoslovakia* (Chicago: University of Chicago Press, 1975) p.247.
37. H.A.L. Fisher (ed.), *Background and Issues of the War* (Oxford: Oxford University Press, 1940) p.17.
38. A.L. Coolidge, 'Ten Years of War and Peace', *Foreign Affairs*, Vol.4 No.1 (September 1924) p.13.
39. Larry Wolff, *Inventing Eastern Europe: The Map of Civilisation on the Mind of the Enlightenment* (Stanford, CA: Stanford University Press, 1994) p.3.
40. *Guardian*, 9 September 1993.
41. Paula Franklin Little, 'US Policy Toward the Demise of Yugoslavia: The Virus of Nationalism', *East European Politics and Society*, Vol.6, No.3 (Fall, 1992).
42. *Guardian*, 8 March 1996.
43. *Guardian*, 5 April 1997.
44. Stephen Castles and Mark J. Miller, *The Age of Migration* (London: Macmillan, 1993) p.125.
45. Ibid. p.11.
46. *Forum*, November 1991.
47. *New Republic*, 4 February 1991.
48. Andrew Convey and Marek Kupiszewski, 'Keeping Up With Schengen: Migration and Policy in the European Union', *International Migration Review*, Vol.XXIX, No.4 (Winter 1995) p.94.
49. *Guardian*, 14 March 1997.
50. Raymond Pearson, 'Nationalism and the Dissolution of Communist Eastern Europe', *Nations and Nationalism*, Vol.1, Part 1 (March, 1995) p.71.
51. *Guardian*, 25 May 1993.
52. Quoted in *Guardian*, 8 November 1992.
53. *Evening Standard*, 5 March 1996.
54. *Guardian*, 22 September 1993.
55. Wolff, *Inventing*, p.3.
56. Daniel Nelson, 'Europe's Unstable East', *Foreign Policy*, No. 82 (Spring 1991) p.139.

57. Dennis P. Hupchick, *Conflict and Chaos in Eastern Europe* (New York: St Martins Press, 1995).
58. Janusz Bugajski, *Nations in Turmoil: Conflict and Cooperation in Eastern Europe* (Boulder, CO: Westview Press, 1993) p.4.
59. *European*, 10 September 1992.
60. *London Review of Books*, 25 February 1993.
61. *Guardian*, 28 August 1992.

Chapter 3

1. James Kurth, 'The Shape of the New World Order', *National Interest*, No.24 (Summer 1991) p.5.
2. Rebecca West, *Black Lamb and Grey Falcon* (London: Macmillan, 1942) p.23.
3. John Feffer, *Shock Waves: Eastern Europe After The Revolutions* (Montreal: Black Rose Books, 1992), p.11.
4. Robin Okey, 'Central Europe/Eastern Europe: Behind the Definitions', *Past and Present*, No.137 (November 1992) p.102.
5. Tony Judt, 'The Rediscovery of Central Europe', *Daedalus*, Vol.119, No.1 (Winter 1990).
6. Okey, 'Central Europe', p.104.
7. *London Review of Books*, 19 December 1991.
8. Larry Woolf, *Inventing Eastern Europe: The Map of Civilisation on the Mind of the Enlightment* (Stanford, CA: Stanford University Press, 1994) p.15.
9. Ivan T. Berend, 'The Historical Evolution of Eastern Europe as a Region', *International Organisation*, Vol.40, No.2 (Spring 1986) p.330.
10. Gerard Delanty, *Inventing Europe* (London: Macmillan, 1995) p.53.
11. Anthony D. Smith, 'National Identity and the Idea of European Unity', *International Affairs*, Vol.68, No.1 (January 1992) p.69.
12. D. Hay, *Europe: The Emergence of an Idea* (Edinburgh: Edinburgh University Press, 1957) p.21.
13. Mihaljo Crnobrnja, *The Yugoslav Drama*, 2nd edn (London: IB Tauris, 1996) p.69.
14. Hay, *Europe*, p.37.
15. Ibid. p.50.
16. Grigore Gafencu, 'Eastern Countries and the European Order', *International Affairs*, Vol.XXIII, No.2 (April 1947) p.161.
17. Quoted in Delanty, *Inventing*, p.17.
18. Pim den Boer, 'Europe to 1914: The Making of an Idea', in Kevin Wilson and Jan van der Dussen (eds) *The History of the Idea of Europe*, 2nd edn (London: Routledge, 1996) p.19.
19. den Boer, 'Europe', p.35.
20. Ibid. p.64.
21. Ibid. p.62.
22. Ibid. p.58.
23. Ibid. p.70.
24. Ibid. p.69.
25. Ibid. p.70.

26. Ibid. p.71.
27. Okey, 'Central Europe', p.120.
28. See N. Pounds (ed.) *Geographical Essays on Eastern Europe* (Bloomington: Indiana University Press, 1961).
29. A. Komjathy, *The Crisis of France's East Central European Diplomacy 1933–1938* (New York: Columbia University Press, 1976) p.1.
30. Eric Hobsbawm, *The Age of Revolution* (London: Abacus, 1977) p.32.
31. Hugh Seton Watson, 'What is Europe, Where is Europe?', *Encounter*, Vol.LXV No.2 (July 1985) p.16.
32. Smith, 'National Identity', p.70.
33. *London Review of Books*, 25 January 1996.
34. Smith, 'National Identity', p.69.
35. William Woodruff, 'The Burden of Power in a Fragmented World – An American View', *The World Today*, Vol.48, No.6 (June 1992) p.105.
36. P. J. O'Rourke, *All the Trouble in the World* (London: Picador, 1994) p.246.
37. Samuel Huntington, *The Clash of Civilisations and the Remaking of World Order* (New York: Simon and Schuster, 1996).

Chapter 4

1. See Samir Amin, 'Imperialism and Culturalism Complement Each Other', *Monthly Review*, Vol.48, No. 2 (June 1996).
2. Quotes from Marshall G.S. Hodgson, 'The Interrelationships of Societies in History', *Comparative Studies in Society and History*, V (1962–3) p.235.
3. Arnold Toynbee, *A Study in History* (London: Oxford University Press, 12 vols, 1934–61).
4. R.G. Collingwood, 'Oswald Spengler and the Theory of Historical Cycles', *Antiquity*, Vol.1 (September 1927) p.318.
5. Collingwood, 'Oswald', p.324.
6. Ibid. p.318.
7. Ibid. p.324.
8. Gordon Childe, *What Happened in History?* (New York, Penguin, 1946) p.1.
9. Childe, *History*, p.180.
10. Ibid. p.180.
11. Ibid. p.16.
12. Hodgson, 'Interrelationships', p.249.
13. Ibid. p.234.
14. See numerous articles from the 1920s and 1930s in the *American Anthropologist* which became a mouthpiece for the Boasian school.
15. W.R. Jones, 'The "Barbarians" in World Historical Perspective', *Cultures*, Vol.4, No.2 (1977) p.104.
16. Owen Lattimore, *Studies in Frontier History: Collected Papers 1928–1958* (Oxford, Oxford University Press, 1962) pp.504–5.
17. Jones, 'Barbarians', p.103.
18. Ibid. p.107.

19. John Hale, *The Civilisation of Europe in the Renaissance* (New York: Atheneum, 1994) p.33.
20. Jones, 'Barbarians', p.105.
21. Ibid. p.115.
22. For an interesting example of the 'masses' component of the 'barbarian' challenge – in France, see Philip Spencer, 'Barbarian Assault: Fortunes of a Phrase', *Journal of the History of Ideas*, Vol.16, No.2 (April 1955) pp.232–9.
23. Hodgson, 'Interrelationships', p.232.

Chapter 5

1. Edward W. Said, *Orientalism* (London: Routledge and Kegan Paul, 1978).
2. Luis del Corral, *The Rape of Europe* (London: George Allen and Unwin, 1959) p.11.
3. John Hale, *The Civilization of Europe in the Renaissance* (New York: Atheneum, 1994) p.20.
4. Quoted in ibid. p.43.
5. Quoted in ibid. p.42.
6. Maxime Rodinson, *Europe and the Mystique of Islam* (London: I.B. Tauris, 1988) p.48.
7. Ibid. p.65.
8. Ibid. p.60.
9. J. Feffer, *Shock Waves: Eastern Europe after the Revolutions* (Montreal: Black Rose Books, 1992) p.11.
10. Piotr Wandycz, 'The Treatment of East Central Europe in History Textbooks', *American Slavic Review*, Vol.XVI (1957).
11. Robin Okey, 'Central Europe/Eastern Europe: Behind the Definitions', *Past and Present*, No.137 (November 1992) p.114.
12. Andrew C. Janos, *The Politics of Backwardness in Hungary 1825–1945* (Princeton, NJ: Princeton University Press, 1982) p.46.
13. Daniel Chirot, *The Origins of Backwardness in Eastern Europe* (Berkeley, CA: University of California Press, 1989) p.3.
14. Janos, *Backwardness*, p.38.
15. Ibid. p.45.
16. Robin Okey, *Eastern Europe 1740–1985*, 2nd edn (London: Routledge, 1992) p.21.
17. See Janos, *Backwardness*, p.49.
18. Joseph Caillaux, 'Economics and Politics in Europe', *Foreign Affairs*, Vol.1, No.2 (15 December 1922) p.32.

Chapter 6

1. Paul G. Lewis, 'Contours of the Shadowlands: The Trials of Transition in Eastern Europe', *Journal of Communist Studies and Transition Politics*, Vol.11, No.2 (June 1995) p.199.

2. J. Feffer, *Shock Waves: Eastern Europe after the Revolutions* (Montreal: Black Rose Books, 1992) p.xv.
3. Quoted in Johnathan Sunley, 'Post-Communism: An Infantile Disorder', *National Interest*, No.44 (Summer 1996) p.4.
4. *Financial Times*, 15 April 1996.
5. *International Herald Tribune*, 15 January 1997.
6. J.F. Brown, 'Uneven Progress. Eastern Europe: The Revolution So Far', *RFE/RL Research Report*, Vol.2, No.1 (1 January, 1993) p.70.
7. Quoted in D. Hupchick, *Conflict and Chaos in Eastern Europe* (New York: St Martins Press, 1995) preface.
8. Thomas W. Simons Jr, *Eastern Europe in the Postwar World* (London: Macmillan, 1991) p.238.
9. Ibid. p.235.
10. Hugh Seton Watson, 'Differences Between East and West', *The Listener*, 19 August 1948, p.274.
11. Henry L. Roberts, 'Eastern Europe and the Historians', *Slavic Review*, Vol. XX (1961) p.511.
12. Quoted in *London Review of Books*, 19 December 1991.
13. Ibid.
14. *Prospect*, April 1996.
15. For argument over history, or contemporary responsibility between Kaplan and Noel Malcolm see letters, *National Interest*, No.33 (Fall 1993) pp.109–11.
16. John R. Bowen, 'The Myth of Global Ethnic Conflict', *Journal of Democracy*, Vol.7, No.4 (October 1996) p.9.
17. David A. Lake and Donald Rothschild, 'Containing Fear: The Origins and Management of Ethnic Conflict', *International Security*, Vol.21, No.2 (Fall 1996) p.41.
18. Michael Walzer, 'The New Tribalism', *Dissent*, (Spring 1992) p.164.
19. Jacques Rupnik, *The Other Europe* (London, George Weidenfeld and Nicolson, 1988) p.21.
20. Ibid. p.20.
21. P. Longworth, *The Making of Eastern Europe* (London: Macmillan, 1992) p.60.
22. Joseph Held, *Columbia History of Eastern Europe in the Twentieth Century* (New York: Columbia University Press, 1992) p.2.
23. H. Schwartz, *Eastern Europe in the Soviet Shadow* (New York: Abelard-Schuman, 1973) p.11.
24. Vladimir Baranovsky and Hans Joachim Spanger, *In From The Cold: Germany, Russia and the Future of Europe* (Boulder, CO: Westview Press, 1992) p.277.

Chapter 7

1. Quoted in G.J. Bobango, *The Emergence of the Romanian National State* (New York: Columbia University Press, 1979) pp.305, 10.
2. N. Pease, *Poland, the US and the Stabilization of Europe* (Oxford: Oxford University Press, 1986), p.9.

3. Thomas Carothers, *Assessing Democracy Assistance: The Case of Romania* (Washington: Carnegie Endowment, 1996) p.38.
4. Ted Galen Carpenter and Amos Perlmutter, 'Strategy Creep in the Balkans', *National Interest*, No.44 (Summer 1996) p.53.
5. Quoted in Bob Deacon and Michelle Hulse, 'The Making of Post-Communist Social Policy: The Role of International Agencies', *Journal of Social Policy*, Vol.26, Pt.1 (January 1997) p.49.
6. *Guardian*, 7 September 1996.
7. *Guardian*, 14 September 1996.
8. *Guardian*, 28 August 1992.
9. Carothers, *Assistance*, p.47.
10. *Guardian*, 20 January 1997.
11. *Guardian*, 28 January 1997.
12. Quoted in *Guardian*, 5 February 1993.
13. Quoted in *Time*, 21 September 1992.
14. R.D. Kaplan, 'The Clairvoyance of Rebecca West', *The National Interest*, No.26 (Winter 1991/1992) p.69.
15. Anne Orde, *British Policy and European Reconstruction After the First World War* (Cambridge: Cambridge University Press, 1990) pp.119, 123.
16. *The Times*, 30 May 1913.
17. David C. Gompert, 'The United States and Yugoslavia's Wars', in R.H. Ullman, *The World and Yugoslavia's Wars* (New York: Council on Foreign Relations, 1996) p.137.
18. F.R. Bridge and R. Bullen, *The Great Powers and the European State System 1815–1914*, (London: Longman, 1980) p.45.
19. *Newsweek*, 22 June 1992.
20. R. Okey, *Eastern Europe 1740–1985* (London: Routledge, 1992) p.148.
21. Quoted in *Guardian*, 27 November 1995.
22. Quoted in *Guardian*, 6 February 1996.
23. *Time*, 11 March 1996.
24. *Observer*, 5 November 1995.

Chapter 8

1. Carlton J.H. Hayes, *Essays on Nationalism* (New York: Macmillan, 1926) pp.74, 92.
2. Ibid. p.55.
3. Royal Institute of International Affairs, *Nationalism – A Report* (Oxford: Oxford University Press, 1939) p.xiv.
4. Louis L. Snyder, *The Meaning of Nationalism* (New York: Greenwood Press, 1954) p.viii.
5. Ibid. p.3.
6. Ibid. p.121.
7. Walter Kolarz, *Myths and Realities in Eastern Europe* (London: Lindsay Drummond, 1946) p.213.

8. Rudolf Schlesinger, *Federalism in Central and Eastern Europe* (London: Butler and Tanner, 1945) p.432.
9. *Observer*, 12 November 1995.
10. Misha Glenny, *The Fall of Yugoslavia* (Harmondsworth: Penguin, 1993) p.140.
11. Quoted in Stephen Iwan Griffiths, *SIPRI Research Report No.5 Nationalism and Ethnic Conflict* (Oxford: Oxford University Press, 1993) p.1.
12. T. Simons, *Eastern Europe in the Postwar World* (London: Macmillan, 1991) p.237.
13. On Magosci and debate about such projects, see Chris Hann, 'Intellectuals, Ethnic Groups and Nations: Two Late Twentieth Century Cases', in Sukumar Perival (ed.) *Notions of Nationalism* (Budapest: Central European University Press, 1995).
14. Mykola Musinka, 'The Rusyne – Ukrainian National Minority in Slovakia', in Jana Plichtova (ed.) *Minorities in Politics* (Bratislava: Czechoslovak Committee of the European Cultural Foundation, 1992) p.223.
15. Ibid. p.225.
16. Kolarz, *Myths*, p.30.
17. Luis del Corral, *The Rape of Europe* (London: George Allen and Unwin, 1959) p.222.
18. David C. Gompert, 'The United States and Yugoslavia's Wars', in R.H. Ullman, *The World and Yugoslavia's Wars* (New York: Council on Foreign Relations, 1996) p.126.
19. Charles G. Boyd, 'Making Peace with the Guilty', *Foreign Affairs*, Vol.74, No. 5 (September/October 1995) p.34.
20. Quoted in *Guardian*, 9 August 1993.

Chapter 9

1. Quoted in R. Okey, *Eastern Europe 1740–1985* (London: Routledge, 1992) p.71.
2. D.S. Luft, *Robert Musil and the Crisis of European Culture* (Berkeley, CA: University of California Press, 1980) p.214.
3. Ivan Berend, *Crisis Zone of Europe* (Cambridge: Cambridge University Press, 1986) p.22.
4. Quoted in Peter Bugge, 'The Nation Supreme: The Idea of Europe 1914–1945', in K. Wilson and J. van der Dussen (eds) *The History of the Idea of Europe* (London: Routledge, 1996) p.85.
5. M. Rodinson, *Europe and the Mystique of Islam* (London: I.B. Tauris, 1988) p.71.
6. Quoted in Maurice Muret, *Twilight of the White Races* (London: T. Fisher Unwin Ltd, 1926) p.30.
7. See 'The Weak Ramparts of the Permissive West', *New Perspectives Quarterly*, Vol.10, No.3 (Summer 1993).
8. André Siegfried, 'The French Democratic Tradition', *Foreign Affairs*, Vol.17, No.4 (July 1939) p.662.
9. Alfred Weber, *Farewell to European History* (London: Kegan, Paul, Trench, Trubner and Co., 1947) p.ix.

10. Geoffrey Barraclough, *History in a Changing World* (Oxford: Basil Blackwell, 1955) p.183.
11. See Alan Milward, *The Reconstruction of Western Europe 1945–51* (London: London University Press, 1984) p.3.
12. Geroid T. Robinson, 'The Ideological Combat', *Foreign Affairs*, Vol.27, No.4 (July 1949) p.530.
13. Arnold Toynbee, 'The Present Point in History', *Foreign Affairs*, Vol.26, No.1 (October 1947) p.191.
14. It is not possible to communicate here the extent to which the Anglo-American world view was dominated by race before the Second World War. For the best discussion of this question see Kenan Malik, *The Meaning of Race* (London: Macmillan, 1996).
15. A. Janos, *The Politics of Backwardness in Hungary 1825–1945* (Princeton, NJ: Princeton University Press, 1982) p.168.
16. See Frank Füredi, *Mythical Past, Elusive Future* (London: Pluto Press, 1993) Chapter 6.
17. B. Ward, 'Europe Debates Nationalisation', *Foreign Affairs*, Vol.25, No.1 (October 1946) p.53.
18. Walter Kolarz, *Myths and Realities in the New Eastern Europe* (London: Lindsay Drummond, 1946) p.7.
19. *The Economist*, 14 June 1947.
20. *The Economist*, 13 December 1947.
21. Bela Fabian, 'Hungary's and Romania's Nazis in Red – Hitler's Graduates Staff Stalin's New Order', *Commentary* (May 1951) p.470.
22. Frederick Hertz, *Nationality in History and Politics* (London: Kegan, Trench, Trubner and Co., 1944) p.258.
23. John Gaddis Smith, 'The Ghost of Hitler: Lessons of the Past', in T. Paterson (ed.) *The Origins of the Cold War* (Lexington, MA: D.C. Heath and Co., 1974) p.235.
24. Marcel Hoden, 'Europe Without the League', *Foreign Affairs*, Vol.18, No.1 (October 1939) p.28.
25. Robinson, 'Combat', p.538.
26. Joyce and Gabriel Kolko, *The Limits of Power: The World and American Foreign Policy 1945–54* (New York: Harper and Row, 1972) p.191.
27. *The Economist*, 3 April 1948.
28. Elizabeth Wiskeman, *Europe of the Dictators* (London: Collins, 1966) p.255.
29. Hubert Ripka, *Eastern Europe in the Postwar World* (London: Methuen, 1961) p.83.
30. Paul Latawski, 'What To Do About Nationalism? The Recurring Dilemma of Western Policy in East Central Europe', in Paul Latawski (ed.) *Contemporary Nationalism in East Central Europe* (London: Macmillan, 1995) p.176.
31. Ibid.
32. Joseph Rothschild, *Return to Diversity*, 2nd edn (New York: Oxford University Press, 1993).
33. Latawski, 'What to do', p.177.
34. *Sunday Telegraph*, 22 September 1991.

Chapter 10

1. Miklos Haraszti, 'Animal Farm Scenarios', *Constellations*, Vol.2, No.1 (1995) p.89.
2. Quoted in *Prospect*, January 1997.
3. Quoted in Simons, *Eastern Europe*, p.266.
4. G.F. Treverton, 'The New Europe', *Foreign Affairs*, Vol.71, No.1 (1991/1992) p.98.
5. *International Herald Tribune*, 3 March 1997.
6. *Guardian*, 15 March 1997.
7. Misha Glenny, *The Rebirth of History*, 2nd edn (Harmondsworth: Penguin, 1993) p.236.
8. Mihaly Vajda, 'East Central European Perspectives', in John Keane (ed.) *Civil Society and the State* (London: Verso, 1988) p.333.
9. Ronald H. Linden, 'The New International Political Economy of Eastern Europe', *Studies in Comparative Communism*, Vol.XXV, No.1 (March 1992), p.3.
10. Quoted in S. Borsody, *The New Central Europe* (New York: East European Monographs, 1993) p.285.
11. Ivo John Lederer (ed.), *Western Approaches to Eastern Europe* (New York: Council on Foreign Relations Press, 1992) p.10.
12. Mike King, *Fortress Europe*, Occasional Paper (University of Leicester: Centre for the Study of Public Order, 1994), p.9.
13. *Prognosis*, 21 January–3 February 1994.
14. See my article 'Minority Rights and the Civilising of Eastern Europe', *Contention*, Vol.5, No.2 (Winter 1996) pp.17–37; for a discussion of this 'who's more civilised than whom' discussion.
15. Quoted in *Prague Post*, 20–26 April 1994.
16. Robert M. Bigler, 'Back in Europe and Adjusting to the New Realities of the 1990s in Hungary', *East European Quarterly*, Vol.XXX, No.2 (Summer 1996) p.209.
17. Keitha Sapsin Fine, 'Fragile Stability and Change', in Abram and Antonia Handler Chayes (eds) *Preventing Conflict in the Post-Communist World* (Washington: Brookings Institution, 1996) p.573.
18. *Evening Standard*, 9 October 1996.
19. *Prague Post*, 17–23 March 1993.
20. Chayes and Chayes, *Preventing Conflict*, p.541.
21. Fine, 'Fragile Stability', p.543.
22. Ewa Lés, *The Voluntary Sector in Post-Communist East Central Europe*, (Washington: Civicus, 1994), p.51.
23. Ibid.
24. Fine, 'Fragile Stability', p.559.
25. T. Carothers, *Assessing Democracy Assistance: The Case of Romania* (Washington: Carnegie Endowment, 1996) p.123.
26. David Samuels, 'At Play in the Fields of Oppression', *Harpers*, Vol.290, No.1740 (May 1995) p.54.
27. Ibid. p.51.
28. C.A. Macartney, *National States and National Minorities* (London: Oxford University Press, 1934) pp.489, 490.

29. See my 'Minority Rights'
30. *Newsweek*, 4 December 1995.
31. Samuels, 'At Play', p.49.
32. Kevin F.F. Quigley, 'Philanthropy's Role in East Europe', *Orbis*, Vol. 37, No.4 (Fall 1993) p.594.
33. Carothers, *Democracy Assistance*, p.97.
34. Ibid. p.71.
35. Fine, 'Fragile Stability', p.573.
36. Carothers, *Democracy Assistance*, p.94.
37. Fine, 'Fragile Stability', p.563.

Chapter 11

1. *The Economist*, 26 December–8 January 1993.
2. August Pradetto, 'Germany and Her European Neighbours', *German Monitor*, No.37 (1996) p.192.
3. Quoted in Charles G. Boyd, 'Making Peace with the Guilty', *Foreign Affairs*, No.5 (September/October 1995) p.22.
4. Ibid. p.23.
5. Pradetto, 'Germany', p.202.
6. T. Garton Ash, *In Europe's Name* (London: Vintage, 1994) p.396.
7. *The Times*, 22 January 1997.
8. *Newsweek*, 2 December 1996.
9. *Prospect*, January 1997.
10. T. Carothers, *Assessing Democracy Assistance: The Case of Romania* (Washington: Carnegie Endowment, 1996) p.v.
11. Ken Jowitt, 'Dizzy with Democracy', *Problems of Post Communism*, Vol.43, No.1 (January/February 1996) p.7.
12. Juan J. Linz and Alfred Stepan, 'Toward Consolidated Democracies', *Journal of Democracy*, Vol.7, No.2 (April 1996) p.15.
13. Krishan Kumar, 'Civil Society: An Inquiry into the Usefulness of an Historical Term', *British Journal of Sociology*, Vol.44, No.3 (September 1993) p.377.
14. *International Herald Tribune*, 21–22 May 1994.
15. William Pfaff, 'A New Colonialism?', *Foreign Affairs*, Vol.74, No.1 (January/February 1995) p.1.
16. *London Review of Books*, 19 December 1991.
17. Abram Chayes and Antonia Handler Chayes, 'After the End', in R.E. Ullman, *The World and Yugoslavia's Wars* (New York: Council on Foreign Relations Press, 1996) p.212.
18. Nora Rathzel, 'Aussiedler and Auslander: Transforming German National Identity', *Social Identities*, Vol.1, No.2 (August 1995) p.276.
19. Peter O'Brien, 'Germany's Newest Aliens: The East Germans', *East European Quarterly*, Vol.XXX, No.4 (January 1997) p.465.
20. Ibid. p.464.
21. Hugh Seton Watson, 'Thoughts on the Concept of West and East in Europe', *Government and Opposition*, Vol.20 (Spring 1985) p.157.
22. *Prognosis*, 18 February–3 March 1994.

Select Bibliography

Banks, R. *The Dynamics of Communism in Eastern Europe* (Princeton, NJ: Princeton University Press, 1961).

Baranovsky, V. and Spanger, H.J. *In From the Cold: Germany, Russia and the Future of Europe* (Boulder, CO: Westview Press, 1992).

Barraclough, G. *History in a Changing World* (Oxford: Basil Blackwell, 1955).

Berend, I. *Crisis Zone of Europe* (Cambridge: Cambridge University Press, 1986).

Bobango, G. *The Emergence of the Romanian National State* (New York: Columbia University Press, 1979).

Borsody, S. *The New Central Europe* (New York: East European Monographs, 1993).

Bridge, F.R. and Bullen, R. *The Great Powers and the European State System 1815–1914* (London: Longman, 1980).

Bugajski, J. *Nations in Turmoil: Conflict and Cooperation in Eastern Europe* (Boulder, CO: Westview Press, 1993).

Carothers, T. *Assessing Democracy Assistance: The Case of Romania* (Washington: Carnegie Endowment, 1996).

Castles, S. and Miller, M. *The Age of Migration* (London: Macmillan, 1993).

Chayes, A. and Chayes, A. (eds) *Preventing Conflict in the Post-Communist World* (Washington: Brookings Institution, 1996).

Childe, G. *What Happened in History?*(New York: Penguin, 1946).

Chirot, D. (ed.) *The Origins of Backwardness in Eastern Europe* (Berkeley, CA: University of California Press, 1989).

Cohen, P. *Serbia's Secret War* (Texas: A. and M. Press, 1996).

Corral, L.D. *The Rape of Europe* (London: George Allen and Unwin, 1959).

Crnobrnja, M. *The Yugoslav Drama* (London: I.B. Tauris, 2nd edn, 1996).

Croce, B. *History of Europe in the Nineteenth Century* (London: George Allen and Unwin, 1934).

Dean, J. *Ending Europe's Wars* (New York: Twentieth Century Fund Press, 1994).

Delanty, G. *Inventing Europe* (London: Macmillan, 1995).

European Community *The Community and its Eastern Neighbours* (Luxembourg: EC, 1991).

Faini, R. and Portes, R. *European Trade with Eastern Europe* (London: Centre for Economic Policy Research, 1995).

Feffer, J. *Shock Waves: Eastern Europe After the Revolutions* (Montreal: Black Rose Books, 1992).

Fest, W. *Peace or Partition: The Habsburg Monarchy and British Policy 1914–1918* (London: George Prior, 1978).

Fisher, H.A.L. (ed.) *Background and Issues of the War* (Oxford: Oxford University Press, 1940)

Füredi, F. *Mythical Past, Elusive Future* (London: Pluto Press, 1993).

Garton Ash, T. *In Europe's Name* (London: Vintage, 1994).

Gati, C. *Eastern Europe and the World* (New York: Cliff's Notes, 1978).

Glenny, M. *The Fall of Yugoslavia* (Harmondsworth: Penguin, 2nd edn 1993).

——. *The Rebirth of History* (Harmondsworth: Penguin, 2nd edn 1993).

Gobineau, A. *The Inequality of Races* (Los Angeles: Noontide Press, 1966).

Gregory Campbell, F. *Confrontation in Central Europe: Weimar Germany and Czechoslovakia* (Chicago: University of Chicago Press, 1975).

Griffiths, S.I. *Nationalism and Ethnic Conflict* (Oxford: Oxford University Press, 1993).

Hale, J. *The Civilization of Europe in the Renaissance* (New York: Atheneum, 1994).

Hay, D. *Europe: The Emergence of an Idea* (Edinburgh: Edinburgh University Press, 1957).

Hayes, C.J.H. *Essays on Nationalism* (New York: Macmillan, 1926).

Held, D. (ed.) *Prospects for Democracy* (Oxford: Polity, 1993).

Held, J. *Columbia History of Eastern Europe in the Twentieth Century* (New York: Columbia University Press, 1992).

Hertz, F. *Nationality in History and Politics* (London: Kegan, Trench, Trubner and Co., 1944).

Hobsbawm, E. *The Age of Revolution* (London: Abacus, 1977).

Hockenos, P. *Free to Hate* (London: Routledge, 1994).

Huntington, S. *The Clash of Civilizations and the Remaking of World Order* (New York: Simon and Schuster, 1996).

Hupchick, D. *Conflict and Chaos in Eastern Europe* (New York: St Martins Press, 1995).

Janos, A. *The Politics of Backwardness in Hungary 1825–1945* (Princeton, NJ: Princeton University Press, 1982).

Jowitt, K. *New World Disorder: The Leninist Extinction* (Berkeley, CA: University of California Press, 1992).

Kaplan, R.D. Balkan Ghosts: A Journey Through History (New York: St Martins Press, 1993).

Keane, J. (ed.) *Civil Society and the State* (London: Verso, 1988).

King, M. *Fortress Europe*, Occasional Paper (University of Leicester, Centre for the Study of Public Order, 1994).

Kolarz, Walter. *Myths and Realities in Eastern Europe* (London: Lindsay Drummond, 1946).

Kolko, J. and Kolko, G. *The Limits of Power: The World and American Foreign Policy 1945–54* (New York: Harper and Row, 1972).

Komjathy, A. *The Crisis of France's East Central European Diplomacy 1933–1938* (New York: Columbia University Press, 1976).

Lampe, J. and Smith, P.B. (eds) *East European Studies in the United States: Making its Own Transition After 1989* (Washington: Woodrow Wilson International Center for Scholars, 1993).

Latawski, P. (ed.) *Contemporary Nationalism in East Central Europe* (London: Macmillan, 1995).

Lattimore, O. *Studies in Frontier History: Collected Papers 1928–1958* (Oxford: Oxford University Press, 1962).

Lederer, I.J. (ed.) *Western Approaches to Eastern Europe* (New York: Council on Foreign Relations Press, 1992).

Lés, E. *The Voluntary Sector in Post-Communist East Central Europe* (Washington: Civicus, 1994).

Longworth, P. *The Making of Eastern Europe* (London: Macmillan, 1992).

Lowe, J. *The Great Powers, Imperialism and the German Problem 1865–1925* (London: Routledge, 1994).

Luft, D.S. *Robert Musil and the Crisis of European Culture* (Berkeley, CA: University of California Press, 1980).

Macartney, C.A. *National States and National Minorities* (London: Oxford University Press, 1934).

Malik, K. *The Meaning of Race* (London: Macmillan, 1996).

Milward, A. *The Reconstruction of Western Europe 1945–51* (London: Methuen, 1984).

Moynihan, D.P. *Pandaemonium: Ethnicity in International Politics* (Oxford: Oxford University Press, 1993).

Muret, M. *Twilight of the White Races* (London: T. Fisher Unwin Ltd, 1926).

Nato *Status of Economic Reforms. Colloquium 1995* (Brussels: Nato, 1996).

Okey, R. *Eastern Europe 1740–1985* (London: Routledge, 1992).

Orde, A. *British Policy and European Reconstruction After the First World War* (Cambridge: Cambridge University Press, 1990).

O'Rourke, P.J. *All the Trouble in the World* (London: Picador, 1994).

Paterson, T. (ed.) *The Origins of the Cold War* (Lexington, MA: D.C. Heath and Co., 1974).

Perival, S. (ed) *Notions of Nationalism* (Budapest: Central European University Press, 1995).

Pease, N. *Poland, the US and the Stabilization of Europe* (Oxford: Oxford University Press, 1986).

Plichtova, J. (ed.) *Minorities in Politics* (Bratislava: Czechoslovak Committee of the European Cultural Foundation, 1992).

Pounds, N. (ed.) *Geographical Essays on Eastern Europe* (Bloomington: Indiana University Press, 1961).

Ripka, H. *Eastern Europe in the Postwar World* (London: Methuen, 1961).

Rodinson, M. *Europe and the Mystique of Islam* (London: I.B. Tauris, 1988).

Rosenberg T. *The Haunted Land* (London: Vintage, 1995).

Rothschild, J. *Return to Diversity* (New York: Oxford University Press, 1989).

Royal Institute of International Affairs, *Nationalism – A Report* (Oxford: Oxford University Press, 1939)

Rupnik, J. *The Other Europe* (London: Weidenfeld and Nicolson, 1988).

Said, E. *Orientalism* (London: Routledge and Kegan Paul, 1978).

Schlesinger, R. *Federalism in Central and Eastern Europe* (London: Butler and Tanner, 1945).

Schwartz, H. *Eastern Europe in the Soviet Shadow* (New York: Abelard-Schuman, 1973).

Sells, M.A. *The Bridge Betrayed: Religion and Genocide in Bosnia* (Berkeley, CA: University of California Press, 1997).

Siebert, H. (ed.) *Overcoming the Transformation Crisis* (Tubinger: JCB Mohr, 1993).

Simons, T. *Eastern Europe in the Postwar World* (London: Macmillan, 1991).

Snyder, L. *The Meaning of Nationalism* (New York: Greenwood Press, 1954).

Stoker, B. *Dracula* (Hertfordshire: Wordsworth, 1993).

Tismaneanu, V. *Reinventing Politics* (New York: Free Press, 1993).

Toynbee, A. *A Study in History* (London: Oxford University Press, 12 vols, 1934–61).

Ullman, R.H. *The World and Yugoslavia's Wars* (New York: Council on Foreign Relations, 1996).

Weber, A. *Farewell to European History* (London: Kegan, Paul, Trench, Trubner and Co., 1947).

West, R. *Black Lamb and Grey Falcon* (London: Macmillan, 1942).

Wilson, K. and Van der Dussen, J. (eds) *The History of the Idea of Europe* (London: Routledge, 1996).

Wiskeman, E. *Europe of the Dictators* (London: Collins, 1966).

Wolff, L. *Inventing Eastern Europe: The Map of Civilization on the Mind of the Enlightenment* (Stanford, CA: Stanford University Press, 1994).

Journals

American Anthropologist
American Slavic Review
Antiquity
Aussenpolitik
British Journal of Sociology
Commentary
Communist and Post-Communist Studies
Comparative Studies in Society and History
Constellations
Contention
Cultures
Daedalus
Dissent
East European Politics and Society
East European Quarterly
The Economist
Encounter
Foreign Affairs
Foreign Policy
Forum
Geography
German Monitor
Government and Opposition
Harpers

International Affairs
International Migration Review
International Organisation
International Security
Journal of Communist Studies and Transition Politics
Journal of Democracy
Journal of the History of Ideas
Journal of Social Policy
The Listener
The London Review of Books
Millennium
Monthly Review
Nationalities Papers
National Interest
Nations and Nationalism
New Left Review
New Perspectives Quarterly
New Republic
Newsweek
New York Review of Books
Orbis
Past and Present
Problems of Communism/Post Communism
Prognosis
Prospect
Radio Free Europe/Radio Liberty Research Report
Slavic Review
Social Identities
Studies in Comparative Communism
Time
Transition
Wilson Quarterly
World Today

Index